Dear Reader:

The book you are about to read is the latest bestseller from the St. Martin's True Crime Library, the imprint *The New York Times* calls "the leader in true crime!" Each month, we offer you a fascinating account of the latest, most sensational crime that has captured the national attention. St. Martin's is the publisher of Tina Dirmann's VANISHED AT SEA, the story of a former child actor who posed as a yacht buyer in order to lure an older couple out to sea, then robbed them and threw them overboard to their deaths. John Glatt's riveting and horrifying SECRETS IN THE CELLAR shines a light on the man who shocked the world when it was revealed that he had kept his daughter locked in his hidden basement for 24 years. In the Edgar-nominated WRITTEN IN BLOOD, Diane Fanning looks at Michael Petersen, a Marine-turned-novelist found guilty of beating his wife to death and pushing her down the stairs of their home—only to reveal another similar death from his past. In the book you now hold, ALL-AMERICAN MURDER, Amber Hunt takes an in-depth look at a controversial case that has made national headlines.

St. Martin's True Crime Library gives you the stories behind the headlines. Our authors take you right to the scene of the crime and into the minds of the most notorious murderers to show you what really makes them tick. St. Martin's True Crime Library paperbacks are better than the most terrifying thriller, because it's all true! The next time you want a crackling good read, make sure it's got the St. Martin's True Crime Library logo on the spine—you'll be up all night!

Charles E. Spicer, Jr.
Executive Editor, St. Martin's True Crime Library

D0838342

TITLES BY AMBER HUNT

Dead but Not Forgotten

All-American Murder

from the True Crime Library of St. Martin's Paperbacks

ALL-AMERICAN MURDER

AMBER HUNT

St. Martin's Paperbacks

ALL-AMERICAN MURDER

Copyright © 2011 by Amber Hunt.

All rights reserved.

For information address St. Martin's Press, 175 Fifth Avenue, New York, NY 10010.

EAN: 978-0-312-54106-4

Printed in the United States of America

St. Martin's Paperbacks edition / September 2011

St. Martin's Paperbacks are published by St. Martin's Press, 175 Fifth Avenue, New York, NY 10010.

10 9 8 7 6 5 4 3 2 1

For those who've been silent

Acknowledgments

When a murder case touches as many lives as that of Yeardley Love, I, as a human first and journalist second, can't help but pay attention. My professional background is mostly in gritty Detroit, where enough lives end in violence each year that reporters simply can't keep up. Not every victim gets a newspaper mention, much less a book.

Some have already argued that Yeardley is no different from, nor more deserving than, the hundreds of victims who die prematurely each year in Baltimore, the big city next door to Yeardley's small-town roots in Cockeysville, Maryland. Largely, those people are right. But every now and then a crime comes along from which some good can come, and it seemed to me that Yeardley's case had that rare potential. The details in this book come from hundreds of hours spent examining police and court documents, conducting interviews, collecting first-person data, reviewing video footage, and verifying published media reports.

It has not been an easy story to tell.

The case against the suspect in this death is ongoing, as of my deadline. As such, the lawyers and law-enforcement officials connected with it were predictably unable to comment. But far beyond that, I was met with a silence I could not have anticipated. The silence in this case became part of the story. It was more than frustrating; it was frightening, and it went beyond protecting the criminal case.

My primary motivation for telling this story was to help ensure that Yeardley was known as more than a college lacrosse player who died a much-publicized death. She had hopes and dreams and flaws and family, just like everyone else. She was not merely a fleeting headline to those who knew her.

As my research unfolded, I repeatedly reminded myself of a simple journalistic truth: Not everyone wants the story told, but that doesn't mean you shouldn't tell it.

Luckily, I had a great deal of help. For starters, I owe huge thanks to Sarah MacKusick, my sister-turned-research-assistant, who helped push me along at the project's start. Toward its end, I turned to Nick DiMarco, a talented reporter and editor with the Lutherville-Timonium Patch (an online news organization). DiMarco was crucial in helping me research Yeardley's younger years in Catholic school.

I also owe thanks to Brendan Fitzgerald, reporter with *C-VILLE Weekly* in Charlottesville; Megan Pringle, anchor for WMAR's *Good Morning Maryland*; Liz Seccuro, author of *Crash Into Me*; Matthew Power, freelance writer and contributing editor for *Harper's Magazine*: and Nick Perry, *Seattle Times* reporter and coauthor of *Scoreboard, Baby!* Additionally, I send props to the *Washington Post*, the New York *Daily News*, the *New York Times*, and the other daily newspapers whose works are credited in these pages. My bias here is unapologetic and undeniable: Without newspapers, the truth would too often be lost.

On a personal front, I (once again) owe undying gratitude to Elijah Van Benschoten, my partner and backbone. (Shirley and Bryan are pretty swell, too.) For a variety of reasons, I also thank Missy, Allison, Madeleine, and Rachel, my sisters; Pat and Larry MacKusick, who treated me as family even after we technically weren't; Jane Dystel, my agent and morale booster; Allison Caplin, my editor and cheerleader; Charles Spicer, my publisher (who only had to give me one pep talk); Jim and Wendy House; and the many friends, both past and present, who helped shape me even if they don't know it: Jonathan Wallace; Alexa Capeloto; Megan Pennefather; the whole Batcher clan; Todd Bowser; Joe Swickard; and too many others to mention this time around.

Finally, I owe a great deal of sanity and self-discovery to my friends at the University of Michigan's Knight-Wallace Fellowship, where I spent 2010–2011 growing as a journalist. I got a mental boost from my extraordinary fellow Fellows, who are without question among the best journalists in the world. In addition to Matthew Power and Nick Perry, thanks go to Laura Daverio, William Foreman, Antonio Gois, Je-Seung Lee, Todd Leopold, Alec MacGillis, Ted Mellnik, Ana Laura Perez, Justin Pope, Emily Richmond, Christopher Sherman, Harry Siegel, James Thomas, Liu Tianzhao, and John Walton. Hats off as well to Charles Eisendrath, Birgit Rieck, and the amazing women behind the curtain.

PART I

"She Didn't Deserve to Die"

Chapter 1

The call for help was panicked and vague. Caitlin Whiteley, a twenty-two-year-old University of Virginia student, had returned home to her cookie-cutter apartment in Charlottesville to find her roommate unresponsive. It was early Monday morning, the end of a typically hard-drinking "Sunday Funday" on campus, and Caitlin couldn't grasp what was wrong. She'd walked home with Philippe Oudshoorn, a friend and fellow athlete, to find Yeardley Love facedown on her bed and a hole kicked through her bedroom door. Something about the way Yeardley's hair lay seemed awkward and unnatural, so Caitlin pushed it aside and gently shook her friend's shoulder. No response. Then Caitlin noticed some blood.

Oudshoorn hurriedly picked up the phone and told the nine-one-one dispatcher that something was amiss—a message that somehow was translated to "possible alcohol overdose" when patched through to nearby police cars—before lifting Yeardley's body from her bed and attempting CPR. By the time detectives arrived to the second-floor apartment on Charlottesville's narrow 14th Street Northwest, the bloody scene looked nothing like the bender gone awry they had anticipated. Medics were bent over the battered body of Yeardley, a pretty and athletic twenty-two-year-old, and were frantically trying to breathe life back into her.

They were failing.

Charlottesville police officer Lisa T. Reeves was among the first to respond, arriving at the four-bedroom apartment in an off-white building at about 2:30 a.m. May 3, 2010. The apartment was on the second floor, the entrance to which was reachable by a staircase in the middle of the building. She hunted for unit No. 9 and entered.

The front door to the apartment was open and untampered, but the door to the bedroom around which all the activity was now centered—Yeardley's bedroom, Reeves would quickly surmise—was splintered, as though someone had punched a hole straight through it. Reeves spotted Yeardley and immediately saw the blood. A pool had saturated the pillow and sheets beneath the girl's head, and smears of red discolored the bed's comforter. Even the bed skirt was stained crimson.

As the officer examined her more closely, she saw bruising on Yeardley's cheek. The young co-ed's right eye was swollen shut, and a large bruise spread down the side of her face. *Blunt-force trauma*, Reeves would soon describe in her police report, her cop voice kicking in. *There is a pool of blood on her pillow*. The girl's face was surrounded by long brown hair sopping with blood. *Probable cause exists that Yeardley Love was murdered*.

Officers arriving at the apartment quickly cordoned off the area. This was no alcohol poisoning; this was a crime scene. Reeves relayed to her superiors the grisly news: The victim, a star lacrosse player on the university's women's team, was dead, pronounced while still in her apartment, wearing nothing but the panties in which first responders had discovered her. The death was clearly violent. Officers quickly descended on the scene and began gathering evidence. They started by interviewing Whiteley, Yeardley's longtime friend, roommate and teammate, and Oudshoorn, a player on the UVA men's tennis team who was along for the gruesome discovery.

Violent crime was rare enough in Charlottesville, with fewer than 250 cases reported in 2009, but violent death was rarer still, stirring in the police force a mixture of shock and curiosity. Reeves tried to tease details from Yeardley's inconsolable roommates, one of whom had rushed to the front yard and was wailing on a cell phone to a friend. The story they weaved in between tears was like something out of a *Lifetime* movie: Yeardley had been in a rocky relationship, they said, and things had gotten progressively worse in recent days; you need to talk to her boyfriend.

Yeardley had been dating twenty-two-year-old George Huguely V, a handsome, six foot two midfielder on the men's lacrosse team, for about two years. Friends knew their relationship had foundered lately, and some felt Huguely was becoming unhinged. He texted Yeardley often, keeping tabs on her when she was out of town with teammates. Rumors circulated that he had punched a fellow lacrosse player for walking Yeardley home one night, possibly offering a goodnight kiss, and others had to break up a fight between the couple that had gotten so ugly, Yeardley had hit Huguely with her purse.

Yeardley had broken off the relationship a few weeks prior, but to some, it was hard to tell. The two hung out in the same crowd at the same bars, and when one friend asked Yeardley the night before she died how things were with George, Yeardley had replied vaguely that things were the same as always.

As Reeves set out to find Huguely, Charlottesville Police Sgt. Steve Dillon, a forensic detective, took photos of the scene, a typical bedroom in a nondescript apartment building situated about half a mile from the heart of campus. Yeardley's room largely looked like any other college student's, complete with strewn-about clothing. Dillon carefully documented each angle he could think of, taking special care to photograph the hole in the bedroom door, which Dillon noticed had little bits of hair clinging to its jagged edges. Reeves, meanwhile, learned that Huguely lived on the same street, just one building down. The roommates' story had been a little hard to follow, but what the officer gleaned was this: Yeardley had tried to call off their relationship because Huguely would sometimes drink too much and get violent. Huguely, Reeves gathered, didn't like that plan.

Officers had no trouble finding Huguely just a building away, in his apartment inside a brick building on 14th Street Northwest, near its T-junction with Sadler Street. It was still dark outside, still the middle of the night, when he agreed to answer questions at the police department. He wore a black T-shirt ironically adorned with a police logo on the front and back, his brown flip-flops and blue Nike shorts appropriate for the spring Charlottesville weather. It had reached 82 degrees the day before; even when bar hopping after sunset, the college kids often left their jackets behind and simply wore T-shirts. After reaching the police department less than two miles from his house, George waived his Miranda rights, saying he was willing to talk. Police secretly set up a video camera to record the conversation. He acknowledged that he had the right to an attorney and the right to keep silent; he invoked neither, Reeves would report. He seemed shaken and distressed, and as he began to tell his story, he admitted that he had been to see Yeardley. As he described the night's events, he used the passive language that cops so often hear from culprits—damning enough to admit some culpability, but distant enough to shirk full blame.

Yes, he'd fought with Yeardley, George told Reeves. He said the couple had ended their relationship of about two years, and the last few days they had chatted primarily over e-mail. George said he had gone to Yeardley's apartment and kicked her bedroom door in, but he had just wanted to talk. Things got out of hand. He shook her, and her head hit the wall. He noticed blood pouring from her nose. He pushed her onto the bed and left. He didn't know she was seriously hurt, he said. He had been injured himself, he said, motioning to scrapes along his right leg—the type that one would get by kicking in a door. Reeves noticed some other scrapes and bruises on George's arms and hands. He shook those off—they were from lacrosse, not the fight, he claimed. It was impossible for Reeves to know if George was being completely forthcoming. When confessing, criminals often downplay their crimes, turning intentional acts into accidents and using slippery language to minimize their involvement. George could have been doing the same. He didn't bang Yeardley's head against the wall; rather, her head "repeatedly hit the wall" as he shook her. George did, however, admit to stealing an Apple laptop from Yeardley's room and tossing it in a Dumpster. Reeves asked him where, so officers could retrieve it when the interview was over.

Huguely repeatedly asked Reeves how Yeardley was, defense lawyers told a judge months later. An hour into the interrogation, Reeves finally told him that Love was dead.

"She's dead, George," Reeves said, according to the lawyer. "You killed her."

Huguely was shocked, his attorney said, and replied, "She's dead? She's not dead . . . You guys said she had a black eye. I never did anything that would do that to her."

With his statement, Reeves knew she had plenty of probable cause to arrest George Huguely V on suspicion of murder. By the interview's end, she likely sensed, too, that the case seemed tailor made for media consumption. Reporters had already gotten word about the story, and local scribes had gathered down the street, trying to interview neighbors over the sirens and wails that shattered the early-morning calm. Yeardley's friends clutched each other and cried in disbelief.

The first news release on the death was distributed by the Charlottesville Police Department before sunrise. Its contents were sparse:

On the morning of May 3rd, 2010, at 0215 hours, City Police were called to 222 14th ST N.W. apartment number 9 for a possible alcohol overdose. Officers arrived and found a female University of Virginia Student unresponsive in the apartment. Police Officers and Rescue personnel who were called to the scene attempted to revive the victim but were unsuccessful.

Police are treating the case as a homicide investigation at this time.

Victim identification is being withheld at this time
pending notification of next of kin. Further information
will be released later today. Until such time, no other
information will be made available to the public or the
media.

The release ended with a bolded plea for people with information to either call police or the Crime Stoppers tip line.

Local reporters with Charlottesville outlets got that initial
word and headed straight to 14th Street Northwest. A reporter
and photographer from the *C-VILLE Weekly*, a 24,000-
circulation alternative weekly largely dedicated to arts and
entertainment in the lively college town, but whose reporters
kept readers abreast of breaking news online, were quickly on
the scene. Reporter Brendan Fitzgerald wasn't sure what type
of story the paper would want when he joined the coverage by
mid-morning. The sketchy information released by police so
far raised far more questions than answers.

"It's hard to predict what kind of coverage you're gearing
up for, but it raises a different set of questions that inform
possible stories when you hear it's a homicide rather than an
alcohol overdose," Fitzgerald later recalled.

The ambiguity didn't last long. Shortly after noon, the
media received an update: George Huguely V had already
been questioned and was in custody. That news release had
more information—including Yeardley's name and standing
at the school:

Regarding the death of a University of Virginia student
occurring this morning at 222 14th ST N.W. Apartment
Number 9, the victim has been identified as 22 year old,
Yeardley Love. Ms. Love was a fourth year University of
Virginia student from Cockeysville, Maryland and is on
the University's Women's Lacrosse Team.

Preliminary investigation by detectives revealed that
Ms. Love is the victim of an apparent homicide. She suffered visible physical trauma, however the specific cause
of her death is undetermined pending an autopsy.

George Huguely, 22, a fourth year student at the University of Virginia from Chevy Chase MD has been charged with First Degree Murder and is in custody at the Charlottesville/Albemarle jail. He is a player for the University's Men's Lacrosse Team.

According to witnesses, Huguely and Love had a past relationship.

Charlottesville Police are continuing to investigate the case and will provide more details as they become available

About 12:30 p.m., an update was posted to *C-VILLE*'s Web site, including a photo of city police vehicles surrounding the scene at 14th Street Northwest. Fitzgerald, who had been helping to weave coverage at a desk, left to join colleague Chiara Canzi at the scene soon after. The local media had long been gathered, chit-chatting as they waited for the scant updates.

"There were a few camera crews awaiting across the street from Yeardley Love's apartment building," Fitzgerald recalled, "and we all made a couple of attempts to speak with people on the street, people walking by. Not a lot of people were talking."

Fitzgerald didn't know then just how silent the campus would become.

While reporters awaited word, detectives behind the scenes were beginning to fill out the obligatory paperwork for search warrants, using the stilted language in which officers are trained to write. In a court request asking for permission to search George's black Chevrolet Tahoe, Reeves wrote: *Your affiant knows from training and experience that persons involved in crimes of domestic violence often view property that was given to a partner being forfeited back to the giver at the termination of the relationship.* Reeves wanted to check inside the SUV to see if George had any of Yeardley's belongings inside. The request was quickly granted. George's apartment was searched, as was Yeardley's bedroom. By day's end, officers had collected dozens of items as evidence, including swabs of red stains in Yeardley's bedroom, her cell phone, and her digital camera. They bagged a note on Yeardley's bureau in which Huguely apologized for an earlier fight and wrote, "You are my best friend." They also recovered her laptop from the Dumpster where Huguely said he had tossed it, and from Huguely, they took DNA samples, fingernail scrapings, his clothing, and his keys.

Charlottesville Police Chief Timothy Longo and Lieutenant Gary Pleasants tag teamed to field the dozens of media queries that flooded the police department, a small force housed in a brick building connected to the district court on Market Street. When appearing on television, their updates were brief and heartfelt. Clearly, the discovery of Yeardley's battered body was unlike anything the officers had seen before.

Asked by reporters if he had experienced a death scene like Yeardley's before, Longo somberly answered, "In the nine years that I've been privileged to serve as chief of police in this community, I have not."

The questions reporters posed were predictable: Why had Yeardley's roommate reported that she might have passed out from heavy drinking? Did alcohol play a role in the death? Why would George have attacked the young woman? Were there any warning signs that went unheeded? Longo and Pleasants answered obliquely, citing the early stages of the investigation and their desire not to screw it up.

"We're not going to go into any specifics," Pleasants told reporters. "There are too many accounts, and we have half a dozen detectives working on it." Longo, meanwhile, told a Baltimore radio station that he couldn't speculate on why Whiteley first reported alcohol overdose when she found the body. Yeardley's injuries were obvious to officers who responded, he said, but he added that by the time officers arrived, Yeardley's body had been moved. It was no longer face down in a pillow, and there was no hiding the bruises and blood on her face.

By early afternoon, the story already had reached far beyond Charlottesville. Interview requests came pouring in from national media outlets, and television personalities such as Nancy Grace and Dan Abrams were beginning to opine about the case. Charlottesville police were inundated with questions wanting to know whether Huguely could be characterized as cooperative, remorseful, or reticent.

"He was upset by the situation he found himself in but was cooperative with police," a department spokesman told reporters.

Reporters tracked down the phone number for Yeardley's family home in suburban Baltimore, where a woman identifying herself as a designated spokesman politely repeated that the family had no comment. Sharon Love, Yeardley's mother, immediately drove to Charlottesville with daughter Lexie, Yeardley's older sister. Longo told reporters that Sharon was in a state of shock.

"She was very gracious and thankful to investigators," he told one New York–based reporter. "The family wants to be left alone to grieve and mourn . . . I can only imagine what Ms. Love is going through."

Huguely's parents were also believed to be headed to Charlottesville, so reaching them by phone would be next to impossible. But the *Washington Post* managed to reach his grandfather, George Huguely III, by phone. "He was a wonderful child and he was going to graduate," the elder Huguely said. "Hopefully he will be graduating. That's all I can tell you, OK? I'm sorry."

John Casteen III, the university's president, released a heartfelt statement that described the anger welling in many at the senseless death. He described Yeardley as a student with "uncommon talent and promise."

"That she appears now to have been murdered by another student compounds this sense of loss by suggesting that Yeardley died without comfort or consolation from those closest to her," Casteen said. "We mourn her death and feel anger on reading that the investigators believe that another student caused it."

Yeardley didn't deserve it, he continued.

"However little we may know now about Yeardley Love's death, we do know that she did not have or deserve to die—that she deserved the bright future she earned growing up, studying here, and developing her talents as a lacrosse player," he said. "She deserves to be remembered for her human goodness, her capacity for future greatness, and not for the terrible way in which her young life has ended."

By Tuesday, as reporters packed a cramped courtroom to catch their first glimpse of a young man charged with first-degree murder, this much was clear: Yeardley Love's death would impact far more than her family or even just the thousands in and around Charlottesville, Virginia. Her name and her story were destined to reverberate throughout the country.

Chapter 2

At 3 a.m. Tuesday morning, when journalist Megan Pringle arrived to work at ABC affiliate WMAR in Baltimore, she knew she had a long day of broadcasting in front of her. Pringle, a petite and pretty anchor and reporter for *Good Morning Maryland*, was briefed on Yeardley's death. A one-man band—meaning a reporter equipped to do his own video work as well—had already been sent to Charlottesville and would be on hand to cover the day's anticipated arraignment, whenever that might occur. Pringle recognized the story as heartbreaking and newsworthy, but it was her co-anchor, Jamie Costello, who remarked, "This is going to be huge."

By the end of the day's broadcast, Pringle knew he was right.

"It very quickly took on a life of its own," she said.

Tuesday afternoon, reporters crammed inside Charlottesville's small district court for the arraignment police had promised would come. It seemed an impossibly tiny space. The building, situated on East Market Street near 6th Street Northeast, had long prompted complaints from county workers as being far too small for even its normal traffic. Now, with it being the first stop for one of the biggest news stories in the country, it was clear that the general district court was ill equipped for the media onslaught to come.

As has become the trend nationwide, Huguely was set to appear for a video arraignment rather than appearing in person—a move that cuts transportation costs and helps avoid unnecessary delays. As such, it was via closed-circuit television that journalists got their first look at the beefy athlete, whose team roster estimated his weight at about 205 pounds—nearly twice as much as his petite ex-girlfriend. The previous day, officials had released Huguely's official lacrosse team photo, revealing an attractive, shaggy-haired college student dressed in his team's blue and orange. Now, he wore the gray and white striped uniform assigned to him by the Albemarle-Charlottesville Regional Jail. His already bushy hair looked even more mussed than usual; his face, drawn and empty, seemed lined with exhaustion. He appeared nervous as he waited for word from the lawyers his parents had quickly retained for him. District Judge Robert Downer spoke briefly with defense attorney Francis McQ. Lawrence, then postponed a bail review hearing until June 10.

Huguely's only words during the minutes-long hearing: "Thank you, Your Honor." His parents and stepfather, who sat in the back of the courtroom, ignored reporters' requests for comment as they left.

Lawrence, looking polished in a black suit and canary tie, stepped outside the brick courthouse and approached a make-shift podium piled with media microphones and tape recorders. Most of the reporters gathered knew little about the Charlottesville lawyer. His name had appeared a few times in *C-VILLE*'s pages—once as the lawyer representing Richard Neal Willetts, a man convicted on federal sex assault charges in 2007. Another time, Lawrence made news when he helmed efforts to have an area in Darden Towe Park near the Rivanna River declared a historic site on which he hoped to build a center dedicated to Lewis and Clark. Other than that, Lawrence was to most a high-priced attorney readying to represent his biggest client to date.

After the arraignment, he looked focused and solemn as he spoke into more than a dozen recording devices. He declined to answer questions, instead reading from a prepared statement drafted on behalf of the Huguely family.

"Because this case involves an active ongoing investigation, any comment on the specific facts would be inappropriate at this time," said Lawrence, his words deliberate. "Until more information becomes available, it is our hope that no conclusion will be drawn or judgment made about George or his case. However, we are confident that Ms. Love's death was not intended, but an accident with a tragic outcome."

Reporters scribbled furiously.

George was withdrawing from UVA, Lawrence added, and would remain in jail for the foreseeable future. He concluded: "Grief has descended on this community as we attempt to understand what happened and why. Our thoughts and prayers are with those who grieve this terrible loss."

The commonwealth's attorney for the city of Charlottesville, Warner D. "Dave" Chapman, rebuffed reporters' requests for comment, saying that he planned to do all of his talking about the case in court. His graying hair matching his suit, he quietly walked past photographers as they snapped his image. Local reporters, at least, weren't surprised by his silence. Chapman, who preferred going by his middle name, Dave, rather than his given name, was known as the Limelight Dodger. In his more than fifteen years as the commonwealth's attorney, he had worked on many of the area's high-profile cases and was an active member of the local Democratic Party. He once told a *C-VILLE* reporter that he knew he was doing his job well when he managed to stay out of the public eye.

"Many times a prosecutor's office is not doing its job well when it's especially visible," Chapman said in the 2007 story. And, he added, he intended to continue his "no comment" refrain when it came to ongoing cases: "We do not try our cases on the courthouse steps."

His round face obscured by a bushy beard, Chapman was unapologetically humorless in public. In 2005, he balked at a softball question posed as he ran unopposed for his attorney post. Asked by *C-VILLE* to describe his favorite snack, Chapman responded that the question was "completely inappropriate." The newspaper replied by printing the cranky response alongside a lighthearted jab: "Man, somebody get this guy a snack!"

But the Yeardley case was far more than a fluff question in an already decided political race. A young woman was dead and a young man's fate dangled precariously. Lawrence had laid out exactly what battle Chapman would be facing. While the prosecution gathered evidence to justify the first-degree murder charge against Huguely, the defense would strive to paint the death as, at best, an accident contingent on external factors—alcohol, perhaps?—and, at worst, a crime of passion. The difference in legal terms was night and day: First-degree murder comes with a life sentence—and, in Virginia, some cases even warrant the death penalty—while second-degree could mean far less time behind bars. If the defense succeeded and secured a manslaughter conviction, Huguely could be freed by his mid-thirties. If they *really* succeeded, he could walk away altogether. In short, Chapman wanted Huguely in prison for as long as possible. The defense, meanwhile, was already underway in its job to set him free.

From the outset, the case was shaping up to be less a whodunit than a whathappened: Huguely admitted he attacked his ex-girlfriend. The question the whole country was asking was, *Why?*

Chapter 3

Yeardley Love was born July 17, 1987, to Sharon (Donnelly) Love and John Thomas Love III at the Mercy Medical Center in Baltimore, Maryland. After a brutal June, the temperatures along the East Coast had settled somewhat, making the final weeks a bit more comfortable—at least externally—for Sharon to finish up her second pregnancy. The day of Yeardley's debut, Baltimore was a breezy 71 degrees. For their second daughter's name the couple chose Yeardley, pronounced Yard-lee; of Old English origins, the name means "enclosed meadow." Yards, as her family affectionately called her, was four years younger than her older sister, Alexis, known by friends as Lexie. Yeardley was immediately in awe of her older sister, a pretty blond with an infectious smile and athletic build.

Yeardley wrote in an essay about her life in 2002, her freshman year of high school, that she liked to do whatever her older sister did. At the time Yeardley wrote the piece, Lexie had just graduated and headed off to Elon University in North Carolina. Yeardley remembered how she always wanted to tag along with her sister and her sister's friends "and not the children my age." Photographs from the girls' youth show Yeardley often at her sister's side, along with children clearly closer to Lexie's age than her own.

"She taught me a lot in life, and she has left me very good examples to follow," Yeardley wrote. "Sometimes I wonder what I could not have done in my life without her."

The Love girls predictably turned heads. They were beautiful and sweet; their parents were both charming and successful. Yeardly and Lexie's father—a man whose glasses and well-kept hair said "corporate," but whose smile had more warmth than most—had worked in finance at Morgan Stanley, according to a coworker who later recalled "Yeardley coming into the office as a young lady to see her dad." Yeardley's mother, Sharon, worked with hearing-impaired students in Baltimore city schools.

Yeardley grew up in Cockeysville, a Baltimore suburb in Baltimore County. It seemed an area of typical suburban sprawl, but in reality, the little town had sprouted up in the midst of a limestone and marble quarry. The Maryland Geological Survey boasts that Cockeysville's "white, crystalline metalimestone" was used for the upper 390 feet of the Washington Monument in Washington, D.C. By the mid-1800s, the marble was a popular accent in- and outside of the row houses built in Baltimore. The Museum of Fine Arts in Boston describes the material as white and fine grained, containing "a brownish mica that can make the stone look slightly gray."

To outsiders, the town today perhaps appears to lack cohesion—a smattering of hotels and restaurants amid industrial-looking complexes. Those who live there know better, however. Children squeal as they splash around the pools and pond at Beaver Dam, nestled, appropriately, along Beaver Dam Road, northwest of Cockeysville Road. Originally a quarry-created swimming hole, Beaver Dam morphed over time into a full-fledged recreational park, complete with picnic areas and basketball courts. Families would gather from late May through Labor Day (depending on weather) and spend entire days swimming, playing sports, relaxing, and grilling. The more adventurous could plunge into the water from a rope swing as friends cheered them on. Teenagers left on their own would engage in typical waterside teen behavior; summer romances began and ended while relaxing quarryside.

Swimmers and sunbathers had their pick between the quarry pond and two chlorinated pools (dubbed the "front pool" and "back pool" for obvious reasons). The Beaver Dam Swimming Club, as it is known, spreads over thirty acres and is a hidden, fun-filled gem that ignites nostalgia in many Cockeysville natives.

Cockeysville shares little in common with the often cash-strapped metropolis eighteen miles to the south. As of the 2010 United States Census, just over 20,000 people lived there, more than seventy-five percent of whom were white. According to a 2007 CNN Money tally, the median income was about $71,200, with an average home price of $350,000. Yeardley was clearly among the privileged. The family's home on Ivy Hill Road hugged lush parkland. According to county records, the Loves bought the 4.25-acre plot in 1986 for $170,000 and built a 4,400-square-foot home. It was a picturesque setting for John and Sharon to raise their daughters.

And the girls were as pretty as their homestead. Both had inherited their mother's high cheekbones, and by their teenage years, their already electric smiles had been perfected by braces. Sharon Love sometimes dressed the girls in matching outfits on special occasions, even pinning their neatly combed, chin-length hair with matching bows. Sharon seemed particularly fond of one outfit—a cute black dress with a cummerbund and a collar embellished with a pink rose dangling delicately at the neck. Both girls had a version of the dress, and in 1992, when Yeardley was about five, her mother took her to an Olan Mills photo studio to have her portrait taken in it. An oversized, floppy pink bow sat atop her head, pulling her hair into a half-updo.

While eulogizing her daughter, Sharon Love said Yeardley had a mischievous side, *People* magazine relayed: "Yeardley would inform her that her outfit looked horrible; Lexie would rush to change. The next day on the computer, Lexie would find pictures of Yeardley dressed in that very same outfit."

Yeardley and Lexie were undeniably sisters, sharing eyes so blue that they were virtually guaranteed to have red-eye in any amateur photograph requiring a flash. They shared, too, the same boisterous laugh, one that could carry across a lacrosse field, not to mention a room. But they had their differences, too: Lexie's look was at times more natural and clean, her blond hair often pulled away from her face and her makeup spare. As Yeardley reached college, she opted to accentuate her already noticeable eyes with mascara lining both top and bottom lashes, and when she wasn't playing sports, her light brown hair often fell loose around her shoulders.

Yeardley was an active and sporty child, and something of a daddy's girl. She began playing lacrosse with her father when she was five. Lacrosse quickly became her favorite sport, and she not only played year round, but sometimes for two teams at once.

Yeardley's first foray into private education was at St. Joseph School, which serves kindergarteners through eighth graders and costs about $5,500 per year. The parish, roughly three blocks down Church Lane off York Road in Cockeysville, is split on both sides of a narrow back road—the chapel on one side, the classrooms and offices on the other. From the school's mission statement:

> Rooted in the teachings of Jesus, our school is enriched by Catholic tradition and lived Gospel values, which are enhanced by the celebration of liturgy, sacrament and prayer. We further the children's knowledge and practice of their faith and guide them to serve others through the use of their gifts and talents. Here at St. Joseph School, we foster a safe and secure environment in which children can grow and learn.

Sister Joan Dumm, a forty-year educator at St. Joseph, taught Yeardley in the second grade. Dumm readied her for the Catholic ritual of First Holy Communion, which symbolizes a child's initiation into the church.

Dumm recalled speaking with John Love, his voice thick with an Irish accent, while he waited to pick up his then-seven-year-old daughter. He was charged with bringing his girls home from school.

"Oh, yes, every day," Dumm said. "We would bring the lines down to the crossing guard to get them across safely, if they were going to the south-side carpool."

John's affection for his daughters was obvious to everyone, she added: "He loved his girls."

Dumm recalled the simple, idle chitchat in the carpool lane that she and John shared as he waited for Yeardley to bound out of the school. The sister described Yeardley as "a happy, lively little girl" whose school life at age seven centered on the sacrament of First Holy Communion, her first reception of the Holy Eucharist—the consecrated bread and wine (or, in a youngster's case, more likely unfermented grape juice) presented as the body and blood of Jesus Christ.

"That's the big thing for the second grade," Dumm recalled.

The students tended to enjoy practicing and learning the ritual because it meant spending time away from the classroom.

"There were never any problems with getting them to go to church," Dumm said of the students. "In fact, they liked to go across the street so they didn't have to do whatever work we had to do in the classroom. So church was kind of a nice place to go."

Sister Georgia Moonis, Yeardley's homeroom teacher in the fourth grade, recalled the girl as "on the quiet side." It was around then that Yeardley played lacrosse at Sky Walkers, a program whose stated mission is to "instill in every girl the confidence that she has no limitations." Players are taught the importance of teamwork over individual performance, and the lessons are meant to carry over from the field into real life. Yeardley was quiet in the classroom, but she was tenacious on the field.

People couldn't help but be drawn to her. She was the type of young woman whose future success seemed predetermined. No one felt a need to worry about her; with her upbringing and self-assuredness, she seemed poised to map

out whatever destiny she wanted. She could take care of
herself, and she was from the type of family that would pick
up any slack were she ever to stumble. She was the unlikeliest crime victim anyone who met her could have imagined.

Kaki Evans recalled her being "vivacious and loving" in
one online post; in another, Grace Caslow marveled at the
"incredible impression" the young woman made.

Friend Catherine Barthelme posted in an online memoriam
that she could never find a better friend than "Yards." She
missed her laugh her smile and her sense of humor "every
single day."

In an online condolence posting directed at Sharon and
Lexie Love, Casey Donohoe, a Jarrettsville, Maryland native, recalled first meeting Yeardley at Sky Walkers in middle
school and playing lacrosse with her in high school. "I remember her with her side ponytail and bright ribbon,"
Donohoe described. She said she admired her kindness and
generosity. Brian Frederick, a coach with the Cockeysville
recreational program, recalled in a letter to the *Towson Times*
that Yeardley wasn't a flashy child "except for that smile,"
he wrote. She was an understated go-getter, Frederick wrote,
the kind of independent and beautiful young woman he
hoped his son would marry someday.

Yeardley and Frederick's daughter, Meghan, were longtime friends, he wrote, having attended St. Joseph from kin-
dergarten through the eighth grade before matriculating at
separate schools. Meg and Yards played against each other
throughout their four years in high school, Frederick recalled.

"God, I looked forward to those games," he wrote. "I knew
I'd get a big 'hello' and that beautiful smile from Yeardley
after the game—win or lose."

While some young adults need time, not to mention trial and
error, to shape their paths in life, Yeardley knew hers from
the time she was in elementary school: She wanted to play
lacrosse throughout high school and college, and she vowed
to attend the University of Virginia, the college her father
had briefly enrolled in before having to leave for the mili-

tary. He never got his degree; Yeardley promised herself that she would attain one for the both of them.

She decided when she was about nine years old that she would go to the University of Virginia, lacrosse stick in hand. After getting her bachelor's degree, she wanted to attend Virginia Law School for three years, she wrote in her high school essay, and after that, she wanted to become a lawyer and raise a family.

"If I had to wish for three things in my life, they would be to go to University of Virginia for college, have a happy and healthy family when I grow up, and to always keep in touch and stay close with my family," she wrote.

Yeardley competed in both field hockey and lacrosse at Notre Dame Preparatory School, a private school in nearby Towson, Maryland, which costs upward of $15,000 in yearly tuition. Lexie had graduated in 2002; Yeardley was four years behind her. In exchange for the hefty tuition, parents are promised a lower student-to-teacher ratio than Maryland's state average (comparing at about 1:9 at Notre Dame to the state's 1:16), as well as access to a slew of sports and extra-curricular activities. While area public schools struggle to keep abreast of even basic requirements, Notre Dame's students bring laptops to use wirelessly in their classes and have access to courses such as Japanese, architectural drawing, and computer graphics. The high-tech bent is balanced by decades-old traditions: The school's uniform hasn't changed since its founding in 1873.

From the time Yeardley began high school, her classes were geared toward college preparation: four credits in English, three credits in history and social studies, three credits in science (including biology and chemistry); three credits in math (including upper algebra and geometry), three credits in sequential levels of a foreign language, one credit in fine arts, two credits in religion, two credits in physical education, three and a half credits in electives, and twenty hours in social service. The latter requirement fell under the school's "service and justice" heading, which, according to the school, was meant to "address a two-fold mandate: in regards to service, to address the immediate needs of underserved populations; and, in regards to justice, to seek ways to change those systems which inherently prove unjust to individuals, societies, and the world." In short, charity work was a requirement for Yeardley to graduate, and her efforts would be rooted in the Gospel. According to the high school's mission statement, the goal was to "prepare women of moral integrity to become more loving, just, and wise."

Yeardley excelled at everything she tried, teachers and administrators at the Catholic school told reporters in the days after her death.

"Yeardley was an outstanding young lady—joyous, spirited, a wonderful person," the school's headmistress, Sister Patricia McCarron, a woman with a kind, round face, said. "I know we all enjoyed watching her on the lacrosse field and seeing her walk the hallways at NDP. We are proud to call Yeardley one of our girls."

Yeardley seemed proud in return. She regularly returned to Notre Dame when she came home on college breaks and kept in touch with Notre Dame's lacrosse coach, Mary Bartel.

"Yeardley was the core of the personality of the team—she was our laughter, a good soul," Bartel said. "She always found an appropriate way to lighten things up. I don't think there is a soul in this building who couldn't say her name without smiling. Yeardley loved NDP and NDP loved her."

If either McCarron or Bartel knew anything about George Huguely, they didn't tell reporters.

Yeardley was giving, too, said those who knew her, volunteering at a soup kitchen and counseling at a summer camp program for children living in housing projects. Neighbors in sprawling Cockeysville remembered her as an ideal mix of kind, ambitious, and intelligent. The advantages she had been given weren't lost on her, either.

Yeardley marveled at a young age at how lucky she was to have a happy, intact family that instilled values in her.

Sadly, the insulation of Yeardley's early years shattered while she was still a budding high school student. Her father,

John, with whom she had played lacrosse since she was five, died of prostate cancer three days after Christmas in 2003—Yeardley's sophomore year—in a loss that would have derailed many bright young lives. Yeardley was devastated, but her friends and family told reporters that she showed strength and grace beyond her years. She and her sister bonded, their mother told *People* magazine.

"Rather than giving in to grief, they vowed to stick together and make their father proud," Sharon told writer Jill Smolowe.

In another account, Molly Ford, a childhood friend, said Yeardley's strength had been inspiring: "She didn't fold when that happened. She was strong to her family and everyone else around her."

Added Casey Donohoe: "She handled everything so graciously and was so strong throughout."

John T. Love's obituary in the Baltimore Sun was simple, direct: "Beloved husband of Sharon Donnelly Love; dear father of Alexis D. and Yeardley R. Love." His funeral mass was held at Immaculate Conception Church in Towson; interment at Druid Ridge Cemetery.

Yeardley, then fifteen, attended the funeral wearing her Notre Dame uniform and black-and-white saddle shoes. She placed a lacrosse ball in his casket.

After her father's death, Yeardley didn't slow down, and her interest in lacrosse seemed to heighten. It's a fast-paced sport with a simple goal: to fling a ball into your opponent's net. Only the goalie can touch the ball; the rest of the players have to manipulate it using the "crosse," a stick with a net attached to its end. Growing up in Cockeysville, where even the local dollar store stocked miniature lacrosse sets, helped fuel Yeardley's passion. On the field, she was petite but fierce, manipulating the lacrosse stick with increasing ease as the years passed. She was a swift defender, making up for being shorter than some teammates with her absolute diligence. In 2004, she earned notice in the *Towson Times,* her local paper, as having netted the only goal in a game against Garrison Forest. In 2006, her senior year, Coach Bartel said that Yeardley was one in a hardworking team. "This is a good group," she said. "We have a lot of team players and hard workers." But Yeardley stood out; that year, she went All-County. After high school, she was determined to play at UVA, not only her father's would-be alma mater, but also the school at which her uncle had been an All-American lacrosse star years earlier. An archive clip from a March 2009 interview with Virginiasports.com revealed just how excited Yeardley had been to finally go to UVA; she called it a "dream come true."

"I had wanted to play lacrosse at Virginia since I was little," she told a reporter at the Web site. She praised Coach Bartel, saying she "always pushed me to work harder. She not only prepared me to play at the college level, but she taught me important life lessons. She always put a strong focus on good sportsmanship and working together as a team."

Many young people with Yeardley's popularity, talent, and looks would have an attitude to match. But she didn't, teammate Casey Donohoe told *People*. Before lacrosse games, Yeardley gave Donohoe gifts—Gatorade sometimes, a favorite snack others. The gift was anonymous, the teammate told the magazine.

"I didn't know till the end of the year it was Yeardley. She was just so thoughtful," she said. "You would think she would be cocky and conceited, but that couldn't be further from the truth. She was humble about everything."

As a senior, Yeardley was recruited by the one school on her radar. When UVA coach Julie Myers offered her a spot on the renowned team, Yeardley beamed, she told a team publication shortly before her death. "That definitely topped the happiest and proudest moment that I will probably ever experience," she said.

Yeardley spent countless hours practicing and playing at UVA's Klöckner Stadium, where soccer dominates in the fall and lacrosse in the spring. The stadium, built in 1992 for more than $3 million, seemed a good luck charm for its athletes. The men's soccer team won national championships there, as did both the men and women's lacrosse teams. By Yeardley's senior year, she lived less than one and a half miles from Klöckner, an easy walk down University Avenue and Emmet Street. Because of its proximity to both the stadium and area bars, the Corner, as locals call the area where Yeardley lived, was a popular spot for both lacrosse and soccer players to call home. Given the tight-knit nature of her lacrosse community, it was no surprise that Yeardley began dating a fellow player about a year into her college career. On the surface, the two made sense, with their overlapping interests and similar backgrounds. They were regularly spotted hanging out with other players at area bars—the Boylan Heights bar in particular, which was a quick walk from each of their senior-year apartments.

As much as Yeardley loved her social college life, she was focused on the future. Poised to major in government and minor in Spanish, she had spent the summer before her senior year interning at a public relations and marketing firm in New York City, and she had a job lined up for after her May graduation—a milestone that, it turned out, she would never reach.

As medics carried Yeardley's lifeless body from her apartment, friends doubled over in tears on the front lawn. One young woman wailed on her cell phone, waking a neighbor with her cries. No one working the police beat has failed to encounter the tale of a boyfriend with a temper, the girl in danger, the realization setting in far too late that a powder keg had long ago been ignited. Still, this case was different than most. Yeardley seemed to have everything, and more than that, she seemed poised to give back to the world. On the field, she was the type to volunteer for extra drills, playing defense against attackers. Off the field, she was determined but gracious, affluent but humble. She was the daughter, the sister, and the friend that people either wanted to have or wanted to be. Now, friends who had been preparing for the rush of finals and the relief of graduation found themselves bracing for an unfathomable funeral instead.

Amy Appelt, a former lacrosse All-America at UVA who graduated in 2005 and founded "onenine lacrosse" to train players, told *Sports Illustrated*'s SI.com that she had coached Yeardley for a season and knew her well.

"You hear that God has a plan for everyone," she mused, "but maybe He messed up this one time."

Chapter 4

As news of Yeardley's death swiftly spread across the campus, the media were given a photograph of the young woman that seemed to symbolize promise cut short. Yeardley looked as all-American as they come, her smile beaming and her face bearing a subtle tan. Blue eyes stared out from an impossibly vibrant face as she stood before a bluish backdrop and wore her lacrosse warm-up jacket. The photo had been taken by the university for the team roster. Yeardley looked perfect. By the time her identity was confirmed, media had already learned and reported the name of the ex-boyfriend fingered in her death. Now, as newspapers released his jailhouse mug shot, the juxtaposition was striking. She appeared on the cusp of greatness; he looked like a defeated criminal.

The photos underlined a heartbreaking reality: Yeardley's life was too soon snuffed out. George's, too, had been full of promise, and now it lay in ruins. They had both been set to graduate the following month. Their dreams crumbled in one fateful night.

As the media coverage continued, it became clear that if Yeardley was the story's damsel, Huguely (pronounced Hueglee) was most certainly its demon. With his pleasant looks and affluent upbringing, he was instantly characterized in media reports as the quintessential spoiled brat who couldn't handle a pretty girl's rejection. Like Yeardley, he grew up in comfort, the grandson of a previous George Huguely who co-founded a prominent building supply company in 1912 that helped build Washington, D.C. George Huguely V was born September 17, 1987, to George Huguely IV and Marta Murphy. His father was a real estate mogul; his mother, a model. The couple divorced in 1998, and George V stayed with his mother, growing up in D.C. suburb Chevy Chase, Maryland (no connection to the actor). His home on Park View Road was visibly more modest than Yeardley's, but his father also owned property on the Outer Banks of North Carolina, as well as an estate reported to be worth between $1 million and $2 million in Palm Beach County, Florida.

George finished the eighth grade at Mater Dei School in Bethesda, Maryland, a Catholic elementary school for boys from first through eighth grades. The school uniform: tan khakis, light blue button-down shirt, school tie, and tan buck shoes or rubber-soled topsiders. "Navy blue sweaters are permitted," according to Mater Dei's Web site. Catholic students historically have been given a break on tuition. The 2010–2011 academic years cost $10,225 for Catholic students, and $11,450 for non-Catholics.

Though George and Yeardley didn't meet until college, their lives until that point were strikingly similar. Both spent high school in private, high-priced institutions. Both were attractive and athletic. Both were considered high spirited and upbeat with bright futures. After eighth grade, George matriculated at Landon School, also in Bethesda, a $29,000-a-year, boys-only school for grades three through twelve. Parents scouting there are assured that their sons will get the best in academics, arts, athletics and character education. Landon, founded in 1929, is non-sectarian and initially employed many retired military men who aimed to instill ethics as well as education in the young boys who enrolled. In the 1960s, Landon students wrote an honor code to guide their actions. Forty-two years later, the school added a civility code. In 2008, after the arrests of some Landon alumni had threatened to tarnish the school's good name, the school formally adopted a code of character that encompassed both the previous codes. The emphasis was on honesty and respect. Instilled in the boys were the following sayings: "I will not lie, cheat, or steal, or tolerate those who do," and "I will treat all people with respect, civility and dignity. I will also respect my school, my surroundings and myself."

As one Landon student declared in a 2010 promotional video online, the boys enrolled at Landon have a different relationship than students in traditional high schools.

"You see the same kids in your English class, and they're in your choir class, then they're on your football team. They're on everything with you," the young man said. "They kind of just become your brothers. It's a different relationship that you have with your friends here."

That comes with the territory in single-sex schools. In a posting called "Why a Boys' School," Landon officials argue that in single-sex environments, boys have "the freedom to thrive academically and socially."

The school isn't alone in its assertions. Same-sex institutions have long argued that boys and girls learn differently from each other, and that teachers are able to cater better to those differences when the students are separated. Landon aimed to tailor its curriculum to its boys' needs based on their ever-changing stages of intellectual, social, emotional and physical development.

Teachers "tap into a boy's natural exuberance," the school claims, and encourage boys to form teams to learn cooperatively.

Proponents of same-sex schools also say that separating males from females alleviates some of the sexual tension and classroom distractions that run rampant in coed institutions. On its Web site, Landon assures parents that "scientific research" has confirmed what Landon has always known: "In a single-sex environment, boys have the freedom to thrive academically and socially."

The research is more divided than that. Some studies suggest that separating the sexes neither improves self-esteem or educational achievement. But Landon disagrees, and it insists on another benefit: family-like bonds among its students.

"Without the distraction of co-ed interactions, boys develop deep and supportive friendships with their peers," according to the school. Some boys stay lifelong friends.

George was a big gun at Landon, named starting quarterback in his senior year and leading Landon to a conference title. And he earned a reputation as a light-hearted jokester. Once he sneaked his coach Rob Bordley's car keys from an office, then drove up to the coach and chatted with him while sitting in the driver's seat until it dawned on Bordley what had happened, a prank immortalized in a 2006 article in the *Washington Post*. The story also highlighted a ballsy bet George had once made with an assistant coach: George would pick off a pass in exchange for a kiss from the coach's fiancée. As he promised, George made the play—then asked for the woman's number.

"He's always in an upbeat mood," Bordley told the *Post* at the time. "Nothing really fazes him. I've asked my assistant coaches if they've ever seen him rattled and they said no. He's just unflappable."

Keeping with Landon's teachings on giving back to the community, Huguely also joined Operation Smile, a children's charity organization founded in 1982 that aims to unite medical professionals with children born with facial deformities such as cleft lip and cleft palate. The effects of the deformities are more than aesthetic. Children are "often unable to eat, speak, socialize or smile," according to the organization's Web site. Huguely was vice president of a student branch of the organization.

Landon had seen its share of controversy, however, specifically with members of its lacrosse team. In 2006, a Landon graduate was one of three Duke University players falsely accused by a dancer of sexually assaulting her at a team party. Though the players were cleared, Bordley told the *Post* that in the scandal's aftermath, he repeatedly warned his team about the risks of alcohol abuse. Huguely was a member of the Landon team at the time.

* * *

George's star dimmed slightly at UVA, mainly because competition was fierce and he lacked the discipline of some of his teammates. As the *Post* reported, he gained weight, prompting teammates to brand him "Fuguely"—"a mashup of his name and a common vulgarity," according to the *Post*. Most of the male players were muscular and lean, conditioned through rigorous exercise to be both fast and long-winded on the field.

"You'd see him walk in . . . with other lacrosse players and you'd think, 'Oh, there goes a bunch of lacrosse players and some other guy,'" a bartender told the newspaper. "He just seemed like kind of an overgrown big kid."

As George would tell police after waiving his Miranda rights, he and Yeardley had been dating on and off for a few years. It wasn't unusual for players from the men's team to date players from the women's team. Their social circles overlapped anyway, as did their schedules. They often hung out together and drank at the same bars. Drinking, in fact, was a common pastime for many players, despite high-profile and longstanding efforts by the men's team to curtail it. In 1999, Coach Dom Starsia adopted a rule that allowed players to drink just one night a week—usually Saturdays. Players who broke the rule were to be suspended indefinitely; players who broke it again were to be dismissed entirely.

"Alcohol and lacrosse have gone hand-in-hand since my days at Brown in the 1970s," Starsia told the *Washington Post* at the time. "Whether it is post-game celebrations or just in general, there was something about the sport and alcohol, and Virginia was no different. I always thought alcohol was an issue here, and it is something we talked about before the season began."

While many applauded Starsia's efforts, others criticized the one-day-a-week green light as a permission slip to binge drink. Some said the young adults would just push their drinking habits underground, making them even harder to rein in if things got excessive. In the days after Yeardley's death, the *Washington Post* reported that eight of the forty-one lacrosse players on the UVA men's team had been charged with alcohol-related offenses during their college careers. The charges included underage alcohol possession, using a fake ID, and driving under the influence. Six of the eight were convicted; two were found not guilty.

Among the guilty, the newspaper uncovered, was George Huguely.

On November 14, 2008, Huguely had been visiting friends at a fraternity house at Lexington, Virginia's Washington and Lee University, about seventy miles from his Charlottesville apartment, when police got a nine-one-one call. Policewoman R. L. Moss and a sergeant responded and found Huguely stumbling into traffic. Moss approached the brawny athlete and asked his name.

"George," he replied.

He wasn't a student in Lexington, he told the officer. The then-twenty-one-year-old was clearly intoxicated. Moss told him she would need to place him under arrest for public drunkenness and asked if his friends at the fraternity could pick him up that night to keep him from having to sleep in a jail cell.

At that point, he became belligerent, Moss later recalled. "He became more aggressive, more physical toward me," she told reporters. He began spewing racist and sexist slurs.

"I told him to stop resisting, that he needed to comply with my orders, that he was only making matters worse," she said.

He didn't. The two tussled, and Moss said she had no choice but to zap Huguely with a Taser. The electrical current caused George to lose control of his muscles, and he went limp long enough for Moss to slap handcuffs on him—but, as the effects of the Taser waned even slightly, he reignited the fight.

"He said, 'I'll kill you. I'll kill all of y'all. I'm not going to jail,'" Moss told reporters. "He was by far the most rude, most hateful, and most combative college kid I ever dealt with."

In another interview, she said: "Am I surprised that he

was involved in another incident involving physical violence? No. Am I surprised to this extent? Yes."

Lexington Police Chief Al Thomas told reporters that Huguely was beyond combative: "He was verbally abusive; he began shouting obscenities; he would not cooperate." At a court hearing a few weeks later, Huguely said he had been so intoxicated the night of his arrest that he couldn't remember any of it—not even being dropped by a stun gun. He was charged with public intoxication, resisting arrest, and public swearing, according to a courthouse clerk.

Ross Haine, his lawyer, was hired by Huguely's family soon after the arrest. The George he met was affable and kind, completely contrary to the vulgarity-spewing drunken mess who had tangled with an officer.

"He did not remember what he did," Haine later recalled. "He was intoxicated to the point where he had some vague memories of what had happened, but he didn't remember the particulars."

Haine, who has worked as an attorney for twenty-three years—the past twenty in Lexington—had seen his share of drunken college-age antics. Huguely's case stood out. The good-looking young man was a star athlete on a lacrosse scholarship, Haine said, and his parents were clearly concerned about him.

"He was a normal college student who had a lot going for him," Haine said. "Really, I liked him."

At the time, both the defense and prosecutor were more concerned about Huguely's vile language than his tussle with Moss, Haine recalled. When the lawyer heard the racist and sexist name-calling Huguely had hurled at Moss, he realized that the young man became a completely different person when he drank. In hopes of shocking Huguely with his own language, Haine set up a meeting with the officer, George, and his parents so that Moss could repeat the words he'd used with her the night of his arrest. Haine hoped George's reaction to the filth he had spewed would both teach him a lesson and mitigate the charges against him. He wanted George's parents to hear as well. They were ~~obviously involved in their~~ son's life, and concerned enough to retain a lawyer and stand by his side during the court hearing.

As George listened to the vitriol, he looked embarrassed and ashamed.

"I'm so sorry, I can't believe I said that," he repeated again and again.

"He never said, 'I didn't say that,'" Haine recalled. "My goal in representing him was to keep him out of jail. I wanted the officer to see how he wasn't bullshitting, that he was sincere. I hoped it would mitigate the offense; I think it did."

Huguely's parents seemed equally shocked by the words their son had unleashed on the officer, Haine said. All of their reactions seemed genuine and sincere.

"It was clear to me he had a drinking problem," Haine said. "He could not believe he had done all that. I've only seen him sober, so what I was hearing about him did not match the person I was talking to. His actions when he was intoxicated were so far away from the person I knew, so completely out of line with his character, it just did not seem to match."

Haine stood alongside his client as George pleaded guilty to resisting arrest and public intoxication and was sentenced to sixty days in jail and ordered to pay $100 in fines. But, as he had hoped, Haine succeeded in keeping Huguely from behind bars: The sentence was suspended, meaning that if George behaved and stayed out of legal trouble, he wouldn't have to serve the jail sentence. As part of the arrangement, Huguely was ordered to perform fifty hours of community service, which he did with the Blue Ridge Area Food Bank in Charlottesville. He was also ordered to attend a twenty-hour substance-abuse assessment program. He successfully completed both, according to court records.

UVA athletes were supposed to report any legal run-ins to the university. George might not have. Athletic Director Craig Littlepage, when pressed by reporters on this point, conceded it was possible Huguely had alerted a coach or told his teammates, but if he had, the information hadn't been passed along to administrators as required. The oversight became another item in the growing list of "what-ifs."

Journalists' uncovering of Huguely's Lexington run-in caught Police Chief Timothy Longo completely off-guard. He said Charlottesville officers had done background checks locally to investigate Huguely's legal history but came up empty. He only learned of the epithet-spewing arrest from the media reports, he told the New York *Daily News*.

Within hours of the arrest in Yeardley's death, Haine learned that a UVA lacrosse player had been identified as her killer. Seventy miles isn't a long way for such news to travel, plus Haine's wife worked in the public defender's office in Charlottesville. It flickered across his mind that he had recently defended a UVA lacrosse player, but he never imagined that the sociable young man he had represented might be the same one now accused of murder.

It wasn't until the next morning, when his phone blew up with calls from reporters across the country, that Haine learned that the young man he represented had gotten into trouble again.

"He's an entirely different person when he's drunk," Haine later said. "I've seen cases like that before, but obviously never that extreme. He's just a different person."

That day, too, reporters dug up details of another police encounter in Florida that occurred just a month after the Lexington hubbub. According to published reports, on December 29, 2008, George and some family members had been aboard the family's forty-foot yacht, named *The Reel Deal*, about a quarter-mile offshore from the glamorous Ritz-Carlton. George V announced that he wanted to go back to the beach. His father refused, saying he would take him home, but not to the beach. Furious, the younger Huguely jumped into the Atlantic Ocean and attempted to begin the quarter-mile swim back to shore. His father radioed for help, and a passing boater safely pulled his son from the salty water. Though the incident was called in as a domestic-abuse complaint, no arrests were made. Sheriff's Deputies for Palm Beach County reported that there were no blows thrown, but "lots of yelling

and screaming." Because police found no evidence of violence, the incident was dismissed as a family spat aggravated
by the young man's temper tantrum.

University officials said they knew nothing of that 2008
incident, either, though George wouldn't have technically
been required to report it because no one was charged. Still,
if the university had been properly notified about the Lexington arrest, and if they had learned of Huguely's tantrum
just a month later, someone within the university might have
seen fit to evaluate him more thoroughly. Instead, the administration apparently remained in the dark, and George's
troubling behavior yet again slid under the radar.

And the allegations kept coming. Another report surfaced that Huguely had punched a sleeping teammate whom
he learned had walked Yeardley home—possibly even kissing her—in February 2009. A bartender who later heard
Huguely describe the assault told the *Post* it was "like some
cheesy action movie, where he stood above the guy while he
was sleeping and said, 'Sweet dreams, punk,' and then just
punched him in the face."

University officials did know about that incident, they
acknowledged to reporters. They said Huguely and his
teammate-turned-punching-bag had approached Coach
Starsia to talk about their scuffle, apparently in an effort to
head off any rumors that might reach the coach first. "They
said they wanted him to be aware of it, but that they had
worked things out and everything was OK between them,"
according to a UVA statement released in the aftermath of
Yeardley's death. Starsia asked Huguely and the other student
if they wanted to talk about it further. Both men passed.
"They told him that they shared the blame for what had happened and had apologized to one another," the university's
statement said.

The final red-flags-in-hindsight that journalists uncovered
were never reported to either university officials or the police. In February 2010, less than three months before Yeardley's death, Huguely reportedly jumped on her and began to
choke her at a party filled with friends. Things got so heated

that one former and two current University of North Carolina lacrosse players intervened to pull George off of her. Yeardley was so upset that one of the UNC players drove her home to Cockeysville to give her time away from George. A former Virginia student said that Huguely was drunk and couldn't remember the attack the next day. That led to Yeardley and George's final breakup, friends told reporters.

"He was really messed up and punched a window of a car on the way over to her apartment" the night of the fight at UNC, the friend told reporters on condition of anonymity.

Huguely tried to get her back, another friend said, but Yeardley was determined to move on.

The incident raised questions: Assuming the university was being forthcoming in denying knowledge of the attack, why hadn't fellow lacrosse players reported the incident? Why hadn't Yeardley reported it herself? Surely, if UVA administrators had learned of a physical attack between one lacrosse player and another—especially one between a dating couple—there would have been repercussions. With the lacrosse culture being so incredibly close-knit, onlookers surmised that the players perhaps didn't want to ruin George's reputation over what they assumed was a one-night, drunken lapse of judgment.

Then, the Tuesday before her death, as Yeardley visited Huguely at his apartment, she confronted him about rumors he had been seeing other girls—specifically two high school lacrosse recruits. Yeardley lost her temper and hit him with her purse, one of her sorority sisters later testified. The handbag flew open and its contents spilled out. Yeardley and Elizabeth McLean, whose boyfriend, Kevin Carroll, lived with Huguely, hurriedly gathered the scattered belongings. McLean later testified that she walked Yeardley home that night "because she was upset." But in Yeardley's haste, she had left her camera and her cell phone, and later asked a friend to go back to Huguely's apartment to retrieve them. The friend found the camera, according to police reports, but she couldn't find the cell phone. Yeardley tried to orchestrate its return several times via email, friends said.

The allegations that surfaced baffled people who knew
Huguely growing up in tony Chevy Chase. Peter Preston told
reporters that his children grew up playing with the Huguelys.
"Georgie," as he knew Huguely, was "just a wonderful, charming, polite young man. . . . George is not a monster."

George's mother, Marta Murphy, was clearly at a loss.
An attractive blond with chin-length hair, she had confidently
stood by her son at his arraignment, clutching her husband's
hand as they quietly passed reporters. Her relationship with
George's father—George IV, who disguised a receding hair-
line with a subtle comb-over—had not always been easy, but
now they found themselves intertwined, having to wade
through legal proceedings as a united front. Neither Murphy
nor Huguely IV spoke with the media at their son's arraignment, but Murphy finally broke her silence when she sent an
anguished e-mail to news media calling Yeardley a "sweet,
wonderful young woman with a limitless future" who had
become a part of her boyfriend's family's lives. According
to friends, Yeardley had spent time chatting with Murphy
during a recent family's day at the university. The two sat
together at a bar and grill and chatted. Huguely stopped by
occasionally, but largely left the women to talk alone.

"I got to know her as George's mom," Murphy wrote in her
e-mail to media. "We also know her mother, Sharon. The pain
she and her family are suffering is something that no family
should have to endure. No parent should have to bury a child
and not a moment goes by when they are not in our thoughts
and our prayers. It has been difficult to remain silent during
this dark, tumultuous time. Along with my family, I am devastated and confused. We are all trying to understand and
cope as best we can. As a mother, I never expected to be in a
situation like this. Though my pain is great, it can never come
close to the anguish felt by the Love family."

Another Huguely family friend told the *Post*, "Every time
I see Yeardley's face on a magazine, I want to die. None of us
can believe this actually happened. It doesn't click. It doesn't
jibe. It doesn't work. The George we knew wasn't capable of

that. There had to be a different George that was inside that head."

But as the details of his stormy temper emerged, it became harder for people following the case to see how Huguely was anything more than a time bomb whose history of violence had been shrugged off because of his wealth. Nationwide, the same question was posed again and again: Just how many people knew Yeardley was in danger?

Police Chief Longo fielded media questions about all the reported scenarios. Some, such as the Lexington run-in with the policewoman, he could confirm, but when it came to the reported incidents involving Yeardley, he simply shook his head.

"We're looking into what, if any, threats were made," he told reporters. "We've heard exactly what the entire community here has been hearing. The difference is that we have to prove it."

That would be an ongoing concern for law enforcement as the case slowly unfolded. Longo didn't say so at the time, but surely he knew as early as May 4 that his city, statistically homicide-free in 2009, would be mired in this new deadly scandal for many months to come.

Chapter 5

Charlottesville, Virginia, is as much Southern charm as it is college town, infused with a humidity-drenched hipness that attracts students worldwide. The city is steeped in history, the former home of founding fathers such as Thomas Jefferson and James Madison, and its origins can be spotted on the facades of its buildings, with sturdy white pillars and sprawling front porches—the trademarks of late-1700s Southern architecture.

Named after the motherland's Queen Charlotte, the settlement was formed within Albemarle County in 1762 along a trade route called Three Notch'd Road that connected Richmond to the Great Valley. Unlike many early towns, it lay slightly inland, away from the estuaries and river runoffs on which plantations of the time relied. Hugged by the Rivanna River, a tributary of the James, Charlottesville grew in a ten-mile chunk just west of the Southwest Mountains. Soon, a courthouse was built on a hillside overlooking Three Notch'd, and businesses began cropping up nearby—taverns, tailors, a gunsmith, and a jeweler. The heart of the town lay not along Charlottesville's main drag, but rather just above it, next to the 1803-built courthouse. But as the early 1800s rolled by, the development began slowly to shift from so-called Court Square back to the trade route. First, there were houses. Next came the businesses. As the decades passed, Three Notch'd Road morphed into present-day Main Street.

Thomas Jefferson, the colonial revolutionary and former United States president who by then was at the end of his accomplished career, saw the town as a perfect spot for higher-minded academics, but he envisioned the University of Virginia as having a separate identity from the rest of Charlottesville. He picked a site atop a small hill about a mile from the town center and, in 1819, founded his Academical Village, as he famously called it. There, daily life was to be infused with shared learning. Faculty would live in upstairs quarters of stately pavilions; downstairs, there would be classrooms. He envisioned ten pavilions, each assigned its own subject and serving as home to the professor who taught it. While other universities placed a chapel at its heart, Jefferson placed a library, one built with a dome reminiscent of Rome's Pantheon, which, according to the university, was symbolic of the enlightened human mind. Jefferson considered true enlightenment so unattainable that he declined to call uppermost class members "seniors." Rather, they were dubbed "fourth years"—a tradition that continues today.

Jefferson envisioned a university that adhered to a student-policed honor system, much like the one he had written in 1779 for his alma mater, the College of William & Mary. The idea was simple: Students agreed to act honorably, promising not to lie, cheat, or steal, or they would be subjected to the harshest of academic sanctions—expulsion. Jefferson believed in self-government, both on campus and off. In fact, one of UVA's main objectives was to produce leaders for a self-governing people.

In March 1825, the university officially welcomed its first batch of students, a class of sixty-eight. The institution was the first nonsectarian university in the country, and the first to allow students to choose elective courses. Jefferson, himself an architect, writer, inventor, and horticulturalist, put his many interests and talents to use by planning the curriculum and recruiting the faculty from all over the world. He designed the Village as a green space hugged by academic and residential buildings with gardens mixed throughout. The Pantheon-inspired Rotunda is regal and elegant, with perfect wood floors and ornate pillars encircling the dome room. As if its appearance weren't quieting enough, those who speak inside are greeted with a stately echo that inspires one to hush in reverence.

Jefferson got to enjoy his creation for a year, regularly hosting events at his Monticello plantation manor, located a few miles from downtown. By the time he died on July 4, 1826—the fiftieth anniversary of the Declaration of Independence signing (and, in a famous coincidence, the same day John Adams, the United States' second president, died)—he had declared the university his greatest achievement. (Monticello, too, still stands as a designated historical site just outside of city limits, and its image has appeared on the back of U.S. nickels since 1938, save for a brief hiatus between 2004 and 2005. Monticello also appeared on the reverse of the long-discontinued two-dollar bill.)

Charlottesville continued expanding, and, in 1850, welcomed the Virginia Central Railroad (first called the Louisa Railroad, and later called Chesapeake and Ohio) as its first railway. Its tracks cut through the south end of town, below Main Street. By decade's end, it connected with the Shenandoah Valley by cutting through the Blue Ridge Mountains. The new line allowed for a boom in shipping as goods and raw materials could more directly reach and pass through Charlottesville. In 1863, with the introduction of the Southern Railroad, the face of the area changed. The crossing railways divided the town into quadrants, with the university in its southwest portion, while the downtown lay northeast.

As shipping expanded, Charlottesville rooted itself as a full-fledged city, holding its first mayoral election in 1854. Its expansion briefly stalled during the Civil War, when many young men were sent into battle. The city itself fared better than many in the conflict, though canal locks were destroyed and buildings burned in Scottsville to its south. The only battle fought in Charlottesville was the Skirmish at Rio Hill, in which Brigadier General George Custer led thousands of

Union solders toward the city on February 26, 1864. It was a decoy, meant to distract Confederate soldiers from separate efforts to free prisoners of war that were being held about seventy miles to the southeast in Richmond. The skirmish did not end well for Custer: He was disoriented by an incidental artillery explosion and chased out of town by opportunistic Confederate troops. Custer got his revenge the next year, when he occupied the town for three days in March. In April 1865, the Army of Northern Virginia surrendered in the Battle of Appomattox Court House, and Charlottesville was spared the blaze that had already engulfed many of its Confederate brothers.

Today, nods to that history still stand. Statues of Generals Robert E. Lee and Stonewall Jackson are displayed in Charlottesville's public squares. Most noticeably, though, are the buildings that remain, the majestic brick-and-plaster structures that whisper reminders of the country's origins, struggles, and potential. James Monroe's Ashlawn-Highland and James Madison's Montpelier continue to draw millions of tourists each year.

But the city offers more than history lessons. In 2004, Charlottesville was ranked the best place to live in the United States by *Cities Ranked and Rated*, a book by Bert Sperling and Peter Sander. The authors weighed cost of living, climate, and quality of life. Similar honors have been bestowed by other publications for decades: *Kiplinger's Personal Finance Magazine* ranked it the fourth-best place to live in the country in 2009; the same year, *Forbes Magazine* declared it the eleventh-best town to find a job; Farmers Insurance has rated it in the top twenty safest mid-sized cities in the United States; even the AARP ranked it one of the top ten healthiest places to retire in 2008. As of 2007, the city had about 41,000 residents, according to a census update. Statistically, Charlottesville is a safe place to live. From 2007–2009, fewer than one hundred aggravated assaults were reported to the Federal Bureau of Investigation, which releases annual statistics on cities nationwide. In 2009, property crimes had crept slightly higher than the year before (from twenty-three to thirty-five), and burglaries rose from seventy-nine to eighty-eight, but the increases were modest. The city's biggest problem historically has been rape: In 2009, 247 were reported. Murders and manslaughter are exceptionally rare, with fewer than a handful a year. None reported in 2009.

Though the university continues to be a huge employer and revenue stream, the area is also drawing attention for its respectable wine industry. The Monticello Wine Trail declares itself the "birthplace of American wine," and the area's nearly yearlong humidity typically helps lock grape-pleasing moisture in the soil.

Incoming University of Virginia freshmen are routinely reminded of the university's history and prestige. It's no small feat to be accepted at UVA, especially for students coming from out-of-state high schools. In recent years, the college has accepted between twenty and twenty-five percent of its out-of-state applicants (compared to more than a forty percent acceptance rate for Virginia residents). In analyzing its incoming class of 2014, university officials said that the "middle 50 percent scored between 1300 and a 1480 on the reading and math portions of the SAT," according to the *Cavalier Daily*. "The majority of these students—93.8 percent—were also in the top 10 percent of their high school classes."

And, predictably, the academics are tough to beat: *U.S. News & World Report* ranked UVA second in "best public universities" in 2011 (tied with UCLA), and it's tied for twenty-fifth when looking at both public and private national universities. Its McIntire School of Commerce is ranked fifth in the nation; its law school, tenth; and its English department, tenth. The University of Virginia Medical Center is one of fifteen major teaching hospitals ranked in the nation's top one hundred, according to Thomson Reuters' "100 Top Hospitals: National Benchmarks" study.

In short, UVA students are expected to be among the best in the country—and they know it.

Once settled in to campus life, students ready to shed their high school personas seem to gravitate toward the city's downtown mall, a quaint pedestrian-only stretch dotted with more than 120 shops and thirty restaurants, based on a city-released count. Many eateries offer outdoor seating, making the mall both people- and pet-friendly. The stretch even has a movie theater and pavilion for outdoor concerts from spring to fall.

Yeardley had been eyeing the University of Virginia since childhood. It was the only college in her sights, and its down-home appeal differed from her small-town upbringing in the best possible ways. Teenagers in Cockeysville largely relied on the nearby Hunt Valley Towne Centre for outings. The outdoor mall boasted a slew of higher-end restaurants, a bookstore, a movie theater and a sporting goods store with a well-stocked lacrosse section. At night, the area teemed with teens—until, that is, curfew set in and youngsters were required an adult escort. In Charlottesville, the fun was spread out citywide. From her 14th Street apartment smack dab in The Corner—a seven-block cluster of restaurants, university bookstores, and bars—Yeardley could walk to grab a burger from Mellow Mushroom, some Vietnamese from Lemongrass, or a beer from Boylan Heights. Boylan Heights boasts burger fare with a twist, and is a popular place for students—athletes especially—to kick back with a beer or gather for post-class revelry.

Chaney Kent, who owned the Corner Market on University Avenue, told a reporter that Yeardley stopped by a few times each week to buy a twelve-ounce can of Diet Coke. The store was a block and a half from her apartment.

"She couldn't be nicer, more pleasant, outgoing," Kent recalled. "When a girl has a name like 'Love,' you don't forget."

George Huguely had also set his sights on Virginia. Considered one of Landon's premiere lacrosse players, he was a natural fit there, both aggressive and agile. His roots in Chevy Chase no doubt made his transition to Charlottesville different than Yeardley's. His town was more consolidated, with a downtown dotted by quirky venues such as American City Diner, a twenty-four-hour soda fountain–style joint that aired nightly film classics like *Niagara* and *Dr. Strangelove*. Huguely's hometown felt upscale but down-to-earth, as though its inhabitants were from older money that they enjoyed spending on good times. Certainly Chevy Chase was more similar to Charlottesville than Cockeysville; Chevy Chase was a mix of laid-back mom-and-pop stores that made college shopping so eclectic. Cockeysville, on the other hand, relied largely on upscale chain outlets.

Despite differences in their upbringings, on paper, Yeardley and George seemed far more alike than not. As they each wrapped up careers at single-sex private high schools, they continued their immersion in lacrosse culture—one inherently married to privilege and pedigree. The sport, of Native American origin, is today an expensive one to play. Though the sport is similar in rules to soccer, players must invest in far more than just cleats and a ball. A typical lacrosse setup calls for a stick (both shaft and head), shoulder pads, rib pads, arm guards, slash guards, gloves, mouth guard, and either eye protection or full-on helmet. Depending on the make and style, each component could easily cost upward of $200. After the gear, there is the traveling. Love and Huguely routinely traveled throughout high school and college, both to play and to watch other teams in action.

The sport required vigorous training from both. Though lacrosse isn't known as one of the country's most popular sports, it's definitely gaining ground, and lacrosse aficionados say its players must possess strength, power, speed, agility, and endurance in spades. Scientific studies indicate that the average lacrosse player must have the aerobic capacities of basketball and football players matched with hefty muscle mass—high bodyweight but low body fat—to endure aggressive physical contact. Thus, a lacrosse player might appear in size similar to a hockey or football player, but his body fat is typically lower.

When training, most lacrosse players focus on developing explosive power and endurance. Training calls for lifting lower-weight loads with more repetitions and faster movements. Unlike with other strength training, explosive power training doesn't require athletes to perform to exhaustion, but rather a typical power session would call for an athlete to lift up to forty percent of his lifting capacity, then stop his repetitions shy of exhaustion. Players are told to rest between two and five minutes between sets, with the goal of performing between three and five sets per session. Many UVA athletes hit the gym up to five times a week.

Speed and agility drills are crucial in lacrosse training as well. For speed, athletes are encouraged to work on "rolling starts," or sprints that begin as jogs, then pick up the pace about halfway through the drill. These are done on flat land, as well as up- and downhill to really push the athlete's endurance. In agility drills, players are sometimes told to weave between a series of cones, turn around, then sprint back. The exercise mirrors the dodging and darting players have to do while passing their competitors on the field in pursuit of the ball.

Because lacrosse calls for such sudden bursts of speed and power, players' muscles are flooded with lactic acid. Lactate tolerance training helps athletes tolerate higher lactate levels, allowing them to recover more quickly from those successive bursts. Shuttle runs—where an athlete springs about ten yards, then sharply turns and springs back—are typical for such training. Athletes typically rest for just thirty seconds between sprints, then cool down with a two-minute walk after wrapping up several sets.

But lacrosse—nicknamed lax—is set apart from other sports by more than how its athletes work up their sweat. It's a complicated intersection of privilege, heritage, and pride.

Journalist Jamie Stiehm for years lived among lacrosse lovers and wrote about the "close-knit, privileged lacrosse culture" in a piece published the week Yeardley died.

"As a former reporter at the Baltimore *Sun* who lived near a lacrosse field and museum, I am familiar with the intense devotion to this sport," she wrote. "Art, books, the theater: All are pretty much dead between March and May.

Believe me when I tell you that in these circles, lacrosse is very nearly the only thing—you go to a game every weekend, home or away, including some far-off place like Providence or Ithaca."

Parents are as immersed in the youth lacrosse scene as the children. Players with natural ability become town heroes. Their names are spread from one lacrosse hotbed to the next. They're scouted as youths by college coaches.

"In college lax, the spring [schedule] becomes the main event of the season, with parents travelling to home and away games, having picnics and tailgate parties—reinforcing the sense that there is nothing more important going on than lacrosse in their lives," Stiehm said in an interview.

"It's a very old-moneyed culture. It was for men for decades, and then girls got into the game . . . It almost by definition excludes people who don't have the means or the money to send their kids to private clubs or buy the expensive equipment. Usually it's a private school thing. It has gates all around it."

Stiehm, who worked for the *Sun* for ten years, mostly covering city news and general-assignment stories, found herself invested in the sport on April 18, 1998, when she was sent to the Brooklandville home of a nineteen-year-old high school lacrosse player who had committed suicide the previous night.

Alexander "Alec" Schweizer was an honor student and star player at St. Paul's School. As starting goalie on the school's team, he had been recruited to attend Syracuse University in New York. Newspapers typically don't cover suicides, but Schweizer's was a "society death," Stiehm recalled. When she arrived at his upscale home, some 300 people had gathered in mourning. They talked openly about the young man's aspirations and talents, and the *Sun* ran Stiehm's piece in its Sunday edition.

More than a decade later, as Stiehm learned of Yeardley Love's death, some of the lessons she had gleaned in her temporary immersion in the lacrosse culture came rushing back. The column she wrote for *Politics Daily* was starkly titled: "Yeardley Love Slaying: Is Lacrosse's Close Culture Complicit?" Stiehm, now a journalist in Washington D.C., offered a resounding "yes" as the answer.

"This young woman was clearly being tormented, harassed, and abused, but because he belonged to a club that protects their own, she was ultimately a victim of that," Stiehm later said. "They let her die in plain view. They ignored what was in front of them. And she didn't bring it out into the open."

As she wrote in her column: "If the entire lacrosse culture around Love had activated to protect her from a threat of violence, even if it came from someone from posh Chevy Chase, then she would be alive today."

The piece outraged some readers, who sent Stiehm angry e-mails calling her a terrible person who, as an outsider, had no right to opine about the inner workings of lacrosse.

"Some of the comments were screams of pain," Stiehm later said. "It was fury, but a little bit of guilt was at play, too."

For a lacrosse-loving college student, the University of Virginia had natural appeal. The Virginia Cavaliers, also called the Wahoos or 'Hoos for short, had won six national lacrosse titles for men and three for women. In 2006, the year Yeardley and George graduated high school and headed for Charlottesville, the men's team won its fourth NCAA Men's Lacrosse Championship, defeating the University of Massachusetts in the title game. The record audience of nearly 50,000 made it the first lacrosse crowd to surpass the attendance of the men's Final Four basketball championship. The Cavaliers were on fire, finishing the season with a perfect 17–0 record. Huguely, that year an All-American player, was expected to be a valuable midfielder, both muscular and capable of running the full length of the field many times per game. The midfielder's job is strategic at its core.

Yeardley was ecstatic when she learned she was accepted to her uncle's alma mater, her neighbors told reporters. In the fall of 2006, she packed up her belongings and drove the mountainous 172 miles to her new home—ready for her life to begin among the dogwoods and white oaks that canopied the campus. But while she was perhaps exactly the type of well-rounded and eager-to-learn student Jefferson had envisioned, surely her fate was not one he would have wished for in his academic Xanadu.

Chapter 6

The reputation Yeardley had earned in high school as bright eyed and big hearted only grew as she began college life. She was known for being quiet in big groups but lively in smaller ones, as well as for her contagious smile and quick laugh. Like about one third of the university's undergraduate females, she opted to join a sorority. Her pick was Kappa Alpha Theta, founded in 1870 as the first Greek-letter fraternity for women. Its vision statement emphasizes its core purposes—to support its members to learn and excel—while its core values are personal excellence and the development of friendship and sisterhood. The Delta Chi chapter at the University of Virginia boasts a slideshow of pictures of young, attractive girls smiling and goofing for the camera. Every year, the chapter holds a pancake breakfast to benefit the Court Appointed Special Advocate Association, or CASA, an advocacy group for abused and neglected children. For Yeardley, the sorority environment wouldn't have differed much from her experience with lacrosse: Both were close-knit and insulated. Those accepted were lifelong sisters—but acceptance was the key.

Maggie Thompson, in signing an online remembrance for Yeardley, said her husband, Nevada, was the cook for the sorority and became friends with Yeardley "during the year

she lived at the house." ~~Jayne Donohoe, Casey Donohoe's~~
mother, said in the same online remembrance that Yeardley
shined in high school and blossomed at UVA.

Courtney Schaefer, the sorority's president in Yeardley's
last year, declined to describe sorority life to reporters, saying that her bylaws and pledges forbade such discussion. But
one long-graduated member, who had belonged to the Duke
University chapter, said that much about the Kappa Alpha
Theta hasn't changed over the years. They're expected to have
good grades, they tend to be pretty, and they have a secret
handshake. (When one outsider posted a question in 2008
on an online blog hoping to learn the secret handshake, she
got an icy response: "You find the answer . . . once you become a member of the sorority.")

Greek life at UVA, like on any campus, is viewed with
nausea by some, reverence by others. In one online student
review, a UVA student acknowledged that "Greek life dominates the social scene . . . Many are bitter about this and
find it superficial, costly, obnoxious and over-prevalent. Those
involved in Greek life, however, love the people they have
met and the relationships they have formed." Outsiders find
the exclusivity and secrecy of it all frustrating, the reviewer
acknowledged.

This much is known: Yeardley found in her sorority a
group of friends whom she considered family. As a Kappa
Alpha Theta (KAO) member, Yeardley's circles would have
overlapped with other sororities as well as the more than
thirty fraternities on campus. The Greek events abounded:
formals, semi-formals, frat parties. Between her sorority sisters and her lacrosse teammates, Yeardley never had to be
alone unless she wanted to be.

As the years passed, Yeardley's lacrosse skills continued to
improve. After the first season launched in spring 2007,
Yeardley—proudly wearing her #1 jersey, the same number
she had worn at Notre Dame Prep—nabbed her first collegiate goal in a game against Virginia Tech. She played in
eight games that season, according to her team biography.

The next year, she went up to nine games, and in 2009, she played in sixteen games, starting in nine of them. Her shining moment came in a game against Richmond, when she nailed two goals. In her final year as a fleet-footed defender, she started in fewer games but was on pace to play in more. She'd seen playing time in fifteen games, as a starter in three. On the field, Yeardley was focused and toned, her hair pulled back in a ponytail or braid as she nimbly maneuvered her blue-and-orange lacrosse stick. Even while wearing awkward eye protection and a mouth guard, her pretty features shone through: delicate nose, piercing eyes, fit physique.

Academically, Yeardley zeroed in on political science, declaring government her major. Bill Quandt, a professor in the university's political science department, told the weekly Charlottesville-based newspaper *The Hook* that even in a class of 250, Yeardley stood out.

"She seemed like a very bright, dynamic, energetic young woman," Quandt told the paper of his experience with Yeardley in a Middle Eastern politics course. "She exuded self-confidence."

Meg Heubeck, a university advisor, told the *Today* show that Yeardley was "absolutely the epitome of the University of Virginia student. Thomas Jefferson would be proud of having such a young woman at the University of Virginia studying. She was just lovely in every single way."

Huguely, meanwhile, became an anthropology major and befriended many in Delta Kappa Epsilon, established in 1852 as the University of Virginia's first fraternity. Despite reports to the contrary, Huguely was not a member there, according to fraternity officials. Rather, he was friends with members, some of whom were fellow lacrosse players. On the team, he was regarded as a big, tough player with an excellent field sense, according to the profile compiled on him by the university's athletics department. When he and Yeardley began dating, they seemed a natural fit, orbiting the same social circles and coming from similar backgrounds. They made an enviable couple—both were charming, well-liked, attractive, and talented.

Yeardley was the team's smile, "the player who made everyone feel better," Coach Julie Myers said after her death.

And Yeardley was occasionally a goof, quick to stick out her tongue and contort her face to make her friends laugh.

"As genuine, kind, and gentle as she was, she was also tough as nails on the lacrosse field," Myers later eulogized. "She played with a heart of a lion."

While George was still known as a prankster, the easy-going part of his reputation began to diminish as he was introduced to the heavy-drinking element of college life. Like many college students, Huguely imbibed. But unlike many, he had taken it to such extremes that he got violent and blacked out. The Lexington incident in 2008 that landed him in a jail cell overnight was one example, but friends told reporters that it wasn't an isolated incident. Several media outlets reported that friends, speaking on condition of anonymity, had heard that Yeardley was fed up with her boyfriend's hard-drinking ways, and that she was especially shaken after he attacked her one night but couldn't recall the incident in the morning. It was one of many rumors that Police Chief Longo declined to address.

After Yeardley's death, Huguely's neighbors talked in hushed voices about the couple's drinking. Both were regularly seen with their lacrosse teammates indulging far more often than once a week, as men's coach Starsia had so publicly instructed against.

The lacrosse players were "known for partying," one fourth-year student told *People* magazine. "They have parties three times a week," said another. "The day after the murder, I saw them with a twelve-pack of beer, a cheap one—that's all they ever drank."

The New York *Daily News* quoted unnamed friends as saying Huguely "partied really hard and when he was drunk or fucked up, he could be violent. He would get out of control." He used text messages to obsessively keep tabs on his girlfriend, the sources continued, and on the night of Yeardley's death, he'd been spotted breaking bottles at a party and saying that he was going to go to her apartment to "get her back." Yeardley reportedly had been at Boylan Heights just a short walk from her apartment in an area of town dubbed the Corner. One Boylan employee said that both university lacrosse teams regularly visited the bar, with some members of the men's team stopping by several times a week.

"They usually come in about midnight," Brett Harder told the *C-VILLE Weekly*. "They're usually pretty drunk when they get here because they've been pre-gaming all afternoon. They hang out. Each of them will have a couple rounds, a couple shots. And then they usually roll out about the time we have to throw them out."

Harder said he had seen Huguely and Love at the corner joint many times.

"Occasionally, I'd see them together," he said. "Most of the time, I'd see them with their respective friends."

No one reported having seen any violence between the two, making the descriptions of Yeardley's death all the more unfathomable.

Based on police reports related to Huguely's interview with Officer Lisa Reeves, the violence he unleashed on Yeardley was tremendous. He went to her apartment and found the front door open. He walked inside and discovered the door to Yeardley's bedroom locked, so he kicked it in with his right leg, scraping his calf in a drunken rage. He had simply wanted to talk, he told Reeves, but it's unclear if anything was said before he grabbed Yeardley and shook her as her head repeatedly bashed into a wall. At some point, he noticed blood pouring from her nose, but, he claimed, he had no idea how badly she was hurt. His fury left behind crimson stains. Within hours, those stains would be swabbed by forensic investigators aiming to piece together what led to the young woman's death.

Parts of Huguely's story troubled police from the start. He told Reeves that when he left, Yeardley was clothed. However, her roommates reported that she was lying facedown and topless on her bed when they arrived. Huguely, too, said he visited just to talk, but when he left, he stole Yeardley's computer—which Reeves would soon learn contained Yeardley's response to an angry e-mail Huguely had sent.

The unavoidable imagery of Yeardley's lifeless body, her pretty face battered and bruised, was too much for many to bear.

"Just to hear that anybody in the UVA community could be suspected of that, regardless of the relationship, does give you a sense of unease," Drew Cook, a twenty-two-year-old senior, told the Associated Press. "Everybody's kind of taking a wait-and-see approach."

Yeardley's sorority sisters weren't the only ones hurting. Young men—both in overlapping fraternities, and members of the men's lacrosse team—seemed dumbstruck. They were big men on campus, both literally and figuratively, and yet they had failed to protect someone who needed help. They had lost one friend at the hands of another.

"I'm sure the boys are suffering just as much," friend Amy Appelt told a reporter. "I'm sure they loved Yards just as much as we did."

Chapter 7

After two days of stunned agony on campus, hundreds of University of Virginia students gathered on the Lawn, the heart of Jefferson's Academical Village, in a show of tearful unity Wednesday night. They sat shoulder-to-shoulder, spread out across the pasture-like setting that in just three weeks was to be the site of a joyous graduation—in which Yeardley Love was supposed to get her degree in political science. Young, tear-streaked faces were illuminated by the dull glow of votive candles. The vigil began with an a cappella version of the Pretender's "I'll Stand By You"—setting the we're-in-this-together tone for the evening.

Outside the university's amphitheater, volunteers plucked white ribbons from overflowing baskets and passed them out to people as they arrived. White ribbons have been adopted by domestic violence awareness advocates to put a spotlight on violence against women.

Ashley Twiggs, then a Charlottesville resident and freelance photographer, crouched on the lawn with her camera, scanning the crowd with her lens. She had first heard about the tragedy while getting her car's oil changed Monday. She and a few others were watching television as they waited for their cars to be returned.

~~"I think I live right near there,"~~ one of the nearby men uttered in surprise.

As a photojournalist regularly handed freelance news assignments, Twiggs immediately knew that she'd soon be asked to help cover the slaying. She was right; *C-VILLE Weekly* first asked her to take an image of Huguely's and Yeardley's apartments to show just how close they were. Twiggs at first tried a shot on the same side of the street so that one of the buildings sat in the foreground with the other in the background, but the angle seemed wrong. So she crossed 14th Street Northwest, attached her 17–55mm lens, and shot wide. The image illustrated perfectly that a single building separated the victim from the accused. Even more, it highlighted how carefree things had been just before the death: blue and orange balloons dangled from the FOR RENT signs outside of Yeardley's building.

Now, as mourners gathered at the evening vigil, Twiggs again pressed viewfinder to eye to capture the story. She snapped images of young adults huddled, their faces solemn and drawn, as they sat cross-legged on the grass.

"It was very somber, very heavy," Twiggs later recalled. "There were a lot of people there, and there was, at that point, a sense of just shock. No one really knew what was going on, but what they did know was bad."

Twiggs, who was then pregnant with her first child, had anticipated that hundreds would show up, so she had her husband drop her off and pick her up from the event. It was a wise move; the turnout was even bigger than she had expected. She steadied her camera as the light grew dim to capture the orange glow of the candles. From a distance, she heard someone sobbing. The sound was enveloped by the amphitheater around which the students had gathered, then echoed back into the crowd. Twiggs couldn't pinpoint the source. It sounded as though everyone, and no one, was crying at once.

As the Virginia Belles, the university's female a cappella group, sang the Pretenders' chorus—"I'll stand by you/ won't let nobody hurt you"—the song seemed both appropriate in tone and ironic in message, given that Yeardley had died alone, allegedly at the hands of a man who was supposed to care for her. Twiggs snapped more photographs as the women, all wearing black knee-high dresses, harmonized on stage.

Sarah Elaine Hart, president of the fourth-year class, approached a microphone inside the amphitheater and verbalized the anger that welled in many.

"What was done to Yeardley was the most egregious violation of trust," she said. "This is a community that is founded upon and believes in honor, but there was no honor in the violent attack that took her life."

"The way in which we have lost Yeardley has shaken us," Student Council President Colin Hood said. "We find ourselves with more questions than answers."

Casteen, the university's president, also stepped to the podium. He began to speak somberly, deliberately, his voice strained with emotion. As he looked across the packed lawn, he lamented them having to be there. It was supposed to be a time for renewal and new beginnings, he told the hushed crowd, but instead, the hundreds had gathered to grieve the ending of a life cut far too short—one "full of promise and high prospects," he said. A life that was not unlike any other student's at UVA.

University students had seen Casteen speak before—usually at press conferences about tuition rates and campus expansions. That Casteen seemed different than the one standing before them now. Before he was stoic; now, he seemed doleful.

"I want to talk tonight about Yeardley Love, and I want to talk about you, and about this community, about us. Some of what I have to say is very hard. Bear with me, and listen," he implored.

Little was yet known about Yeardley's death, he said. The prosecutor had charged a classmate with murder, and a defense lawyer had described her death as an accident. But those details were scant and piqued more questions than provided answers. Besides, Casteen said, this evening's gathering wasn't the forum to analyze evidence and weigh guilt. All that would happen in due time in the courtroom.

Instead, he said, this forum was to acknowledge "what

we do know," he said. That was that Yeardley had accomplished a lot in her short life, that she was respected by those around her—classmates, faculty mentors, coaches and sorority sisters, but most of all her family—and that she excelled in everything she strove to do in life. Yeardley did nothing to deserve being attacked and beaten, as the police reported she had been, he said. In fact, no woman—no person—deserved such cruelty.

Casteen paused, then turned his focus to the countless gathered before him.

"My hope for Yeardley, and for you, is that her dying inspires an anger, a sense of outrage . . . and wherever Yeardley's name is recognized that no woman, no person in this place, this community, this state, our nation need either fear for her safety or experience violence for any reason—not because of her sex, not because of her size, not because of an attacker's advantage or arrogance or mindless sense of right to abuse, to harm, perhaps to kill; and then that memory of Yeardley's name, her personal strengths, her successes, her human worth may survive the memory of the dying about which we ache tonight, and that you and we and all who know the story of Yeardley Love will learn the lessons of her living, of her life."

Casteen took a breath, then changed focus. He wanted to talk about the students who sat before him, he said. They'd sprawled on the Lawn, and by now, Yeardley's teammates and Coach Julie Myers couldn't hold back the tears. Their faces contorted with grief, they listened as Casteen asked each in the audience to walk away from the event empowered. He asked that they take away a determination to speak up for themselves, to act when they see or hear about others suffering from abuse or violence. He beseeched those in unhealthy relationships to seek help—to talk to a faculty member, the police, a family member, or to even seek out Casteen himself.

"If you fear for yourself or for others any form of violence, act," he said. The support belonged to them already; it was theirs inherently. They had the right to demand support, to expect it. They had an innate right to respect and assistance, and they had a duty to reach out to friends in need.

"Don't hear a scream, don't watch abuse, don't hear stories of abuse from your friends and keep quiet," he said. "Speak out."

Some huddled on the grass nodded in agreement. The air was heavy, weighed down by countless what-ifs and should've-beens. Not a week ago, the average student's biggest concern was cramming for finals. Now, all that seemed trivial. Now, they listened to a man whom most had revered and some had feared. And he was promising to take them to the police if they ever were in danger.

He asked that they leave the Lawn that night with the knowledge that the blows and abuse Yeardley had apparently endured in her final moments threatened the community as a whole. Left un-confronted, it could end more than individual lives; it could destroy a culture. The best way to honor Yeardley and her life was for the students to move forward and protect each other, to preserve the community of trust. Choose to recognize the evils in the world and confront them, he implored. Promise that in the years to come, you'll remember this loss, he told them, and "tuck away in your soul the knowledge that neither Yeardley Love nor any woman ever attacked has deserved it." No one has to die such a senseless, vicious death, he said. He asked those gathered to protect themselves and each other, not just now but for the rest of their days.

Before Casteen stepped away from the mike, he closed: "May God bless Yeardley Love."

Even journalists who sat quietly among the students found themselves moved by the event. For Brendan Fitzgerald, Casteen's words reverberated strongly. He had never seen Casteen so emotional.

"He appeared very choked up," Fitzgerald recalled, "and having been to numerous events where he offered speeches, to hear his voice waver was a novel experience for me. It was something I hadn't anticipated."

Looking around at the grief-stricken students, Fitzgerald

said he "wasn't deaf to the students who had a very difficult
time remaining stoic."

Twiggs's chest weighed heavy as she looked at the sea of
somber faces.

"It was profoundly sad," she recalled. "I live in the community. You can remove yourself from stuff [as a journalist],
but at the same time, I live here. I could feel it."

As dusk turned to nightfall, members of the university's
male a cappella group, the Virginia Gentlemen, silently filed
on stage. A low, amber-hued stage light cast tall and eerie
shadows on the wall behind them as they began, quietly at
first, to sing. A few words in, the song was recognizable—
Pink Floyd's "No More Turning Away"—as soloist Daniel
Bennett (UVA '10) mustered more power behind his vocals.

In the second stanza, Bennett was joined by thirteen Gentlemen, all wearing matching khakis, sports coats and bow ties,
in the somber song, and as Charles Dyer (UVA '10) stepped
forward for a brief harmony, the gravity of the lyrics was undeniable.

The song's words described the "pale and downtrodden" as
being speechless, uniting in a wordless alliance. Though the
song doesn't specifically address violence against women, the
repetition of the haunting title—"no more turning away"—
seemed eerily appropriate.

As the men sang, the sky turned from deep lavender to
nearly black.

"It's not enough just to stand and stare," the men sang. "Is
it only a dream that there'll be no more turning away?"

When the song ended, the only audible sounds were hushed
sobs from the Lawn. And with that, the men bowed their
heads, and slowly left the stage.

Chapter 8

Before Yeardley's remains could return home to Maryland, doctors first needed to examine her lifeless body one last time. It would be a crucial step in evidence gathering, as medical examiner William Gormley noted not only the young woman's height, weight, ethnicity, and injuries, but also searched for clues that might shed light on her last minutes alive.

Gormley, a well-respected pathologist who graduated from the Medical College of Ohio in 1977, worked as an assistant chief medical examiner in Virginia's Richmond-based Central District. Not every death in Virginia requires an autopsy, but many do—those who die in state mental facilities or people who appeared to be in good health and die while unattended by a physician, for example. As someone who died from what appeared to be traumatic injury, Yeardley certainly qualified.

Virginia was one of the first states in the country to institute a statewide medical examiner system in 1946, abolishing its previous coroner system. The difference is significant: Coroners are politicians who win their posts by election. They often have no background in medical or forensic science. But medical examiners are licensed to practice medicine, and most are trained in forensic pathology. They're schooled specifically in determining both cause and manner of death—the former being the specific method of death, the latter being an umbrella category. In simpler terms, "gunshot to the head" is the cause of death; "homicide," the manner.

Medical examiners conduct medicolegal death investigations, which require an eye for both medical and legal detail. They typically begin with external observations, then shift to the inside of the body. In Yeardley's case, many details would have been noted, and many photographs taken, to enumerate the injuries to her face that Reeves had so quickly spotted upon entering the 14th Street bedroom. Undoubtedly there were other autopsies to conduct that day—Virginia opens about 6,000 death cases per year, the autopsies for which are spread among just four facilities—but none would have been more pressing. Statewide, there's just more than one murder a day—on par with an average year in the city of Detroit—very few of which make national headlines. Yeardley would have become the state's top priority.

Gormley no doubt checked for the types of clues that help solidify a prosecutor's case, such as using tape to lift any fibers from Yeardley's body or panties and checking under her fingernails in the hope of discovering her attacker's skin cells. He likely examined her neck for evidence of bruising, a sign of strangulation. Internally, he would have dismissed as "unremarkable" her organs, which appeared normal for someone her age, and taken notes highlighting any abnormalities he encountered. All of this would have been standard procedure for Gormley, but in Yeardley's death, he would have had to spend far more time inside her head than most, taking notes and photographs on the damage done to her brain. Surely Gormley could have predicted, even without Lawrence's "accidental death" comment, that the defense would attempt to minimize the damage George had done when he slammed Yeardley's head against a wall.

While Gormley documented his findings, Yeardley's family made arrangements for her funeral. Sharon Love planned a Saturday funeral in Towson, a few minutes' drive from their hometown of Cockeysville, close to Notre Dame Prep. The mass and preceding visitations were announced in newspaper obituaries:

> LOVE, Yeardley R. On May 3, 2010 Yeardley Reynolds Love, beloved daughter of Sharon Donnelly Love and the late John Love; devoted sister of Lexi [sic] Love . . .

The family asked that memorial contributions be made to The Yeardley Love Memorial Fund at Notre Dame Prep, or to the Yeardley Love Women's Lacrosse Scholarship Fund for the Virginia Athletic Foundation.

In today's world of online obituaries, Yeardley's, which ran on the *Baltimore Sun* Web site, reached thousands more people nationwide than it would have in pre-Internet days. And the impact was huge. More than 500 people signed her online guest book to express condolences, with posters listing their hometowns from across the country—Georgia, Florida, California, Wisconsin. One poster, from Austin, Texas, wrote: "What a tragic loss not only to your family, but even to us who did not know Yeardley." Another poster from Columbus, Georgia, wrote: "May God wrap you in his arms in this time of sorrow. Yeardley was such a beautiful young woman.

Some directed their notes to Sharon and Alexis directly. They asked that the women hold tight to their Christian faith and recognize that Yeardley was now with Jesus. Some identified themselves as belonging to the UVA community— either past graduates or current students—while others were parents of college-aged young women and men who described the ordeal as a "parent's worst nightmare." Others still had lost loved ones to the hands of a batterer—nieces and daughters taken from them too soon.

But the virtual guest book was for more than catharsis for strangers. Several people who said they knew Yeardley left heartfelt messages, clearly using the forum as a place to commiserate with others in grief.

"She was such a kind, sweet girl and her beautiful smile and eyes will live on forever," wrote Tiffany Hales, who claimed to be a former co-worker of Yeardley's father. "She is in heaven with her dad."

Brian Frederick, Yeardley's former Cockeysville rec coach, posted the same letter that was to appear in the *Towson Times*. He had to miss Yeardley's funeral, he explained, because his own daughter was graduating college, and he believed Yeardley would prefer he celebrate with her friend rather than mourn at her interment.

Sharon Donnelly Love asked that the media not attend her daughter's May 8 funeral service, but some reporters attended the visitation beforehand and described the dark wooden casket in which Yeardley was laid to rest, and the pink flowers with green stems that covered it. Visiting hours were held at the Ruck Funeral Home, and thousands arrived to pay their respects. Many had never met Yeardley, but they were touched nonetheless, brought to tears by the description of the tragedy of her final moments. Women who themselves had been battered, trapped in dangerous relationships with volatile men, wondered if they had been spared a similar fate. Despite some family members' quiet comments that Yeardley was no "shrinking violet" who would have tolerated physical abuse, the young woman's broad smile still was destined to become entwined with domestic violence.

"This isn't easy," one friend said to another as they approached Yeardley's casket at the funeral. A newspaper reporter overheard.

Photographs of Yeardley in happy times—dressed in Halloween costumes, celebrating victories with her lacrosse teammates—were strewn about the funeral home and displayed on a laptop slide show. Flowers and cards sent in sympathy came from those closest to Yeardley, as well as from complete strangers. One came from CNN's *Larry King Live*. The funeral service program passed out the next day featured a photograph of Love as a child dressed as an angel. Underneath the image was this quote: "Truly great friends are hard to find, difficult to leave, and impossible to forget"—her senior quotation from her 2006 yearbook. On the program's back cover was the essay Yeardley had written during her freshman year of high school. Its final line read, "So far my life has been filled with joy and happiness, and I hope to keep living my life that way."

Filling the pews were Yeardley's friends, family, and sorority sisters from Kappa Alpha Theta. UVA president John Casteen attended as well. Each was handed a booklet that included the now-haunting essay.

Though the funeral mass was private, nearly a dozen television cameramen lined up across the street, along with many more photographers. Reporters from some outlets donned muted outfits to quietly sit among the mourners who attended. Some speakers told of Yeardley's goofiness and her generosity, and more than one commented on her contagious smile.

But it was UVA's lacrosse coach who led the congregation in a cheer.

The Cavaliers, she explained, took turns before each game leading teammates in a pregame chant. "One, two, three, together, 'Hoos!" they would cry, invoking the team's nickname. One day, as Love led the cheer, she accidentally counted to four.

This Saturday morning, as Myers' remembrance caused laughter to mix with mourners' tears, Myers counted to four. On cue, the congregation responded in one voice: "Together, 'Hoos."

From then on, Cavaliers would always count to four, Myers said.

The massive Cathedral of Mary our Queen, built in 1959 and visited by Pope John Paul II some 36 years later, seated 1,400 people, which on this day was far too few. Congregants spilled from the pews into the aisles. More mourners still gathered outside, watching as a solemn sea of orange and blue—the Cavalier colors—followed out the casket in hushed respect. Some Notre Dame students wore their uniforms—the same attire Yeardley herself had donned six years earlier to her father's funeral. Others wore blue and black ribbons and Yeardley's initials: YL. Yeardley's mother and sister sat in the front. Had May 3 never happened, they instead would have been preparing to attend Yeardley's graduation. One photographer snapped an image of Lexie, Yeardley's older sister, with a tissue pressed to her cheek, her mother's hand resting compassionately on her left shoulder.

But there were moments of levity as well. Julie Myers described Yeardley as a girl willing to ham, sometimes goofing around with propeller hats to make others laugh. She recalled when Yeardley tried to cook French bread after moving into an apartment with roommates. The attempt was a total failure, and the scorched bread filled the apartment with smoke, setting off fire alarms.

Yeardley was a rare mix of toughness and charm, she said.

"Yeardley Loves don't come around very often," she said. "She was truly remarkable, not because she tried to be, but because she just was. It came easy for her to be great, to be kind-hearted, welcoming, encouraging and engaging to all who knew her. She was legitimately awesome."

After Myers asked the congregation to hold hands and chime, "1-2-3-4, together 'Hoos!" the gathering broke into applause.

But a shadow hid behind every smile. Nuns dressed in white sweaters, navy skirts, and black habits, who had carefully arranged the delicate floral spray before mourners filed into the church, watched somberly as Father Joseph Breighner began the Mass.

"Every one of us is in a state of shock," said Breighner, known affectionately as "Father Joe" and author of a few spiritual paperbacks, including *When Life Doesn't Make Sense*. On the book's cover, Breighner looks pensive, his clerical collar peeking out from beneath a green windbreaker.

In his homily, he said Yeardley's friends and family could honor her life by living theirs the way she would have.

"She never made fun of anyone," Breighner said. "She always wanted others to feel good. . . . In memory of Yeardley, make the better choices from now on. Choose kindness instead of cruelty. Choose forgiveness instead of vengeance. Choose love instead of hate. Choose the right thing instead of the wrong thing."

Fr. Breighner, joined at Mass by Auxiliary Bishop Denis Madden, never mentioned George Huguely by name, but he reminded the congregation that Jesus preached forgiveness.

"At some point, we will have to forgive someone," he said. "Today may not be that day. It may not come for many days. But we will have to forgive, because it is the only way to heal."

He added that Yeardley's surname was apt.

"Two thousand years ago, a young Jewish rabbi named Jesus died a senseless, violent death. All he did and all he preached was love," the reverend said. "This past week, a woman has died a senseless, violent death. Her name was Love. And love is what her life is all about."

PART II

"This Guy Has Robbed Her"

Chapter 9

Within twelve hours of Yeardley's death, Charlottesville swarmed with local reporters. By the next night, Chief Longo—a broad-shouldered cop with a graying crew cut—had appeared on national talk shows hosted by television personalities such as Nancy Grace and Jane Velez-Mitchell. The interviews would be replayed often in the days that followed as more information trickled out about the case, no matter how minor.

Longo had started his career in Baltimore, graduating with a law degree from the University of Baltimore and being admitted to the Maryland Bar in 1993. For nearly twenty years, he worked on the Baltimore police force, rising through the ranks until he retired as Colonel in charge of Technical Services. After that, he accepted the top-cop post in Charlottesville. Longo was used to public speaking, regularly headlining lectures on ethics and professional standards for law-enforcement agencies. He also taught as an adjunct professor at Towson University, less than three miles from Notre Dame Prep, and served as law and business guest lecturer at the University of Virginia.

Despite his smarts and obvious speaking skills, Longo's words occasionally weighed him down as he tried to make sense of the tragedy on national television. It was a tough case even for a twenty-five-year law-enforcement veteran.

Grace repeatedly described Yeardley as "scrubbed in sunshine," a flowery turn of phrase perhaps not surprising from a prosecutor-turned-legal-commentator-turned-author, who in recent years had begun writing crime novels.

"Breaking news tonight," Grace boomed, her voice dripping with her Macon, Georgia roots. "Beautiful, talented star athlete, scrubbed in sunshine, just days before twenty-two-year-old co-ed Yeardley Love set to graduate UVA, her body found, likely still warm, battered, beaten, facedown in a pool of blood in her own bed, her life, so full of promise, cut short."

Grace called the case a "bombshell," and seemed outraged at the prospect of a bad guy with such stellar social standing.

"Oh, no, not a parolee, not a violent felon, not a drifter with a record! Suspect No. 1, another UVA athlete, a college lacrosse star turned killer."

Grace's overly animated vexation—and her quickness to convict—mirrored the country's. The George Huguelys of the world weren't supposed to turn into murder suspects. Even as reporters dug into his background looking for the dark triggers that might have precipitated such an evil turn, the most they uncovered was an idyllic childhood marred slightly by divorce. His legal run-ins had begun just two years prior, and while they were troublesome, they had never foreshadowed murder.

Courtney Stuart, the senior editor of the weekly newspaper *The Hook*, explained how the heartbreaking tale spread across the campus:

"We got word yesterday that there was a student that had passed away," said Stuart, who paused her own coverage of the case to appear on Grace's show via Skype. "At first, it was presented . . . as a possible alcohol overdose, but by the middle of the day yesterday, they had announced her name and also the arrest of George Huguely, both, of course, lacrosse players. Then over the course of the next twenty-four hours, details have been coming out . . . They've been pretty horrific."

Longo elaborated little on what he had already said publicly to reporters.

"Suffice it to say that investigators very quickly began looking at Mr. Huguely in this particular case, perhaps because of his relationship with Ms. Love and information that they began to gather from potential witnesses," he said. "They contacted him initially at his apartment."

By then, search warrant affidavits had been obtained by some media outlets. In them, Huguely was described as having made incriminating statements after waiving his Miranda rights. As he referenced the beating Yeardley endured, Longo's measured façade seemed to waver.

"The facts are horrific," said Longo, who was interviewed by phone. "They're shocking. They're incomprehensible. They're unthinkable. And to witness that, and particularly as a parent, to look at the body of a young girl who, as you said, you know, had so much to look forward to—it's just a terrible situation. And to have to sit here tonight and to hear the graphic description of how her body was discovered and to think, at home in a hotel room somewhere here tonight in Charlottesville, her mom is hearing that, is just completely troubling. And this is a very sad, sad set of circumstances for an entire community."

Longo declined to speculate on a cause of death, saying the autopsy was still pending, though some reporters had incorrectly begun reporting that Yeardley was strangled.

Grace, having invited a forensic pathologist, defense attorney, and prosecutor on the show, hammered Huguely's lawyer for his statement outside of the courthouse. "I couldn't believe my ears, so I got a printout to make sure 20/20 and 20/18 got it right," she said, referring in folksy manner to each of her eyes. She read Lawrence's statement declaring the death an "accident with a tragic outcome."

Grace cried bull.

"She was beaten to death. That is not an accident," she said, exasperated. "That is one blow, another blow, another blow, another blow until she bled through her nose, ears, and mouth."

Grace wasn't alone in her disbelief: Velez-Mitchell, also on CNN, declared it impossible for Yeardley's death to have been accidental. She called the slaying another incident in the "war on women," and invited law-enforcement analyst Mike Brooks to weigh in on the case.

"There's no way there's an accident here," Brooks said.

Velez-Mitchell incredulously asked Stacey Honowitz, a sex crimes prosecutor, how Huguely's lawyer could try to claim the death was accidental when the beating was apparently so vicious.

"Well, listen, he's not going to stand up and tell you that he intentionally killed her," Honowitz replied. "Then he'd be confessing, basically, on behalf of his client. So what he's trying to do is probably ease, you know, into people the notion that it was just a tragic accident in the hopes, maybe, that the prosecutors will re-look at this case and think about the relationship that they had, and maybe try to downfile it from a first-degree murder."

Predictably, the speculation had begun. And not just on the national stage.

Back in Charlottesville, defense lawyers who knew Francis McQ. Lawrence quietly dissected his first public statements about the case. Some thought it was too soon to declare anything accidental. After all, by saying Huguely didn't mean to kill her, Lawrence was implying that she indeed died at his client's hands. Perhaps that point wouldn't matter in trial, where comments made to reporters weren't likely to be repeated. But Lawrence's peers wondered if he had already dealt his client a fatal blow in the court of public opinion.

For Brendan Fitzgerald, the *C-VILLE Weekly* reporter, Yeardley's death wasn't the isolated incident that it had been portrayed to be by some national reporters. In fact, Yeardley was the seventh UVA student to die that academic year—making it an unusually tragic year.

"There wasn't similar national presence for previous instances," he said.

The deaths were all different. One student, twenty-two-year-old Stephanie Jean-Charles, had returned to her home in Haiti and was killed in the catastrophic January 12, 2010 earthquake that killed an estimated 230,000 people. Another student, twenty-six-year-old John Jones, was spelunking in November 2009 when he became stuck upside-down in Nutty Putty Cave about eighty miles south of Salt Lake City. Twenty-eight hours after he got stuck, he died, becoming the first known fatality at the cave. On December 14, Justin Key, a first-year business student, succumbed to the flu, according to his friends' Facebook memorial page. In January 2010, Scott May—a nontraditional student who enrolled in the university in his forties—died of natural causes after several long-term health problems. Matthew King, a graduate arts & sciences student, died April 19, 2010, in a cycling accident away from campus. Also in April, fourth-year student Joseph Arwood passed away at the University Medical Center after a fraternity brother found him unconscious one morning at their shared Sigma Phi Society house. Arwood's official cause of death has still not been publicly released.

In late April, the university's Student Council voted in favor of a bill to honor the six students who had passed away so far. On a Friday afternoon just weeks before graduation, about 200 students gathered to honor the six. Relatives of each student were invited. The bill, sponsored by Council President Colin Hood, while in reality inconsequential, was symbolically meant to "attempt to improve the rights, opportunities, and quality of life of every student in their honor."

Every college endures heartache and loss. A microcosm of outside society, campuses are just as likely as the non-campus world to have freak accidents, disease, and suicide. In a typical year, UVA might have lost three or four students, university officials said. But seven was unusual, and one being a homicide, allegedly at the hands of another student, was devastating and rare.

And yet, it wasn't the only homicide the Student Council

paused to remember. The remains of Morgan Harrington, a pretty Virginia Tech student, had been discovered in January in Charlottesville. Her case was the only one in the spate of recent tragedies to garner even a fraction of the national attention that Yeardley would receive just months later. She wasn't enrolled at UVA, but her disappearance had haunted many of the young adults on the Charlottesville campus.

Chapter 10

Twenty-year-old Morgan Harrington, a striking blond education major, had traveled to Charlottesville's John Paul Jones Arena for a Metallica concert October 17, 2009. She got separated from her friends when she wandered outside the arena hoping to find a bathroom. Without a ticket to get back inside, she called from her cell phone and told them not to worry about her, that she would find a way home. Witnesses described seeing a woman hitchhiking a few miles from the stadium, but Morgan never made it home. She was last seen walking across a bridge near busy Ivy Road wearing a black mini-skirt, black tights, knee-high black boots, and a Pantera T-shirt.

A few days passed before officials were satisfied that Morgan hadn't simply stayed over with a friend. The search frenzy began. Morgan's purse and cell phone were discovered in a parking lot near the university's track and baseball fields, but there were no signs of a struggle, and certainly no Morgan. Ominously, the battery in her cell phone was missing, a possible attempt by an attacker to keep authorities from tracking her down via pings off cell phone towers.

The search stretched into a nearby valley. Students not only from UVA and Virginia Tech, but also from Shenandoah Valley's James Madison University, combed the targeted areas and passed out flyers alongside law-enforcement agents. Police painstakingly pieced together her movements from the time she left the arena, at about 8:30 p.m., until about an hour later when she was last spotted on the Copeley Road bridge.

Virginia State Police Lt. Joe Rader used the media to issue a plea for information.

"Perhaps you saw someone stop a vehicle," Rader said. "Perhaps you saw this young lady get into a vehicle. Somewhere out there lie the answers or lies the vital link."

The disappearance ate away at the area's college students. How many times had they walked alone in Charlottesville at 9:30 p.m.? Whatever happened to Morgan could have happened to anyone.

While the arena was criticized for refusing Morgan reentry, many who attended the concert were shocked that anything had gone awry. Despite heavy metal's harsh reputation, this particular concert was remarkably placid.

"The thing that surprised me the most of all about this concert was how calm it was and how safe and in control the security was in the venue," one concertgoer said. "There were policemen inside and out."

After Morgan had been missing about a month, police released a description of a Swarovski crystal necklace she had been wearing in hopes of drumming up any new leads. The chunky piece was made up of large crystal chain links, an edgy addition for a planned night of head banging.

The case generated national attention. Morgan was, after all, gorgeous and white, two prerequisites for widespread coverage. And her parents' appeals were too dolorous to ignore.

"Please come home," Dan Harrington, her father, said while fighting back tears. "If someone has Morgan, please let her come home safely."

"She has her Halloween costume picked out, and we'd love to see her walking around in it," said Gil Harrington, Morgan's mother. "She's got a dog that's missing her. Let's bring her back, and she can address all these things, so she can be back with her family."

The anguish was amplified with dozens of Morgan sightings nationwide, not only locally in Virginia, but from as far away as New Mexico. Police couldn't discount the reports, especially considering that in recent years several college students had faked their own kidnappings to get attention. But Morgan's family and friends knew this wasn't in her makeup. She would never intentionally cause her family so much grief. Besides, she did what she was told, her father told reporters: "I called her two weeks ago and told her to get her flu shots. She got it the next day."

As the search dragged on, Gil Harrington took to a blog to regularly post updates in hopes of generating tips for police. Christmas was unbearable, she had written on the blog (www.findmorgan.com) on December 29, 2009:

"Our pain was sharpened by expectations for this holiday season. I found Christmas compromises that were acceptable to me. It was challenging to have a new, different tradition that acknowledges Christmas and still honors our missing Morgan. Our décor was pretty muted, but what has been done is genuine and celebratory of love and caring. It's tricky, though, to find that path. Every time I go into our closet, Morgan's Christmas gifts reproach me from the top shelf. And then despair almost takes me out."

As the weeks continued, Gil Harrington's words alternated between heartrending and hopeful. She balked at the police's characterization of Morgan's disappearance as an "abduction."

"It is soft language," she wrote. "Abduction means to move away from—that is a passive euphemism for what has occurred here. Morgan was not 'moved away' from us—she was *ripped* away, *severed* from us! She was *amputated* from her life. The person who did this *robbed* her from us. I think even the posters could better reflect what has been inflicted on our family—Morgan is not missing—like my frequently misplaced reading glasses—SHE was stolen!!"

That was written January 12, 2010. Three weeks later, Morgan's parents got the nightmarish phone call: A farmer had spotted a skeleton on his rural Albemarle County land about an hour's drive northwest of Richmond. The Harringtons rushed to the area. All that remained were bones, but they were sure it was their daughter. DNA testing eventually proved they were right. (Though authorities determined that she actually died in 2009, near the time of her abduction, the remains' January discovery placed the homicide statistically in 2010 for record-keeping purposes.)

In February, Morgan's death was officially ruled a homicide.

Because crime is so rare in the area, and because Morgan, like Yeardley, had been slain in her prime, the case seemed tailor-made for crime-hungry media. The experience left many in Charlottesville disenchanted. It seemed reporters only swooped into town for horrific news, splashing images of the picturesque city alongside gruesome descriptions of tragedy. Morgan's parents seemed to recognize that public attention was a necessary evil in drumming up leads in the case. It was at their prompting that police released a sketch of a possible suspect after DNA testing connected Morgan's remains with the sexual assault of a Fairfax City woman in 2005. Dan Harrington, Morgan's father, said that based on the location of his daughter's makeshift burial spot—farmland that is difficult to reach by car—he was certain the killer was someone local. "Someone has to be comfortable with knowing the area, knowing where to go," he told the *Today Show*. The Harringtons also were vocal in their disappointment at what they perceived as foot-dragging by the Charlottesville police. On January 23, Gil Harrington took to the blog:

"I am concerned about the complacency in Charlottesville. I am feeling a tendency to downplay Morgan's abduction, to protect the idyllic reputation of the city. I bought into that idyllic image until my daughter was stolen there. I understand the reluctance to be associated with this crime. I myself would prefer not to be known as the Mom of a missing girl. Charlottesville would prefer not to be recognized as the location of abduction. But there is no going back."

Despite the offering of $150,000 in reward money— $100,000 from Morgan's family and $50,000 from the band Metallica—Morgan's murder remains unsolved.

Five months after Morgan's bones surfaced, as TV cameras choked the usually peaceful street on which Yeardley and Huguely lived, it seemed like déjà-vu for Charlottesville residents. Frustrated with the negative attention, many passersby ignored reporters' questions and looked perturbed when caught on film for B-roll, or supplemental footage to be interspersed with interviews and talking-head experts opining about the case. One Boylan Heights employee told a reporter she was tired of talking about the case. She had been interviewed three times already that day, she said.

Journalists tried to gobble up whatever morsels of detail they could, talking to people on the street and interviewing area business employees. Those wanting to dig deeper, to find out if Yeardley had any clue she was in danger or to learn if there was a broader lesson to be gleaned from the tragedy, were shut down. Unlike in Morgan's case, where the missing girl's parents invited journalists into her bedroom to ensure she was seen as person and not merely a statistic, Yeardley's loved ones were mum. Surely they were blindsided and overwhelmed by the massive national attention. And unfed journalists become all the more ravenous. It seemed everyone remotely connected to the Loves and Huguelys were contacted in one way or another—by phone, by e-mail, through social networking sites. The less information reporters get on a high-profile, competitive story, the more desperate they become for any tidbit of information. Sometimes the perseverance pays off with someone landing a scoop; other times, it backfires, causing people to clam up. The handful of friends who had been willing to talk to the media were quickly asked by Yeardley's family to quit responding, and they complied. Calls to Sharon and Lexie Love were met with "no comments" and assurances that other people close to Yeardley would decline to comment as well. The only family member to speak, albeit briefly, was Granville Swope, Yeardley's uncle—the UVA alumnus who had once been a star lacrosse player. Known to Yeardley as "Uncle Granny," he called his niece a "delightful lady in every respect."

"She had a great future," Swope told a reporter. He accused Huguely of robbing her of it.

Yeardley's sorority sisters were clearly floored by the loss. They huddled on the front porch of their three-story brick Kappa Alpha Theta home and embraced in tears. Nevada Thompson, identifying himself as the sorority's cook, answered reporters' knock on the front door and somberly said they weren't ready to comment.

"We're in mourning," he said.

A pall hung over the entire university. Normally early May buzzes with end-of-year activities, eleventh-hour cram sessions for finals, and graduation parties galore. For Yeardley's sorority sisters especially, the joy had been sucked out of their final month on campus. Outwardly, they said little, posting a one-sentence mention of the tragedy on their blog that Yeardley was a wonderful person and that her "sisters" were praying for her family. The posting prompted responses from "other Theta sisters" that echoed the sentiment. One woman wrote: "I hope your warm memories of Yeardley carry you through this difficult time."

Courtney Schaefer, the chapter's president, issued a statement: "We are in a state of mourning, and for the respect and privacy of Yeardley and her family are not ready to comment further on the situation." Schaefer and other sorority sisters declined to speak with reporters even months later, saying they had promised Yeardley's family that they would remain silent until after the case went to trial.

Though the public sentiment was in their favor, Yeardley's family didn't want conclusions reached before trial for fear that a potential jury would be tainted. In declining one interview, Sharon Love, Yeardley's mother, said that her primary concern was "doing right" by her daughters, and assured one reporter that answers would come in time.

Chapter 11

Just as Love's death seemed to eclipse all other news in Charlottesville, reporters back in Baltimore saw a community reaction like few others. By the end of May 4's broadcast of *Good Morning Maryland*, reporter and anchor Megan Pringle knew the station would stay on top of the story at every turn—for better or worse.

If someone ever sat down to map the characteristics required for a case to infiltrate the American consciousness, many of its bullet points would coincide with the Yeardley Love homicide. Attractive victim, check. Life full of potential, check. Loving upbringing, check. Unlikely suspect, check. Nothing in Yeardley's background remotely hinted that her life could someday end in such brutal fashion—and that made her a perfect victim for Americans to rally behind.

People immediately began calling WMAR with stories. They knew the Loves, some said, and remembered how devastated Sharon Love had been when her husband passed away a few years prior. Even at gas stations, people talked about the case. They were sickened by the news, and many asked whether funds had been raised to help pay for funeral costs or start a scholarship in Yeardley's name. (There were.) For Pringle, a Michigan native turned Maryland transplant, it was the first time she fully fathomed just how small a town the big city of Baltimore really was.

"Baltimore and the surrounding communities are very close knit," explained Pringle, who moved to Baltimore in 2007. "When people ask, 'Where did you go to school?' they don't mean what college. They mean where you went to high school. It's been a very tough place to meet people. People who grew up here and went away to college come back, and they're still friends with people they went to high school with."

The Baltimore area is specked with private Catholic high schools. Even Pringle's co-anchor sent his daughters to institutions similar to Notre Dame Prep, where Yeardley graduated. Jamie Costello, who has worked for WMAR for twenty-four years, said some parents send their children to private religious schools for the theology. Just as many are looking for the best mix of academics and sports. Increasingly, the private schools' lacrosse programs have become big draws, Costello said, because talented players can secure hefty scholarships for top-rated universities.

Baltimore City Public Schools long ago earned itself a lackluster reputation. In the 1990s, the city and the state of Maryland swapped barbs, each blaming the other for failing students. In 1995, the city even sued the state, saying it had violated the Maryland constitution by failing to give students an efficient education. The state fought back, saying the city had mismanaged the district. After an all-out public brawl, a resolution was finally reached that called for the state to give the district more money and, in exchange, Maryland would have more control in running the city's schools. The plan, as intended, only lasted a few years, but the criticisms lobbed at the district never seemed to stop. Newspaper editorials regularly called on the politicians in power to strengthen the schools. In 2006, for example, the Maryland State Board of Education aimed to revamp the whole system, from instruction to leadership to school management. State Board members said too many schools weren't making the grade.

The public district's mediocre reputation prompted many

in Baltimore and surrounding areas to seek out private institutions. Schools such as the Institute of Notre Dame (pronounced "dahm"), which came before Notre Dame Prep, were deeply rooted in their communities and had stellar reputations. IND, as the all-girl Baltimore institute is called, boasts alumnae such as former U.S. Speaker of the House Nancy Pelosi and barrier-breaking NBC news anchor Catherine "Cassie" Mackin. IND opened in 1847; when it became overcrowded, the School Sisters of Notre Dame opened the Notre Dame of Maryland Collegiate Institute for Young Ladies in 1873. Notre Dame's Towson campus continued to turn out noteworthy graduates, including Susan Aumann, a Republican member of the Maryland House of Delegates representing the 42nd District in Baltimore County.

Students at the various Baltimore-area private schools invariably know each other, either from overlapping during elementary or middle schools, or from competing against each other in high school sports. Many still hang out at the same summer swimming holes and play at the same recreation centers. Jamie Costello said most grow up with lacrosse sticks in their hands. Those who didn't know Yeardley personally felt as though they did, and the sense that the community had lost one of its own was overwhelming. Even more telling, many Baltimore residents knew of the Huguely family because they followed high school lacrosse—never mind that Bethesda-based Landon was nearly an hour's drive from Baltimore.

"When you're here, everybody knows everybody," said Costello, an Overlea High School graduate. "They all play one another—the DC schools play the Baltimore schools. Everyone overlaps."

The outpouring after Yeardley's death was immense, Pringle said, and the station's coverage reflected it. In the first days, *Good Morning Maryland* ran multiple stories. Reporters kept tabs on both the legal turns in Charlottesville and the community reaction back in Cockeysville and nearby Towson. Notre Dame Prep officials spoke briefly and solemnly about the loss, describing it as profound and unimaginable.

Pringle and Costello continued to field phone calls from heartbroken residents, some of whom called more to share their grief than assist with stories. There was a communal sense of loss beyond anything Pringle had experienced in Baltimore before.

Violent death is by no means rare in the big city, which reported 238 murders and non-negligent homicides to the FBI in 2009. Baltimore often ranks alongside Detroit, St. Louis, and New Orleans as having the highest per-capita murder and manslaughter rates in the country. Many of the slayings don't make the news at all simply because the media outlets don't have the staffing to keep up.

"Some people said there are lots of women the same age in Baltimore City who are murdered perhaps at the hands of domestic violence and it doesn't get the same kind of attention," Pringle said. "They said, 'You guys are just doing this story because it's a pretty, rich, white girl.'"

That prompted debate in the newsroom. Did Yeardley's case warrant more coverage than average? It was a tough discussion, Pringle said, in part because the station—like dozens of other media outlets nationwide—could not ignore the community's response to Yeardley's death. It was all anyone talked about. On the other hand, Pringle struggled with thoughts of the many other nameless women whose deaths were going unreported. She couldn't help but wonder whether the outcry would have been as deafening had Yeardley been black or poor.

The newsroom divide reminded Pringle of a similar debate in 2007, when the body of twenty-five-year-old Sintia Mesa was discovered in the trunk of her own car. Mesa, a former Morgan State University student, had been reported missing just days prior. Police found her cell phone and other personal items near a Dumpster. Then came her body. The other big news of the day was the death of racehorse Barbaro, notable in Baltimore especially because of the area's huge horseracing following. Barbaro won the 2006 Kentucky Derby, then shattered a leg two weeks later after a false start in the Preakness Stakes. Six operations failed to properly heal the horse, and it was euthanized January 29, 2007. WMAR producers planned to lead the evening news with the horse, followed by coverage of the gruesome discovery of Mesa's body. Some balked, arguing that a woman's life was worth more than a horse's. In the end, Pringle said it was a split decision: Barbaro led the 5 p.m. newscast, Mesa the 6 p.m.

Pringle's newsroom wasn't the only one contemplating its coverage of the case. The *Washington Post's* Daniel de Vise penned a column titled "Yeardley Love slaying: overplayed?" on the newspaper site's College Inc. blog. De Vise, responding to dozens of reader comments posted beneath the previous days' news stories, defended the case as being worthy of the *Post's* newsprint: It took place where homicides are rare, and the suspect was from an affluent Chevy Chase family. So while Yeardley being a Baltimore resident would perhaps not have elevated the story to warrant eight bylines in the Sunday edition, de Vise reasoned, Huguely's status as a local boy would have.

"What if Huguely were from Baltimore?" de Vise pondered. "I am sure we would still cover the story. But perhaps not on the front page, and perhaps not with seven or eight reporters."

He pointed to the Morgan Harrington homicide as proof that it takes more than a young, white female victim to land on the *Post's* coveted section fronts. Harrington's case had gotten ink, but never section-front ink, he wrote, "because Morgan wasn't local."

In the weeks surrounding Yeardley's death, there were dozens of fatal and nonfatal shootings plaguing both Washington, D.C. and Baltimore. Many weren't reported. In one, a nineteen-year-old pregnant woman was shot March 21. Three months later, a second young pregnant woman survived two bullets to her abdomen. Neither woman was white. Pringle said it was telling that the local news barely followed up on either story, while even the smallest developments in Yeardley's case often led the newscast.

* * *

Historically, stories about young adults slain in college settings have made substantial headlines. Eight months before Yeardley's death, the country was transfixed by another East Coast campus murder—that of twenty-four-year-old Annie Le, a doctoral student at Yale University who disappeared just days before she was to be married. While officials at first wondered if she fled in fear of the lifetime commitment she was facing, her friends and family knew that Annie had been happier than ever and was thrilled to be getting married. The days of worrying came to an end on September 13, 2009, the day she was supposed to walk down the aisle. Le's body was discovered crammed into a wall panel of a research building. She had been beaten and strangled.

Like Yeardley, Annie seemed on the cusp of greatness. She was attractive and intelligent, working in the medicine school's Department of Pharmacology. She wanted to cure cancer.

The media attention was so great that one TV producer ended up crushed in a bum rush at a news conference. *NBC News* producer Alycia Savvides reported that she "saw stars" after a cameraman—one in a throng gathered around a police spokesman—bashed into her with his camera, knocking her to the ground. Afterward, a police sergeant admonished the journalists.

"We don't want anyone getting hurt, all right? . . . Those cameras are heavy," Sgt. Anthony Zona said.

Spokesman Joe Avery reportedly slowly shook his head.

"I've never seen a bunch of people so out of control in my life," he said.

Two days later, the media mob reassembled for word that a suspect had been arrested: Raymond Clark III, a lab technician who worked in the building. On March 17, 2011, Clark pleaded guilty to murder and attempted sexual assault in a deal that called for a 44-year prison sentence. For the first time, prosecutors revealed that he had left behind evidence of a sexual assault and related DNA evidence. Until then, they had not publicly suggested a motive for the killing.

The arrangement, made under Connecticut's Alford Doctrine, allowed him to agree that the state had enough evidence to convict him without admitting he committed the crime.

In reporting Yeardley's death eight months after Annie's, some national outlets drew parallels. But there were other, seemingly long-forgotten cases that more closely mirrored the UVA student's death than that of Annie Le. One such case is that of Kathleen Roskot.

Roskot was a sophomore and star lacrosse player at New York's Columbia University in the fall of 1999 when she met Thomas Nelford Jr. Though Nelford, a struggling artist, had dropped out of school out of fear that academics would interfere with his artwork, he was bright and kind, and the two had much in common—including sports.

Nelford was a wrestler, making a big enough splash his freshman year to be named "one of the top" freshman wrestlers in the Ivy League by the Columbia sports media guide. Roskot, meanwhile, was known as an upbeat, go-get-'em type who often took to the field and told teammates, "It's a great day to get better," a high school teammate recalled at her funeral. Like Yeardley, she was all drive and discipline, and a powerful on-field competitor. With green eyes and dark hair, Roskot, too, had been raised in insularity by still-married parents in an affluent suburb—in her case, Long Island.

Over their six-month relationship, Roskot and Nelford spent a lot of time together, as college paramours tend to do. For Nelford, whose parents had dragged out a nasty divorce, Kathleen was his first real girlfriend. To her friends, Nelford perhaps seemed a little weird—more reclusive and arty than her previous boyfriends—but he never seemed violent.

Still, like Huguely, Nelford provided plenty of red flags in hindsight. Nelford's cartoons, published in the student newspaper, sometimes turned lugubrious. As the *New York Times* described:

In one cartoon, a man and woman trade a series of insults and ugly confessions, culminating with the man saying, "The voices told me to kill you in your sleep."

The woman then screams, "April Fool's!"
The man replies, "That's today?"

Another strip, called *Sid, the Ugly Kid*, described a smart but troubled teenager who fantasized about slaughtering those who ridiculed him for being ugly, according to a New York *Daily News* account. In one panel that later haunted classmates, Sid finds a rope and hangs himself because "that fucking bitch broke my heart."

Roskot was discovered February 5, 2000, in her dorm room with her throat slashed. The security guards who found her naked body had been asked by her lacrosse coach to check on her after she failed to show up to a morning meeting at the school gym. An hour later, Nelford was found dead beneath a subway car uptown. He had his girlfriend's college ID and her wallet. Though the couple had been seen holding hands just hours before Roskot's death, friends said she was trying to end their relationship. It's the only motivation for the murder-suicide that police could offer. Busloads of classmates and lacrosse teammates attended her funeral.

Kathleen Roskot's death was basically in another media era, however, before twenty-four-hour news cycles and lightning-fast Internet communication. There were no Twitter or Facebook updates about her death, and today, only a handful of stories are accessible online. Occasionally, for a few years after her death, Roskot's name and a brief paragraph describing her untimely death appeared alongside a fresher crime for comparison's sake.

At the time, however, the impact was comparable to Love's death. The New York newspapers posed similar questions: What warning signs were missed? Were colleges doing enough to head off potentially deadly problems? *Time* magazine mentioned the case in 2001 in a story about a spate of recent campus suicides—at least two of which began with murders. Those accounts focused on whether campuses were ill equipped to deal with the mental-health issues buried deep inside some students.

But another issue was raised, too. Erica Goode, a *New York Times* writer, penned a piece called "When Women Find Love is Fatal," highlighting three separate domestic attacks that all occurred within the span of a weekend.

Roskot's case was the first. The next day, thirty-nine-year-old Marie Jean-Paul's husband cut her throat with a machete, then set her body ablaze. Soon after, eighteen-year-old Joy Thomas was shot in the head by her ex-boyfriend. Somehow, she survived. Goode's piece highlighted frightening domestic-violence statistics that were true in 1998: 32 percent of nearly 3,500 women killed in the country died at the hands of husband or boyfriend, either past or present. "In comparison, 4 percent of 10,666 male homicide victims in 1998 were killed by current or former intimate partners," she wrote.

"We haven't come close to affecting intimate partner violence and homicide the way we have other kinds of violence and assault," Dr. Susan Wilt, a representative with the New York City Department of Health, told Goode. "It remains a shocking issue that this is the main reason that women end up dead and that it occurs within the context of their home and family, where they are supposed to be safe.

"Women worry when they go out," Dr. Wilt added. "They should worry when they stay in."

Wilt had been tracking homicides by intimate partners in New York since 1990. She found, and other studies had borne out, that many of the deaths occurred either while or soon after the woman tried to leave the man.

"It's absolutely a crime of rage," she said in 2000. "There is a sense of 'How dare you think you can live without me?'"

It's a question resurrected at least once a year with a high-profile domestic violence slaying. Entire true crime libraries are dedicated to cases in which one half of a once-happily married couple kills the other. Domestic violence experts say the statistics can't possibly tell the whole story, either: There are many murders that likely were committed by one's partner that have gone unsolved for lack of evidence. Many of those cases eventually are forgotten by everyone but the victim's family, perhaps a reflection of a "she should have known better" mentality.

But in cases where the killer is known and the victim is a young college student, it seems more likely that people will pay attention. Such was the case with Kristin Mitchell's murder in 2005. And when Mitchell's father learned of Yeardley's death five years later, he felt an immediate connection—and a sinking in his stomach.

Kristin was a pretty, blond twenty-one-year-old studying food marketing at St. Joseph's University in Philadelphia. Like Yeardley, she had attended Notre Dame Prep, though after two years, she felt she didn't relate well with the privileged girls in Towson. She ultimately graduated from Mount de Sales Academy in Catonsville, Maryland, which was still a private institution, but was slightly less expensive. Also like Yeardley, Kristin had been devoted to helping the less fortunate, volunteering for Project Appalachia, which helped build homes for the poor, and spending time in other career-service programs at St. Joe's.

And like Yeardley, she met a guy who, police said, would cut her life short.

Bill Mitchell, Kristin's father, said there were red flags, but her circle of friends didn't know how to recognize them—least of all Kristin. At twenty-eight, Brian Landau, her boyfriend, was several years older, and he seemed to crave control. The text messages were constant. He'd ask her to skip her night classes at school to spend more time with him, then sulk if she said she needed to keep up on her schoolwork. He harped on her to lose weight, then accused her of cheating on him when she shed a few pounds. Brian seemed generous at first, buying Kristin gifts for no reason—but then used the gifts to argue that she owed him her loyalty.

"We learned these things after the tragedy," Bill Mitchell said. "We lived near Baltimore; she lived near Philadelphia. She was almost twenty-two, so you hope she's safe on her own."

She wasn't. Aside from an occasional comment about her

relationship with Landau not being "perfect," Kristin's life seemed more or less normal, and she focused on graduating. She began the joyless task of pursuing job interviews when potential employers set up shop at her college's job fairs in the fall of 2004. She seemed to do well making the rounds, talking with companies such as Hormel and Rubbermaid, but the big job, the one everyone wanted, was with General Mills, her father recalled.

Bill Mitchell coached her through her through several interviews, but they concentrated mostly on the big job interview with General Mills. He helped her prepare for the dreaded "where do you see yourself in five years" types of questions. Bill told his daughter to study the company and its competition. "Go in and win it," he encouraged her. "She had nothing to lose and I wanted her to be as confident as could be," Bill later recalled. "She was always good in an interview setting."

She dressed in power clothes—likely her favorite dark gray business suit—and nailed the interview, landing a job as a sales associate. She was to start her new career on July 8, 2005. Part of Kristin's new beginning, however, included ending things with Landau. She told some friends things just weren't working out. Then, on June 3, police discovered Kristin's bloodied body inside her apartment in Conshohocken, Pennsylvania. Her life had drained out from dozens of stab wounds.

Though the discovery was made in the morning, Bill Mitchell said he didn't learn about his daughter's death until that evening. Police, apparently busy collecting evidence, had trouble finding Bill's cell phone number and called the local police in Baltimore for help. Bill was in the car, driving, when his phone rang. He didn't understand why police would be calling, he recalled, and, suspicious when the officer insisted they talk in person, Bill agreed to meet at a public supermarket, just in case the person on the other end of the line was an imposter. He met the officer near the front doors of a Giant supermarket. The detective asked him to come into her police car, but Bill refused.

"This situation was just so out of place. I wanted to hear whatever the detective had to say right there at the doors of the supermarket," Mitchell later recalled.

The officer hesitated, then told him that Kristin had been killed.

"I walked to her car and sat in the passenger seat and called a detective in the Philadelphia area as I busily wrote notes on a legal pad," Mitchell recalled.

Mitchell had already told his wife that he was meeting with the police. Now he headed home to tell her and their son that Kristin was dead.

Landau, in a dramatic display of what hardened cops call overkill, stabbed his girlfriend more than fifty times. Her throat had been slashed six times; her back stabbed eleven.

He told police that the couple had been fighting, and each had stabbed the other, according to news reports in the days that followed. Though Landau went to a hospital for treatment of his own wounds, the medical examiner determined they were actually self-inflicted. Landau backtracked and said that some of the wounds were from an aborted attempt to kill himself. When the news stories came out, Bill Mitchell was mortified. The media had reported what Landau told police—including a claim that Kristin had slashed him when he rebuffed a sexual advance.

"Talk about insult to injury!" Mitchell said. "Imagine: Your daughter's been murdered and our newspaper sends up the tabloid version of what happened."

Kristin simply would not have grabbed a knife in anger, her father said.

"My daughter would have been panicky if she had a tiny splinter in her finger," he said. "She had no tolerance for pain, whether it be hers or someone else's."

District Attorney Bruce Castor Jr. opted not to seek the death penalty in the case but still charged Landau with first-degree murder, meaning life behind bars without parole. The court proceedings dragged. The trial, originally set for early December 2005, was postponed, leaving the Mitchells to endure their first Christmas without Kristin with no idea when the case would reach court.

"The wait," Bill recalled, "was numbing."

Eventually, a new date was set: June 5, 2006. But before the jury was selected, Landau hedged, pleading guilty to third-degree murder against the advice of his counsel. Facing life imprisonment, he opted instead to plead to the lesser charge and was sentenced to thirty years in prison, making him eligible for parole beginning in 2020.

The Mitchells considered it a victory. Though they wanted Kristin's killer locked behind bars and away from society forever, there was always the possibility of things going terribly wrong in the courtroom.

"A trial would have been devastating," Bill said. His family had already endured what he considered Kristin's character assassination in the days after her death. He never believed her fight with Landau was mutual; it wasn't in Kristin's character to grab a kitchen knife and stab another human being.

"We knew from advice we were given that in the courtroom, first they kill the person, then they kill the person's reputation," Bill said. "Kristin would not be there to defend whatever this man or his attorney would say about her. We would also be at the mercy of the judge."

And then there were the crime scene photographs. Kristin's body, mutilated and bloodied, looking nothing like the sweet-smiled cat lover her family knew and loved.

"It's as if she would have been murdered all over again," Bill said.

Mitchell and his wife, Michele, collaborated with two of Kristin's friends and created the Kristin Mitchell Foundation (www.kristinskrusade.org), a non-profit educational organization meant to raise awareness among young adults about the potential dangers of unhealthy dating relationships. Each year, it sponsors Kristin's Krusade, a 5K run/walk on St. Joseph's campus. The goal, her family said, is to warn young adults about the dangers they face in the hope that another family might be spared their pain.

It was a lofty aspiration, one reinvigorated with the death of Yeardley Love five years after Kristin's murder.

Bill learned about Yeardley through an e-mail from a friend who had attended UVA years earlier. The details released by police rang painfully familiar: A young Baltimore-area woman, well educated and immersed in volunteer work, killed by a boyfriend near graduation time at college. The Mitchells were drawn to the case; they attended Yeardley's wake and extended condolences to family members. It wasn't the first death since their daughters that struck a chord.

Somehow, though, Yeardley's death seemed different than the others. It seemed that this time, the whole world was paying attention.

Chapter 12

Yeardley Love's Death a Wake-Up Call About Domestic Violence
    Domestic Violence While Dating: The Yeardley Love Case
    Yeardley Love's Murder Shines Light on Domestic Violence

So read the headlines in the days after Yeardley's death. The newspapers and Web sites presented them with such fervor that someone who didn't know better would think that the death actually *did* serve as a wake-up call to society. In truth, such headlines have appeared time and again with little impact. Like the batterers they describe, the stories themselves are mired in a cycle, telling readers that this time, things really will get better. But they rarely do.

Even UVA's immediate response implied to some that the administration was viewing Yeardley's death as yet another "she should have known better" situation. Mike Gibson, chief of the university police, sent out an e-mail at 9:18 a.m. May 3 advising students that "the best defense is to be prepared and take responsibility for your own safety and for that of your friends and fellow students."

Among the "reminders" he laid out: Trust your instincts

~~and call nine-one-one if you're uncomfortable; avoid iso-~~lated areas and walking alone at night; keep your doors and windows locked; don't allow strangers to follow you into a locked building; never prop open card-reader doors; alert the police if you spot someone peeping into a residence or see someone watching, photographing, or filming an area.

None of the suggestions would have helped Yeardley the night she died. One student complained to a reporter that the advice consisted entirely of strategies to avoid stranger danger. "Locking doors and walking home with a friend will do little if that friend is the one who will later beat or rape you," the third-year student said.

In 2008, the Violence Policy Center, a nonprofit violence educational foundation, released a report titled *When Men Murder Women: An Analysis of 2008 Homicide Data.* Among the findings:

- For homicides in which the victim-to-offender relationship could be identified, 92 percent (or 1,564) of female victims were killed by someone they knew.
- Of those, 64 percent (or 997 women) were wives or otherwise intimately involved with the killers.
- "Women face the greatest threat from someone they know."

The only upside to the statistics was that the number of homicides across the board had been declining for years; however, the likelihood appeared even greater in 2008 than a decade earlier that a murdered woman had died at the hands of someone who had professed to love her. (Of course, the domestic crimes weren't limited to homicide. According to the National Institute of Crime Prevention, intimate partners commit more than one-quarter of rapes and sexual assaults, while strangers are responsible for about one in five sexual assaults. Most of the others are committed by acquaintances.)

Love and Huguely's case was considered more shocking than many, not only because both victim and accused were rich, popular, and successful, but because in hindsight, Huguely seemed wrapped in warning signs. Bob McDonnell, Virginia's governor, released a statement sending his "thoughts and prayers" to the Love family.

"Yeardley Love was a young woman of terrific talent and promise; her innocent young life was taken far too soon," the governor said. "While there are no words that can properly convey the sadness and pain that so many are going through, it is heartening to witness the positive way in which the student body of UVA has come together to remember Yeardley Love, mourn her passing, and help each other through this difficult time."

McDonnell closed the statement by saying he had asked UVA president John Casteen to meet with him "to study and fully consider every possible idea that could help prevent such a senseless crime from taking place in the future." The governor also took to *Good Morning America* to call for changes to how criminal records were reported. Yeardley's death could have been prevented if someone had spoken up, he said.

"There's ways to get information to administrators obviously from police, from court records, but it brings the larger question of the obligation to all of us in our society [that] if we see things that look wrong or strange behavior or violent behavior, to really be more involved," he said. "Particularly in domestic-related situations, can other people intervene because they see things going on . . . Maybe this could have been prevented."

By the time of the May 12 interview, McDonnell had already met with Casteen to talk about what legal steps could be taken to ensure that administrators learn of a student's violent history—either on or off campus. The governor said he wanted to avoid what he called a repeat of an "unprecedented tragedy."

"There's reviews going on now," he said. "We're conducting our own look at the facts after all the investigation is done. When the general assembly comes back next year, we can make those changes."

The case even grabbed the attention of Phil McGraw, better known to TV audiences as Dr. Phil. Three women a day die from domestic violence, he said, and women between twenty and twenty-four years old are in the highest risk group.

"This is a serious problem. These intimate relationships . . . are fueled by so much jealousy," he told *Good Morning America*. "It gets a lot of attention when it's a star athlete, but this is something that permeates every area of our society."

While Huguely's history of violence should have been noticed by school officials and coaches, McGraw didn't blame either for missing the warning signs. He did, however, call on schools to start teaching girls how to spot the risks and warning signs of an abusive relationship.

"This type of violence is preceded by emotional control, threats," he said. "If you're in a relationship like this, the last thing you want to do is confront your abuser. . . . Talk to somebody that you trust, somebody responsible that can help you find an exit strategy."

Ironically, that message had been delivered to UVA students just three weeks before Yeardley's death. Liz Seccuro, the founder of STARS—Sisters Together Assisting Rape Survivors—had been invited to the campus to talk about sexual assault at her alma mater. In 1984, as a freshman at UVA, Seccuro, still a virgin, was drugged and gang raped by three members of the Phi Kappa Psi fraternity. She didn't know any of her attackers, and, because of the drugs coursing through her system, could only remember one of the rapes graphically. The next day, she awoke on a sofa wrapped in a bloody sheet. Determined to learn her rapist's name, she foggily sifted through his mail before fleeing his apartment. Armed with his identity, she reported him to the then-Dean of Students. The dean's callous response still causes her to shudder: "Are you sure you didn't have sex with this man and you don't want to admit that you aren't a 'good girl'?"

Seccuro went to the hospital for treatment, then to the university police and to student health. She said she made dozens of reports, none of which went anywhere. The dean told her that the Charlottesville police had no jurisdiction over Phi Kappa Psi, and he said he spoke with her attacker, who claimed the sex was consensual. "I was told, in so many words and actions, to go away," Seccuro wrote in a column published online in the wake of Yeardley's death. "I did not, but my life was diminished. I felt that I did not matter."

Nothing happened in Seccuro's case for twenty years. It was then that she got a letter from her attacker, William Beebe, who wrote to her as part of his Twelve-Step recovery program. He said he got her home address by calling the university's alumni office, and that he had been following her whereabouts for nine years. He was sorry he raped her, he said. Seccuro took the letter to the Charlottesville police, which, as it turned out, did indeed have jurisdiction over the frat house where she was raped. Luckily for her, there was no statute of limitations on filing a rape charge.

It was during the lead-up to trial that Seccuro learned of Francis McQ. Lawrence and Rhonda Quagliana. The duo—known locally as Fran and Rhonda—represented Beebe. In March 2006, she faced her attacker in person and gave two hours of testimony at a preliminary hearing. The judge ruled there was enough probable cause for the case to go to trial.

Instead, Beebe pleaded guilty to the lesser charge of aggravated sexual battery. He had struck a deal with prosecutors: He would provide them with information leading to the arrests of the two other fraternity brothers who had raped Liz before his attack, and in exchange, he would be sentenced to ten years with all but eighteen months of the sentence suspended. Beebe began serving his prison time in March 2007; he was released less than six months later. The other two suspects have not been charged in the assault.

The experience turned Seccuro into a victims' rights activist. She founded STARS in 2006 in hopes of helping rape survivors and secondary victims (friends and family) through education and Web-based resources. One major facet of the organization's mission is to help colleges and universities revamp their responses to rape and sexual assault. Twenty years may have passed, Seccuro said, but much has stayed the same on campuses nationwide.

In April 2010, just three weeks before Yeardley's death, Seccuro returned to UVA. She was invited to speak at the annual Take Back the Night Rally, which highlights violence against women. The twenty-one-year-old event, peppered with local bands, speakers, and free food, was designed to give a voice to survivors and encourage people to take steps to prevent sex crimes. It would begin with a rally, followed by a march across campus, and wrap up with a "speak-out" at the university's amphitheater on McCormick Road.

Seccuro stood alongside Dan Harrington, the father of homicide victim Morgan Harrington, and spoke at the rally of blame and responsibility.

"Blame for sweeping crimes against women under the rug," Seccuro later wrote. "Blaming victims for going to concerts or parties or dating a fellow student. We are, I said, collateral damage, acceptable losses in the University's now-failed PR campaign that they are one of the best, most elite schools in the United States."

Though a lot of her speech was about sexual assault, she preached pointedly about violence between intimates and "the whole 'if you see something, say something' bit," she later recalled. When she learned of the death so soon after her speech, she was both heartsick and angry. She had been told that local law enforcement had created a series of videos for students that addressed an array of problems plaguing the campus: Assault, dating violence, substance abuse, and eating disorders were among the issues. But the videos never made their way to UVA's students because they were deemed inappropriate to show at a student-governed school. Seccuro wanted to scream.

"I had a friend who had been raped her First Year there near the new dorms in total darkness," Seccuro recalled. "When she approached the administration about better lighting, she was told that 'Mr. Jefferson would not have wanted the ugly aesthetic of such lights on the grounds of his Academical Village.' Point blank."

Seccuro was incredulous: "Really? Really??"

Eventually, the lights were installed after both women and men complained that they felt unsafe walking home from the library.

Seccuro, who wrote a book about her ordeal (*Crash Into Me: A Survivor's Search for Justice*), considers UVA's approach to campus violence downright deadly. Violence exists at every college, she said, but UVA, by standing by its status as a student-governed university, has been particularly steadfast in refusing to require that its students have to attend orientation, much less education in sexual assault or dating violence.

The criticism has been leveled before at the university. In 2004, *The Hook* wrote a daring cover article titled "How UVA Turns Its Back on Rape," in which reporter Courteney Stuart described the clandestine Sexual Assault Board that meets, takes testimony in secret and issues rulings in response to rape allegations among students. The story questioned exactly whom the policy was designed to protect, and highlighted the case of twenty-one-year-old rape victim Annie Hylton. Even though the young woman's attacker had been found guilty by the secret committee, his punishment was laughable: He was banned from the first-year dining hall and from the aquatic and fitness center, and he was ordered to attend counseling. He was never booted from campus, and remained at UVA until he graduated in 2003.

"One of the most bitter ironies for UVA rape victims is that the school seems to reserve its harshest penalties not for sexual predators, but for students who violate the Honor Code, an antebellum proscription against lying, cheating and stealing," Stuart wrote. "Honor offenses can include such things as copying a classmate's French homework or stealing a bicycle. Honor violators draw just one penalty: immediate and permanent expulsion."

UVA's honor system is entirely student-policed, meaning that a panel of students is convened to hear allegations against their peers. The panel weighs guilt and innocence, and just one sentence comes with a guilty plea: permanent dismissal.

The first student-run honor system cropped up in the late 1700s at the College of William & Mary. Jefferson envisioned something similar at his academical utopia, though it wasn't introduced until after a student shot a law professor on campus in 1840. Professor John A. G. Davis died of a pistol wound while trying to calm a disturbance between students on the university's lawn, according to UVA's history of its honor system. "This incident resulted in the adoption of the Honor Code in 1842," according to UVA's Web site, and is "one of the school's most venerated traditions. Administered solely by students, the Honor System requires that an individual act honorably in all relations and phases of student life."

However, as the years passed, UVA's system narrowed to highlight just three mandates: no lying, no cheating, and no stealing. Any of those violations meant immediate dismissal. Committing murder, meanwhile, wasn't included on the automatic expulsion list. While UVA's system is unique, it is mirrored in a few other institutions. Princeton University, for example, has boasted an entirely student-run honor code since 1893. On the Ivy League university's Web site, Princeton claims: "Entirely student-run, the honor code has been successful because generations of undergraduates have respected it, and by common agreement they afford it the highest place among their obligations as Princeton students."

UVA's system has made its own slew of headlines over the years. In early May 2001, the university was wracked by controversy after professor of physics Louis A. Bloomfield leveled academic dishonesty charges against 122 students. That was nearly twice as many charges as had been filed against all UVA students during the previous two years combined. Bloomfield, who taught "How Things Work"—a popular introductory physics class—was alerted to possible cheating after a student complained that the grade he had given her was low while others with higher marks had cheated.

Bloomfield created a software program to help him ferret out cheaters. The software would detect similarities of six consecutive words or more between papers submitted to him over the last five semesters. According to an account in the

New York Times, it took the program fifty hours to run through the more than 1,800 papers. It worked. Some of the papers were virtual replicas.

"I expected to see a couple of matches," Bloomfield told the Times. "I was a bit shocked to find sixty."

Bloomfield's experiment turned into a scandal, one that served as the apex for students' increasing complaints about the university's disciplinary unfairness. Some filed lawsuits, including a student whose degree was revoked eight years after he graduated. The trial leading to that revocation was held without the (former) alumnus present.

Thomas Hall, who headed UVA's Honor Committee during the Bloomfield scandal, said at the time that an investigative panel was going through the 122 cases, and that some students were expelled. Others, however, were found to have shared work to help each other out but didn't know the work would be plagiarized. In those instances, the students were allowed to stay.

One student likened the honor system to the "death penalty" because of its black-and-white severity. But despite the growing complaints, UVA students chose to stand by the system, flaws or not. The student body voted in a referendum to reject proposed changes to the code.

Meanwhile, students accused of rape and assault weren't treated with nearly the same obduracy. A student alleging rape could go to the police, but prosecutors have publicly acknowledged that some cases are too he-said/she-said to generate enough evidence for criminal charges. In many campus rape cases, both parties had been drinking, and there weren't any witnesses. Prosecutors can prove there was sex, but proving it was forced is too great a legal hurdle. Accusers in those cases have a university-provided recourse: They can bring their allegations to the University Judiciary Committee and hope for a guilty verdict by a panel of students. But unlike with cheating allegations, there is no set-in-stone punishment.

That discrepancy led to the creation of www.uvavictims ofrape.com, a group created by Susan Russell, the mother of a UVA student who claimed to be sexually assaulted in her dorm room by a man she was not dating or interested in. "The University mandated that she use a weak administrative process to handle this crime of sexual assault," Russell says on the site. "No other type of crime committed on grounds is trivialized in this manner."

Russell launched the site in 2004 and plays off Thomas Jefferson's emphasis on honor. "Is it Honorable for a University to support Zero Tolerance for Cheating but not for Rape?" Russell asks. "Is it Honorable for campus police to refuse to transfer jurisdiction for felony crime to the local police? Is it Honorable to do nothing when you're told by a young woman that she's been sexually assaulted?"

The site, sharp as a knife in its allegations, accuses the university police of mishandling the case and posts photos of various UVA administrators whom Russell deemed complicit in the case. It immediately made headlines, as did Annie Hylton's subsequent civil suit against her alleged rapist.

Hylton, a member of the varsity volleyball team, had been on campus just five months when she went on a date that ended in rape. She went to the hospital and reported the attack to university authorities, then pressed to have her case heard by the secretive Sexual Assault Board, a subcommittee of the University Judiciary Committee. The experience was nauseating, she told a CBS reporter in 2006. The six-hour hearing was in a small conference room, where she sat just feet away from her alleged attacker.

"Even thinking about it now makes my chest get tight," she told a reporter.

The assault board sided with Hylton, agreeing that the man had violated the school's code of conduct, despite his insistence that the sex was consensual. But if Hylton expected to feel vindicated by the ruling, the hope was short-lived. The board didn't even suspend him. Outraged, Hylton went public in hopes of drawing attention to UVA's ludicrous double standard. Cheat on your final? Immediate expulsion. Rape someone? You're banned from the fitness center.

Even worse, Hylton was told that if she spoke about the case, she could face charges of her own from the University Judiciary Committee. But she spoke out anyway, and UVA's mind-boggling disparities became public: In three years, from 2000–2003, thirty-eight students had been booted for cheating—in the same time span that sixty UVA students had reported they'd been sexually assaulted. No one had been suspended or expelled for sexual assault, *The Hook* reported.

Charlottesville prosecutors never brought criminal charges against Hylton's attacker, but she was eventually awarded $150,000 by a jury in her civil suit. More than that, her decision to speak out about the case was rewarded as well: The college safety nonprofit Security on Campus, Inc.—formed in the aftermath of the grisly 1986 murder of Jeanne Ann Clery at Lehigh University—filed a complaint against UVA in late 2008 for mishandling sexual assault cases. The Department of Education ruled that the university had repeatedly violated federal law by threatening victims of sexual assault with punishment if they spoke about their cases. Victims were free to speak—in theory, anyway.

More than seven years after her daughter's attack, Russell still maintains the UVA Victims of Rape site and said she continues to hear from young women looking for support.

"Do I think that anything has changed? Perhaps the school is more clever in how they hide assaults on their campus," Russell said. "The Commonwealth of Virginia is a state of 'good old boys.' There is great opposition to change, and crimes that involve women are treated as though 'she' brought it upon herself."

UVA alums like Seccuro agree the university still has a long way to go. The policies have changed, but the mentality and culture haven't. And it extends beyond rape allegations. Students on campus are implicitly taught to keep quiet, mind your own business, don't sully a classmate's reputation with even a cheating allegation.

For Russell, one of the biggest frustrations was the university police. She wanted to turn her daughter's case over to

Charlottesville police and was surprised to learn that the university department had jurisdiction.

"Many people living in the commonwealth, to include most lawmakers, are under the assumption that local law enforcement has the jurisdiction to investigate any crime that occurs on a college campus," she said. "Unfortunately, that assumption is wrong. Campus police have jurisdictional rights for dormitories and classroom buildings. Local law enforcement may be called in to assist, but unless the University or college transfers jurisdiction to them, campus police retain jurisdiction."

Russell wanted to change that. She sought a sponsor for legislation that would change how felonies would be investigated. The bill, eventually titled Virginia House Bill 2490, was sponsored by Delegate Paula J. Miller and called for university police to be required to contact local law enforcement when a felony occurred on the campus.

Specifically, the bill directs the chief law-enforcement officer of "a public or private institution of higher education" to immediately notify the local law enforcement agency when someone died on the campus or a rape had been reported. "Upon notification, the local law-enforcement agency shall assume responsibility for leading the investigation. The campus police department and all other employees of the institution of higher education shall cooperate."

"Why this bill? Because campus police tend to turn a blind eye to campus rape crimes. They treat them as administrative matters," Russell said. "This bill is not meant to demean the hardworking campus police, but to aid them. It allows the crime to be investigated by the local police, who are highly trained and staffed to handle crimes of this magnitude."

After Yeardley's death, questions swirled about how much university officials knew of Huguely's legal run-ins. Athletic Director Craig Littlepage said neither he nor UVA president John Casteen had been alerted, but Littlepage stopped short of saying that none of Huguely's coaches had been told. Had Coach Dom Starsia been told? Huguely had confessed to him the late-night beating he unleashed on a teammate for allegedly kissing Yeardley. Starsia chose not to report the incident to the school's Judiciary Committee because both young men supposedly had assured him that they shared the blame and had worked things out. But surely someone had noticed after Huguely's 2008 conviction in Lexington that he began fulfilling his community service sentence. Were coaches in the dark, or did they look the other way?

Huguely was supposed to report the run-ins himself. The university's policy required that students self-report any arrests. But those who do face expulsion or probation, making it unlikely that an average student, much less an athlete with everything going for him, would willingly step forward and put a bull's eye on his chest.

As Stetson University law professor Peter Lake told the *Washington Examiner*: "The pressure to win and compete and maintain eligibility is so strong that it actually plays against safety."

Huguely, like seven of his teammates who had also been entangled in alcohol-related charges, opted to overlook the self-reporting rule in favor of saving his own skin. As the media scrutiny mounted, Casteen turned to Governor McDonnell to push legislation that would require police agencies statewide to report student arrests to the university.

So much for the honor code.

In another cruel twist of timing, one week after the Take Back the Night rally, Claire Kaplan, director of Sexual and Domestic Violence Services at UVA's Women's Center, had scheduled a nearly three-hour session for some athletic department staff members to discuss creating a support network to help student athletes deal with domestic abuse.

"I was very excited to have the athletic department involved," Kaplan told a *USA Today* columnist, who wrote that Kaplan was unable to shake the "heartbreaking irony of the timing" of her requested meeting.

"There's not much that shocks me, so I don't know if I was shocked, but I was horrified," said Kaplan, who didn't know Yeardley or Huguely. "It's a hideous wake-up call here. If there was a pattern of violence, did she reach out to anyone at all, did she reach out to friends who didn't know what to do? Or was she stuck in her silence?"

The answers were proving difficult to uncover. Yeardley never reported Huguely to police or campus authorities as someone she feared. Based on police documents, some friends knew there had been spats and discord, but no one was speaking publicly about what warnings should have perhaps been better heeded. If there were lessons to glean from the case, Yeardley's family made it clear they'd have to come out in the courtroom.

"I feel like this whole thing was so preventable," Kaplan told columnist Christine Brennan. "Somebody knew something that they thought wasn't important. Did anyone speak out? Did people say to her, 'Yeardley, you are not safe with this person?'"

Kaplan hoped Yeardley's death would ignite outrage and trigger state-mandated change.

"People can't close their eyes anymore," she said. "They can't pretend it's not happening. I hope there will be more support on a state level and more specifically on each campus for mandatory, thorough education on gender-based violence. In the meantime, if students have friends who are in questionable relationships, they can't stay silent anymore."

Russell isn't convinced that Yeardley would have been saved even if she'd reached out to UVA for help.

"They may say that Yeardley Love should have reported her concerns, but I know firsthand that when those concerns are reported, nothing happens," she said.

By now, it's been so often repeated that domestic violence is about power and control that it sounds more like the moral of an after-school special than a real-life lesson. But, experts say, it's true. And dating violence doesn't always manifest in telltale "I walked into a door" types of bruises, according to Break the Cycle, an organization whose mission is "empowering youth to end domestic violence."

Sometimes there's physical violence, while other times

there's emotional abuse—verbal put-downs, name-calling, mind games. Abusers could use social status to make their partners feel subservient, or they could make threats—anything from threatening to leave or swearing they'll commit suicide.

A week after the Love slaying, Marjorie Gilberg, Break the Cycle's executive director, lambasted Virginia for its shoddy civil protection laws in cases of dating violence. The organization had been tracking states' laws for three years, and for the third year in a row, Virginia received a failing grade because its laws limit the types of behaviors that qualify for a protection order. Even if Yeardley had sought an order, she couldn't have been granted one because she and Huguely had separate apartments.

Journalist Jamie Stiehm, who herself had once been mired in a violent relationship, wasn't entirely surprised that Yeardley hadn't reached out to the university or local police for help.

"She was a very accomplished athlete and student," Stiehm said. "On the outside, she had everything going for her. The encoded message is, something like that doesn't happen to people like us. The elite class sort of comes with the expectation that everything in your life is peachy keen."

By asking for help, Yeardley would have been forced to admit to herself that everything wasn't as perfect as it seemed.

"You're confronting your own sorts of flaws in an otherwise perfect façade," Stiehm said. "These girls are very resilient . . . They're used to cultivating this air of hardiness and great enthusiasm and capability. Yeardley was the girl who had everything."

Dr. Barrie Levy, a psychotherapist and expert in dating violence, said young women in abusive relationships are in too much denial to recognize that they're mired in the type of relationship they've been warned to avoid.

"It's not just the thinking, 'This doesn't happen to people like me,' but it's the denial that it's even happening," said Levy, author of several books, including *Women and Violence*. "You don't call it violence. You just think he gets upset now and then."

Levy, a member of the Women's Studies Department at the University of California at Los Angeles, has heard countless stories of teenagers and young adults who initially mistake controlling behavior as unbridled passion. Levy began researching violence against women in the 1970s, and she worked in prevention education in high schools and middle schools. That's when she first began hearing stories of teenagers whose puppy-love romances had turned tragic.

"That was an eye opener," she recalled. "Some of my colleagues were having the same experience. You think nobody would get trapped in a relationship at that age."

But they do.

While the gender roles are sometimes reversed, the situation typically is this: At first, the young suitor seems romantic and impossibly attentive, wanting the girl all to himself. He calls and sends text messages, shows up at her door unexpectedly, meets her outside of her classrooms. She's flattered and floored by the attention—and far too love-struck to notice as he slowly begins usurping her free time, edging out her friends and family.

"Among girls who haven't been exposed to violence earlier in their lives, they think maybe he's had a troubled past and that she can make it better," Levy said. "They think, 'He'll have a good, healthy relationship with me, he'll learn to trust me and he'll change.' "

Most never see their partner as abusive, especially if he doesn't outright hit. The controlling moments are explained away: "This is the exception, I understand him so well, he doesn't mean to hurt me, he cares about me so much."

The common refrain is that he will change, Levy said.

"But what happens is that she begins to change, he doesn't, and he begins to have an even more powerful effect on her," Levy said. "She becomes more traumatized, more ashamed, more isolated. She's less confident, less certain of her own strength. He may be critical all the time. She starts to avoid doing anything that will get him upset. She thinks, 'I'm just really going to focus on being in this relationship.' "

And if she does decide to leave, she puts herself in great

danger. Domestic violence experts have coined the term "separation violence" to mark the perilous phase in an abusive relationship when one party tries to leave the other. That is when the abused partner is at greatest risk of being killed by his or her abuser.

"Many girls try to break up and the reactions are so much worse than staying together and trying to fix things," Levy said. "He might promise to go into counseling, and she's ever hopeful that he will change. That's what rules these relationships: hope and fear."

To the people who balk at the idea of someone like Yeardley Love—by all accounts a strong, smart, independent woman—stumbling into the role of victim, Levy has a message: "Any one of us could fall in love with someone who crossed that line. It could happen to anyone, no matter how strong or how weak you are."

Yeardley Love's strength perhaps made her a powerhouse on the lacrosse field, but it did nothing to save her life.

Chapter 13

The image of domestic violence is coated in stigma, the woman often assumed to be meek and weak-willed. While women are assured in books and on Web sites that domestic violence crosses all socioeconomic boundaries and is nothing for the victim to be ashamed of, they're rarely provided with testimonials from women professionals—lawyers, doctors, highly educated go-getters—who have suffered at the hands of their partners. The message is clear: Maybe it *does* happen in affluent society, but you sure as hell don't talk about it.

No doubt, Yeardley Love was taught never to tolerate domestic abuse. Notre Dame Prep, her high school, prides itself on instilling strength in its students, and Yeardley's own academic and athletic achievements indicated that she intended to bust through any obstacle that cluttered her path. By all accounts, she was tough both on and off the lacrosse field.

Maybe too tough for her own good.

Strong, educated women sometimes lull themselves into a false sense of security, domestic violence experts say. These women believe abuse simply doesn't happen to people like them, so those who do experience violence in their relationships shroud themselves in silence. They trick themselves into thinking that the relationship isn't even abusive, much less that it's the type to escalate into one of those grisly stories covered on the nighttime news.

Yeardley seemed to be growing increasingly concerned, according to details in police reports and her friends' accounts in the days after her death. A week before she died, she reportedly shared with a teammate a disturbing e-mail Huguely had written her. She had also gone home for a weekend to get away from George after a particularly heinous fight. To journalist Jamie Stiehm, the red flags were there, but everyone seemed to ignore them.

"They couldn't imagine something so vicious could happen in their circle," Stiehm said of Yeardley's friends and teammates. "It's a lack of imagination and profound elitism as well. That willful oblivion really cost her her life because they didn't protect her."

Affluence and education can work against the victim of an abusive relationship. People shrug off her concerns because they assume she has the means to leave the situation.

Add to that a privileged abuser, and things get even more complicated. The picture of Huguely painted in the wake of Yeardley's death was that of a young man who had been given too many breaks for behavior that would have likely landed most people in jail. Somehow, he had evaded real consequences for all of it.

"George exemplifies the Cavalier culture with a capital C," Stiehm said. "The privilege, the breeding, the sense of entitlement, the thinking that the rules don't really apply to me . . . His teammates, if they weren't protecting him, they were ignoring him."

Women trapped in abusive dating relationships are sometimes hesitant to seek help, experts said. They tend to focus on their partner's better attributes rather than examining the put-downs and the violence they're secretly enduring.

"She sees a good side of him. You don't fall in love with someone who's horrible all the time," Dr. Barrie Levy said. "You see him when he's not being abusive. Maybe he's really loving or has a lot of other qualities you really like."

Yeardley didn't have children or a lifestyle to support, so

she had no solid reason to stay with Huguely—except, perhaps, that she didn't want to put her lacrosse friends in a
tricky situation by breaking up and having to air the couple's
dirty laundry, a development that undoubtedly would have
made the final months of their college careers much less
pleasant.

Maybe that's why some of her friends didn't even know
she had broken up with George.

Court records show that police began investigating whether
Huguely had threatened Yeardley immediately after her
body was found. At the same time, they were gathering
other information—specifically about Huguely's constant text
messaging.

In today's society, cell phones and smart phones mean
people can stay in constant communication. For an emotionally unstable partner, this can provide yet another tool aimed
to tether a couple together. Friends told reporters soon after
Yeardley's death that Huguely was texting her constantly after their break-up. While the contents of the texts weren't immediately released, dating violence experts said they needn't
have been threatening to constitute what's been dubbed as
"textual harassment."

"It's gotten astonishingly worse in the last two years," Jill
Murray, an author of dating violence books, told the *Washington Post* for a 2010 story on the high-tech stalking method.
"It's part and parcel of every abusive dating relationship
now."

The messages perhaps seem benign at first glance: *Call
me. Where r u? Who r u with?* But they arrive at the sender's
will, never mind if it's during class or dinner or a family vaca-
tion. Kristin Mitchell's family said she seemed to get text
messages constantly from her then-boyfriend and killer-to-be.
After her death, detectives discovered an ominous message
on her phone that she had sent to Landau just hours before he
stabbed her to death: *You are being ridiculous. Why can't I do
something with my friends?*

Victim advocates say technology, yet again, is proving a

double-edged sword: With all the convenience attached to being easily found, there's the potential danger of being easily found.

"The advances in technology are assisting the perpetrators in harassing and stalking and threatening their victims," Kacey Kirkland, a victim services specialist with the Fairfax County Police Department, told one reporter.

Charlottesville police were granted a search warrant to examine Huguely's Blackberry smart phone in December to see how many, and what types, of text messages he may have sent Yeardley. Even if the messages had been deleted, a forensic examination of the phone could potentially turn up saved screen shots of the notes. Police would also subpoena cell phone records in hopes of learning just how many of those notes Huguely tended to send out. If the messages themselves were benign, perhaps the quantity would be telling.

As a public service, Break the Cycle posts "ten warning signs of abuse" right on its Web site: checking your cell phone or e-mail without permission; constant put-downs; extreme jealousy or insecurity; explosive temper; financial control; isolating you from family or friends; mood swings; physically hurting you in any way; possessiveness; telling you what to do.

Bill Mitchell is convinced that nothing will change without education. Years after his daughter's death, he hears regularly from people trying to save loved ones from dangerous relationships. The Kristin Mitchell Foundation's Web site spells out ways to get help and highlights the common theme that seems to run through most cases of dating abuse: control.

"I think every time a young woman dies like this, it's the opportunity for everyone to wake up and find out what this is all about. Dating violence is *real*. It happens a lot! It's just that you don't hear about it much."

In the months that followed Yeardley's death, that began to change—much to the apparent discomfort of the university and the slain woman's family.

Chapter 14

As it became clear to local reporters that Yeardley's case would surpass any other they had covered in recent memory, reporter Brendan Fitzgerald said the *C-VILLE Weekly* began to devote more and more resources, because the case raised a slew of questions that authorities did not seem ready—or willing—to answer. One of the biggest questions was that of entitlement.

As word of Huguely's earlier outbursts surfaced, some wondered if the good-looking Landon graduate had been given a pass for behavior that would have landed others behind bars. And others questioned how many of Yeardley's own friends had ignored signs that her boyfriend was unstable—possibly even dangerous. Looking for answers, Fitzgerald knocked on doors lining a half-mile stretch of 14th Street Northwest. Few people answered, and those who did declined to talk. He headed to the lawn outside of the university's rotunda, where students lounged between classes. They sprawled on the grass in T-shirts and shorts, the early May days creeping above eighty degrees.

None talked.

In a world where there's no shortage of people to opine on anything and everything, Fitzgerald was shocked to meet only silence. It was one thing when Huguely's advisor in the anthropology department declined to comment—that was to be expected—but never had Fitzgerald encountered so many tight lips among students.

"It was a surprise to me as a reporter and as a former UVA student to approach a group of half-dozen students to ask for any comment on any respect and have them all decline, and not for lack of words," Fitzgerald said. "It's rare in any of my experiences in UVA that students were hesitant to share their opinions. They are a very bright lot reliably year after year. I expected no shortage of nuanced takes or ideas."

When pondering why this case seemed to trigger silence at UVA when so many others encouraged an outpouring of thoughts and emotions, Fitzgerald came up empty. Finding students to talk about Morgan Harrington's disappearance had never been difficult. But there was something about Yeardley Love's death that left students guarded and speechless. Was it the case itself, the blinding media coverage, or the last straw in a deadly year that left the whole campus emotionally drained? Fitzgerald didn't know.

"To find nothing was startling," he said.

Still, reporters toiled away. Sensationalized or not, Yeardley's case had touched thousands upon thousands of people worldwide. It eventually would grace the cover of *People* magazine, whose average single-copy sales in the first half of 2010 were nearly 1.3 million. Though Sharon Love gave a brief comment to *People,* its coverage, like most other publications, relied heavily on early newspaper accounts, quotes, and information gathered immediately after Yeardley's death. And none of the accounts shed any light on Yeardley's relationship with George.

University officials, in fact, instructed those who knew the couple to keep quiet. One student athlete told a reporter that members of the university's sports teams—not just lacrosse—had been told not only to refrain from making public comments, but to refuse new friend requests on social networking sites such as Facebook in hopes of filtering out anecdote-seeking reporters. Indeed, dozens of UVA students contacted via Facebook and LinkedIn (another social site but with a more professional slant) simply ignored incoming messages asking about Yeardley and George.

Faced with few live sources, reporters turned to paper ones, filing a slew of requests under federal and state Freedom of Information Act laws. Journalists wanted the details: What evidence had been collected at the crime scene? What exactly had Caitlin Whiteley and Philippe Oudshoorn described in the nine-one-one call to police? What crucial information had Huguely tried to trash when he stole Yeardley's laptop and tossed it in a Dumpster? The day after the death, news media were given what they were accustomed to receiving: limited access, but some access nonetheless. In an ongoing investigation, journalists don't expect to be given information that might jeopardize a case, but they do expect to have access to police and court documents that have historically been deemed public by legal precedent. It's a checks-and-balances system, after all: The media can't keep tabs on the government and governmental procedures if the government completely closes its books. Reporters were allowed to review three search warrants linked to the crime, and the contents of those warrants were instantaneously reported in print, on television, and online.

But suddenly and without explanation, the records were sealed in a move that baffled the news outlets. On May 6, three days after Yeardley's death, Judge Cheryl Higgins with the 16th Judicial Court granted prosecution motions asking that warrants for several searches be sealed—specifically, the searches of Yeardley's apartment, of Huguely's apartment, of Huguely's car, and of Huguely himself. Higgins filed four separate orders, each of which was, like the warrants themselves, sealed.

The *Washington Post*, no stranger to waging battles over the public's right to know, joined the *Daily Progress* and *Richmond Times-Dispatch*, as well as the Associated Press, in challenging the Commonwealth of Virginia for sealing the documents.

It wasn't just that some documents weren't available, the media consortium argued, but that Higgins's order failed to say which records were sealed and why—nor did the judge specify for how long they would remain out of view. Attorney Craig T. Merritt argued that Virginia Supreme Court guidelines require that the public be given such specifics so that they have the chance to oppose the action. Higgins's filings were unfairly vague, Merritt argued, and offered no timeline—saying only that the documents would be sealed "temporarily."

Predictably, George's family said little to the media—not an uncommon position for people whose loved one has been charged with a vicious crime and could face life imprisonment. Yeardley's family also remained cloistered, as did her friends. The day-after pleadings for time and space turned into a widespread vow of silence at the request of Yeardley's family. Her likes and dislikes, her goals and dreams, the details that turn a tragic story into a human one, were kept under wraps.

Mary Bartel, Yeardley's lacrosse coach at Notre Dame Prep, told one reporter via e-mail that Yeardley's mother had originally granted her permission to speak to Yeardley's character and history at the school. "Beyond that, we continue to respect the family request that our response to questions be 'no comment.' Thanks for your understanding," she wrote. Others similarly shied from talking, saying that they had promised Yeardley's family their silence.

Somehow, despite the disconnect, Yeardley's story wasn't lost. Within days of her death, several groups on Facebook had been dedicated to her. One online memorial had more than 100,000 members by week's end. Six months later, "In Memory of Yeardley Love: UVA Lacrosse Player" still had 75,960 members.

Another Facebook memorial page, titled "R.I.P. Yeardley Love, May 3, 2010" drew more than 24,000 members.

"Did not know Yeardley personally, but feel free to post on the wall . . ." wrote the page's creator, twenty-four-year-old Benjamin Edmonds of Cooperstown, New York.

"I had no idea that it would get so big," he said later. "I

just happened to be the first person to create it. It started out one by one and soon I was getting thousands of members an hour."

The outpouring on the Internet provided a forum for both friends and strangers. It was a sign of the high-tech times: Just as young adults had begun turning to the Web to create and maintain friendships, they turned there, too, to share stories of grief, to express their outrage and to post poems and songs they had written in Yeardley's honor. Social networking proved it's about more than connecting people in life; it could connect in death as well.

"I never knew Yeardley but this story has really stuck with me," one woman wrote. "A young life taken too soon and so tragically."

Wrote another: "It is critically important that women protect their friends. NEVER allow anyone who is being threatened to remain silent. . . . Yeardley lost her life because of silent acceptance of violent behavior."

Some who posted online were angry, calling on the Commonwealth to pursue the death penalty against Huguely. Others were more tempered. "He deserves a trial," one man wrote. "Get your stuff together before you speak." Thousands reached out to Yeardley's family, offering support and prayers.

Tiffany Danielle, a lacrosse player from Cincinnati, Ohio, put her thoughts to music, publicly posting a dedication video with a nearly three-minute song written for Yeardley. Through a mixture of rap and R&B, she sang that though she didn't know Love, the young woman's death had brought her to tears.

The two shared a mutual love of lacrosse, she sang—"a lax family that we were both part of"—and that commonality made them family. "And when we step on the field, you're the one we think of," she sang, before promising to root for orange and blue.

Phyllis Botti of Los Angeles was one of the countless people who had no connection to the case but found herself drawn to it anyway. Months later, she could recall exactly

Yeardley (left) immediately looked up to her older sister, Lexie. "When I was little, I liked to do whatever my sister did," Yeardley wrote in an essay about her life in 2002, her freshman year of high school. *Photo courtesy of One Love Foundation/joinonelove.org*

After her death, Yeardley was described by many as an angel. As a little girl, she once dressed as one.

Photo courtesy of One Love Foundation/joinonelove.org

Yeardley and Lexie turned heads growing up. Both were athletic, slim, pretty and quick to smile.

Photo courtesy of One Love Foundation/joinonelove.org

In the days after her death, friends told reporters that Yeardley had a goofy side. *Photo courtesy of One Love Foundation/joinonelove.org*

After the death of John Love III, Sharon (Donnelly) Love (far right) grew even closer with her two girls.

Photo courtesy of One Love Foundation/joinonelove.org

Images of a broad-smiling Yeardley, affectionately known as Yards to her friends, helped catapult her story to international news.

Photo courtesy of One Love Foundation/joinonelove.org

The Boylan Heights bar, located just down the street from both Yeardley and George's apartments, was a popular hangout for UVA lacrosse players.

Photo by Amber Hunt

George Huguely V was recruited as a valuable midfielder, both muscular and capable of running the full length of the field many times per game.

Photo by Andrew Shurtleff

In 2008, Huguely was arrested for public intoxication after spewing racist and sexist slurs at a police officer who ultimately used a Taser to control him.

Rockbridge Regional Jail photo

Both George and Yeardley spent countless hours practicing and playing at UVA's Klöckner Stadium, located less than two miles from their separate apartments. *Photo by April Barney*

Charlottesville Police Chief Timothy Longo, formerly a Baltimore cop, speaks to the crush of media who began swarming the city in the hours after Yeardley's death first made headlines.

Photo by Andrew Shurtleff

Police were called in the early morning hours of May 3, 2010, to discover Yeardley's bloodied body in her second-floor apartment. *Photo by Amber Hunt*

George lived just two buildings away from his girlfriend in this brick building. *Photo by April Barney*

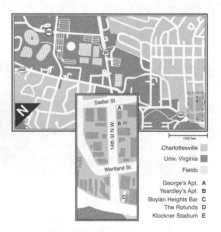

Charlottesville
Univ. Virginia
Fields

George's Apt. **A**
Yeardley's Apt. **B**
Boylan Heights Bar **C**
The Rotunda **D**
Klockner Stadium **E**

Illustration by John James Anderson

Thousands of distraught students, faculty and community members flooded the campus for a candlelit vigil two days after Yeardley's death. *Photo by Eric Kelley*

Members of the UVA women's lacrosse team sob at the vigil.
AP photo by Steve Helber

George looked defeated and drawn in the first mugshot released of him after his May 4 arraignment.

Albemarle-Charlottesville Regional Jail photo

Since his arrest, George Huguely V has been housed at the Albemarle-Charlottesville Regional Jail in a pastoral part of town.

Photo by Amber Hunt

how she first learned of Yeardley's death and admitted that her friends accused her of being obsessed with the case.

"I'll never forget it. It was May 4, I was at work and I see this blurb from AOL saying that this young man was arrested for supposedly killing this young lady," she recalled. "It was odd. I live in Los Angeles and we hear of people getting killed all the time, or kids being kidnapped. I read about those and get sad, but I move on, but this one really got to me. There was something about this case. My friends said, 'Phyllis, you're like obsessed with this story. You act like this is someone from your family.'

"I just think it's her face and her eyes," she continued. "She just looked like an angel on earth to me. Her eyes completely haunted me. It's interesting because before I saw the photo, it still got to me, but when I saw her face . . . She was full of life and promise, and that smile."

It wasn't that Botti identified with the violent ending Yeardley had met, either. The fifty-three-year-old divorced animal rights activist said she's never been abused either verbally or physically. (With a name like Botti and a six foot four father named Bruno, no one would dare, she joked.) It was more that Yeardley's death seemed so pointless and avoidable. She takes to heart the famous Albert Einstein quote: "The world is a dangerous place, not because of those who do evil, but because of those who look on and do nothing."

"It's so tragic that no one did anything and there were all of those signs," she said.

Botti has followed every development. She regularly posts links to updates on her Facebook profile page. She can rattle off the case's twists and turns with ease—the campus vigil, the details of Huguely's past arrest, his reportedly heavy-drinking hours leading up to the death. She found herself in tears talking about the case with friends. She even got in arguments with some who didn't like how the media had focused so much on Yeardley and Huguely's wealthy upbringings.

"I would say that I know it could happen anywhere, but you don't expect it to happen in a place like that," she said.

Yeardley had no shortage of friends through her profile page on Facebook. (It's unclear if George ever had one, or if it was swiftly deleted after his arrest.) In her public photo, she wore a strappy dark top and white pants draped alongside a friend on top of what appeared to be a barroom pool table. The girls, facing opposite directions with their heads propped, were fresh-faced and beaming; Yeardley's arms looked toned and tan.

Friends posted and tagged hundreds of photographs of Yeardley. Some of the pictures, later shared with reporters or posted in video montages elsewhere online, showed her smiling and laughing alongside her friends. Her clothes were flattering and fresh, appropriate for Charlottesville's humid summers. She seemed to favor tops either strappy or strapless, sometimes accented with bold, chunky necklaces. She was known to dress up both for Halloween and New Year's Eve, and while many of her photos were posed and smiley, she wasn't afraid to ham it up for the camera. In one, she looked appropriately goofball, dressed with two friends in rainbow propeller hats and nerdy glasses, complete with thick tape at the bridge. In another, she wore an expression of mock seriousness while dressed in camouflage overalls and a hunter orange vest.

She had more than 1,000 Facebook "friends," though several who responded to journalists' interview requests said they had only peripherally met the young woman. The hefty friend count isn't surprising for a girl Yeardley's age, on the cusp of graduating college, with so many interests. Nowadays, Facebook is used as much to catch up with high school classmates as it is to discover new people with overlapping interests, said Dave Awl, author of *Facebook Me!* which is in its second edition. In his book, Awl describes how people Yeardley's age and younger have different concepts of what friendship is than previous generations. They meet someone either in real life or online whom they deem interesting enough to warrant "friending," and from there, they recalibrate, he said.

Plus, he said, a college student set to graduate is wise to have a huge network (allowing some "friends" more access to personal info than others, he cautioned), as you never know where information about a job might surface. Many of Yeardley's friends were fellow lacrosse players, both male and female, from universities across the country. Many, too, were from the Baltimore area, some of whom she had met just once or twice before they became part of her entrusted online circle.

"If you're outgoing, if you're gregarious, if you have diverse interests and an intellectual curiosity, it's normal to have 1,000 friends online," Awl said.

By all accounts, Yeardley was each of those things.

Within six months of Yeardley's death, her Facebook profile had been deleted. All that remained were the pages created in her memory.

Chapter 15

Immediately after Yeardley's body was discovered and Huguely's arrest had been made public, the fate of the UVA lacrosse season for both men and women was unclear. Both teams had lived up to their stellar reputations in the regular season. The men had dominated in every game, save one conference match against Duke in April. As the quarterfinals neared, the team bounced between first and second ranking nationally. Though the women's season had been peppered with a few losses, they still ranked a more-than-respectable fourth place by April's end, even after coming off of two painful losses to Maryland and Northwestern during the Atlantic Coast Conference Tournament.

About 3 p.m. the day Yeardley died, ESPN's Quint Kessenich turned to social networking site Twitter to drop a lacrosse bombshell: Virginia had canceled the remainder of both the men's and women's seasons, he announced.

Sports Illustrated rushed to confirm, but UVA denied the development, prompting Kessenich to hastily issue a correction. Within hours, Kessenich's entire Twitter account disappeared. ESPN issued a statement on the sportscaster's behalf: "I am sorry for this mistake. While I had heard from two reliable sources that the seasons were canceled, I should've discussed it with my news editors and checked with University of Virginia officials before reporting it. When I discovered it was inaccurate I immediately issued a correction."

To some lacrosse players and fans, the rush to report a rumor was a bad sign that the tragedy unfolding would cast a pall over not just the university and the academic year, but over lacrosse as a whole. Some newspaper columnists and bloggers pointed fingers at the close-knit culture as being complicit in Yeardley's death. The warning signs had been there, some argued, and Huguely's violent tendencies should have been spotted long before he had the opportunity to kill.

On May 7, the *Baltimore Sun* ran an editorial with the headline: "A Shadow on Men's Lacrosse: Sport must deal with persistent reports of violence and sexual abuse." Penned by Peter G. Prowitt, the Sunday piece declared that "if ever there was a wake-up call that the culture of sex and alcohol abuse surrounding the sport of men's lacrosse has spun out of control, the case of Yeardley Love is it."

Lacrosse had seen this type of backlash before. In March 2006, a female student at North Carolina Central University accused three Duke University students of raping her at a party in Durham, North Carolina. The accusation dripped with scandal: The accuser, Crystal Mangum, was a stripper and escort, and she was black. The men she accused were white, and they were privileged lacrosse players. The allegations rocked the collegiate world in general, and that of lacrosse—a sport largely comprising privileged, white players—in particular. Not only were the three Blue Devils players accused of a crime, but of one that was racially motivated. Mangum said the men had called her a nigger, and, in leveling the charges, Durham County Prosecutor Mike Nifong suggested the assault might be a hate crime. The picture painted was of rich white boys feeling so entitled and superior to their black escort that they could justify forcing themselves on her.

The accused men declared their innocence, but the public's perception of them wasn't helped by an e-mail sent by one of the lacrosse players just hours after the party ended. Ryan McFadyen wrote to other players that he planned to

have some more strippers over. The e-mail, rife with punc-
tuation and grammatical errors, read:

> To whom it may concern
> tomorrow night, after tonights show, ive decided to
> have some strippers over to edens 2c. all are welcome..
> however there will be no nudity. i plan on killing the
> bitches as soon as the [sic] walk in and proceeding to cut
> their skin off while cumming in my duke issue spandex..
> all in besides arch and tack please respond
> 41

Forty-one was the jersey number for McFadyen. The
e-mail, quoted in a probable cause affidavit, was used by
law enforcement to secure search warrants related to the alleged attack and bolstered the prosecutor's belief that the
men accused were guilty as sin.

The media latched onto the outrage-invoking story. Pundits opined about such a crime keeping in step with lacrosse's
culture of entitlement. Some went so far as to say they were
shocked not at the alleged behavior of the players, but rather
at the authorities' insistence that these ne'er-do-well rich
kids finally be held accountable. In her show immediately
following the indictment of two of the lacrosse players,
Nancy Grace roasted a guest who suggested that the athletes
might be innocent. "That's your first concern?!" Grace interrupted. "Do you have a sister? I assume you have a mother."
Fewer than eight percent of reported rapes are proven to be
false accusations, she added, so the possibility that the young
men were innocent meant "not a hill of beans in my assessment of this case."

The lacrosse world was rattled—even the Huguelys.
George V and his father were both interviewed for their reactions to the scandal by the *Washington Post*. Huguely's
father told the paper that he'd used the incident as an opportunity to counsel his son about avoiding potentially dangerous situations.

"Regardless of what winds up happening, you have to

learn from this experience and take what you can from it," the elder Huguely said. "You always have to remember and can't let yourself be in a situation where something like this could happen."

Huguely V said he couldn't help but sympathize with the team.

"They've been scrutinized so hard and no one knows what has happened yet," he told the paper. "In this country, you're supposed to be innocent until proven guilty. I think that's the way it should be."

Duke wasn't as cautious in its reaction. The university suspended the lacrosse team for two games in late March, then canceled the remainder of the 2006 season, because of the allegations. Lacrosse coach Mike Pressler, who had helmed the team for sixteen seasons, was forced out. (Though his departure was outwardly presented as a resignation, he was awarded a settlement of an undisclosed amount from Duke in October 2007 for wrongful termination.) As it turned out, the university had perhaps reacted too hastily. In April 2007, thirteen months after the supposed off-campus gang-bang, North Carolina Attorney General Roy Cooper dropped all charges against the three accused players. More than that, he declared the three innocent, which was an unusual move; most prosecutors dismiss charges with prejudice, allowing law enforcement to save face by saying there maybe isn't enough evidence *now*, but we might levy the charges again if we find more evidence. Instead, Cooper said Nifong, the county prosecutor, had gone "rogue," and the North Carolina State Bar filed ethics charges against Nifong that ultimately got him disbarred for "dishonesty, fraud, deceit, and misrepresentation."

Not every word in Mangum's story was a lie: She and another woman had indeed been hired as escorts for a party hosted by several members of the lacrosse team, but she had never been assaulted there. DNA swabs taken from her body did not match up with any of the white Duke lacrosse players. Her motivation to lie was tough to gauge. She might have been under the influence of prescription drugs and possibly alcohol, and she seemed to believe the tales she told, police said. But the damage to the Duke players' reputations had already been done. They would forever be linked to a violent assault that never actually happened.

Though the charges were dropped, the story wasn't over. Pressler moved on, becoming coach of Bryant University's Bulldogs, finally telling his story in 2008 as a contributor to a book written by author Don Yaeger. Mangum's outrageous legal run-ins continued; in February 2010, she was arrested and charged with attempted first-degree murder and arson for allegedly trying to stab her boyfriend and set his clothes on fire in their bathtub. Though a 12-member jury found Mangum guilty of child abuse the following December, they couldn't agree on the arson charge, resulting in a hung jury and mistrial in the case. Some of Mangum's supporters told reporters that she was targeted as punishment for the Duke allegations four years prior.

On April 3, 2011, Mangum was arrested for another fight with a different boyfriend. This time, she was accused of repeatedly stabbing Reginald Daye in the abdomen; the 46-year-old died eleven days later, prompting prosecutors in Durham, North Carolina, to charge her with first-degree murder. As of this writing, she remains in jail awaiting trial.

The details of the Duke case were resurrected every time a new allegation even peripherally linked with alcohol or sex was publicly leveled at a men's lacrosse player—like in 2009, when three players at Sacred Heart University in Connecticut were charged with conspiracy to commit first-degree sexual assault. The charges apparently stemmed from a drunken encounter in which two of the players inappropriately touched an eighteen-year-old girl while she had sex with the third player. Charges were dismissed in 2010 for lack of evidence, but the incident reopened an old wound.

As the case against Huguely unfolded, the wound was more than reopened; it was picked at and salted until it festered and oozed. Some wondered if lacrosse would ever regain its footing as an all-American sport played by clean-cut kids.

"I don't want to repeat the Duke debacle of self-inflicted flagellation, but the [alleged] murder of Yeardley Love by a Virginia lacrosse player . . . brings to mind another dimension that the Duke mess revealed," one blogger wrote. "The culture of lacrosse epitomizes privileged swaggering wealth and elite violence comfortable with its own superiority and confident in its ability to act with impunity."

After Yeardley's death and Huguely's arrest, the divide between those who believed the allegations and those who didn't wasn't an issue, as had been the case in the Duke scandal. There was no denying that Yeardley was dead, and no one questioned—publicly, at least—whether her death was at George Huguely's hands. Even his defense lawyer didn't deny that—yet, anyway. But what hadn't changed between the Duke scandal and this new heartache were the criticisms lobbed against lacrosse.

An opinion piece posted on Opposing Views (www .opposingviews.com) declared that "lacrosse presents a different form of entitlement" than other scandal-ridden sports, such as football and basketball.

"It's a niche sport protected and supported by serious East Coast wealth," the piece said. The sport may be "slumming" now by entering community centers and trying to recruit the middle class, it continued, but it traditionally flourished at posh finishing schools.

For those born and raised in the sport's East Coast hotbeds, lacrosse, with its Native American roots, is considered the most American of sports. Often said to be the "fastest-growing sport on two feet," lacrosse programs have popped up in Florida, California, Texas, and Colorado, as well as some Midwest states. In an article about preventing lacrosse injuries, the Cleveland Clinic, regarded as one of the country's top hospitals, approximated that lacrosse had more than 130,000 high school players in 2010. "It is estimated to have grown faster than any other sport at the high school level over the last ten years, and is also the fastest-growing sport over the last five years in the NCAA," the hospital stated.

It's a sport steeped in history. When played by Native Americans, it was considered stellar military training. Sometimes entire villages or tribes would play against each other, and the goals were separated by miles rather than yards. The players used sticks that looked like a bishop's crosier, and because the ball (then made of hair-stuffed deerskin) was often nowhere near each player, their attacks against each other were strategic and violent. French explorers spotted the game in action in the 1800s and immediately adopted it. It spread quickly in Europe and Canada, and took root in cities dotting the United States' East Coast. The Montreal Lacrosse Club is largely credited with organizing and modernizing the sport, creating the first written rules in 1856. A rewrite followed eleven years later, and the new rules called for twelve players per team (a rule that would later change for men), as well as a hard rubber ball. William George Beers of the Montreal club designed a stick better suited to catching the ball and throwing it with accuracy.

Ice hockey and lacrosse have long been considered siblings. Johns Hopkins University in Baltimore was a major hockey-playing college in the late 1800s. When lacrosse was introduced toward the turn of the century, it caught fire throughout Maryland, prompting the creation of programs for all age groups. Johns Hopkins remains the heart from which the lacrosse lifeblood pulsates: It's home to the Lacrosse Museum and National Hall of Fame, and its men's team has won more than forty national titles.

The rules for men's and women's lacrosse differ in a lot of ways: In the men's game, ten players take the field; in women's, there are twelve. The size of their sticks are different. Even their field sizes can differ. But they deviate most in the physicality allowed: In women's lacrosse, body contact is forbidden. So-called "rough checks"—or swinging your stick at an attacker's stick—are also banned. Both types of contact are fine by men's standards. The differences, which slowly evolved over the past 100-plus years, have inspired criticism: Some say that the differences between the men's rules and women's rules are so great that they should be classified as two different sports altogether. As one player said, plenty of female athletes would prefer the rougher incarnation, while plenty of men would like the challenge of using skill and endurance over size and aggression.

Because of the physical contact allowed, the genders differ in equipment as well. Men must wear helmets with facemasks and four-point chin straps, as well as padded gloves. Women don't have to wear gloves or helmets as they aren't expected to endure as much physical punishment. (The exception is the goalkeeper, who has to wear a facemask, chest protector, and throat protector.) The women are mostly concerned with protecting themselves from the dense rubber ball zipping by, so they tend to wear mouth guards and either goggles or eye masks.

The sport has slowly spread from its New England roots into other parts of the country, fueled largely by people who grew up with it in their hometowns only to be heartbroken when they moved as adults to lacrosse-less parts of the country. The introduction of the sport to some Western states can be directly traced to East Coast transplants. It helps, too, that beginner lacrosse gear has gotten a bit more affordable in recent decades, beginning with the introduction of plastic stick heads in the 1970s. Some athletic companies have begun marketing low-cost starter sets, too, so that parents don't have to drop more than $100 to let their children at least test out the sport.

"The game is the mix of the best attributes of all sports," Matt Cone, president of the Washington Lacrosse Foundation, told the *New York Times* for a 2005 story about lacrosse's booming popularity. "It has grace, finesse, contact, and is a lot of fun to play and watch. People become addicted to it."

Some insist the sport would grow even faster if there were more coaches: "There have been several teams that wanted to start, but weren't able to find a coach, so they didn't happen," Alexis Longinotti, the Northern California chapter president of U.S. Lacrosse, told the *Times*. U.S. Lacrosse oversees both men and women's lacrosse in the United States.

Lacrosse magazine, published by U.S. Lacrosse, boasts a circulation of more than 300,000.

No matter its growing popularity, the sport still draws its share of (sometimes envy-driven) ridicule. In a 2007 episode of the NBC sitcom *30 Rock,* black comedian Tracy Morgan quipped to Tina Fey's character: "I'm gonna have so much money, my great-grandkids are gonna play lacrosse. Lacrosse, Liz Lemon!"

Players gather in online forums to tout lacrosse's superiority over other U.S. sports (baseball seems a particular foe) and to joke about balls, shafts, and heads. But lighthearted though some of the jokes and jabs are, lacrosse's reputation seems to fall under fire every few years—a fact not helped by the dark, anonymous underbelly of the World Wide Web. Separate from the sex and alcohol scandals, some lax players—or those purporting to be as they type behind a cloak of untraceable online handles—seem determined to paint the sport as one played by racist, entitled members of society's upper crust—most of them harboring a "boys will be boys" mentality.

"As my old lacrosse coach used to say, 'They invented soccer because they had to come up with something for the girls to play,'" one online poster wrote in early 2010 beneath video footage of a lacrosse interview. Even that comment was light-hearted compared to countless others.

One far-from-unique example: A young black player posted a video review of his lacrosse shaft and head on YouTube, prompting a slew of racist responses: "Your [sic] black, go play basket ball [sic] with the rest of your people, cause lacrosse does not want you!" wrote one commenter with "lax" in his or her profile name. The comment was mirrored by dozens of others. On other sites, writers said that while sports in general seemed to harbor a "mind your own business" mentality when it came to violence against women— "pro bowl quarterback Ben Roethlisberger receives a slap on the wrist for violence against women while Michael Vick loses his career for violence against dogs," one blogger wrote on OpposingViews.com, referring to the two NFL players—lacrosse presents a deeper-seated sense of entitlement. It's not the type of sport that, say, a poor, urban kid can discover and infiltrate, but rather a niche sport of seemingly impenetrable environs. In short, collegiate sports offer one layer of insulation from the real world, and cloistered deeper still is lacrosse.

Just three days after Yeardley's death, Andrew Sharp, an editor with SBNation.com, wrote a piece anticipating the lacrosse debate in which he provided unique insight into the lacrosse culture and the possible role it played. The case was more personal than most, he wrote, because he'd once met Huguely and shared friends with Yeardley.

"George Huguely went to Landon, my high school's biggest rival," he wrote. "He partied with some of my best friends. In high school he was known as a lacrosse prodigy, and eventually, as the starting quarterback for Landon's football team. His life may not have been 'charmed' on the inside, but from afar, it looked like he had it pretty good. Girls loved him, and guys respected him."

Sharp had braced himself for the lacrosse discussion, then decided to delve in and head it off with a piece of his own. He knew the discussion would come, just as it did in the Duke scandal. For outsiders, the lacrosse culture is as bizarre as it is impregnable. Its male players more often than not fit the stereotype—their hair shaggy, their clothes preppy, their attitudes cocky. They're the top echelon in a sport for the elite, and those who are gifted are treated like celebrities first in high school, and then in college. The excesses start early, too, with adults and community members sometimes looking the other way when a player is caught breaking curfew or drinking underage. With college, it seems the excesses only heighten: more booze, more power, more prestige.

Sharp attended a private and costly boys' school much like Landon, he wrote, and many of his closest friends played lacrosse. Because of that, Sharp grew up alongside a lot of guys who partied hard and "treated a lot of people like crap." Women, non-athletes, and authority figures were all dismissed as lowly creatures.

"Pretty much anyone that wasn't *one of them* either didn't exist, or existed solely as an object of ridicule," Sharp said.

That of course didn't apply to all players or all teams, according to Sharp, but enough to make a real concern of the sense of entitlement some say goes hand-in-hand with lacrosse.

Perhaps George Huguely didn't feel entitled to date Yeardley Love over her objections, Sharp concluded, but it was possible that being immersed in the lacrosse culture helped lead him down a dangerous path where he used alcohol as a coping mechanism and his enviable social status to shrug off any real repercussions for his behavior.

Peter Prowitt, the *Sun* columnist and a Virginia native, said he would "readily defend the virtues" of lacrosse, but he saw a danger in pretending that Yeardley's death was "a freak occurrence."

"Closer study of the culture of sexual misconduct and off-the-field troubles in men's lacrosse reveals a disturbing trend up to Ms. Love's case and suggests that there exists an ugly side to lacrosse, as is often claimed regarding basketball and football."

The editorial indictments kept coming. Author and columnist Michael Kimmel wrote a story called "Lacrosse and the Entitled Elite Male Athlete" two weeks after Yeardley's death. In it, he described Huguely as a "rich preppy jock at one of America's richest and preppiest schools."

"To some, Huguely was simply a monster, a deviant psychopath," Kimmel wrote, then dismissed that as a minimizing assessment leveled by "us 'normal' folk . . . Others, though, pointed out how unbearably common and 'normal' such attacks actually are: In the United States alone, three women are murdered every single day by their intimate partners and more than a million are physically assaulted every single year."

The pundits pointed out how violent lacrosse is, questioning whether Huguely was drawn to it because of his own violent tendencies, or if the sport actually created the violence. While women's lacrosse is no-contact, it's common in men's lacrosse for one player to hack at another with his stick. Pretty much all forms of attack are green-lighted, short of from-behind shoves and head shots.

But some in the lax world said too much was made of Yeardley and Huguely's lacrosse ties. On one lacrosse forum, one poster—identified as "3rdPersonPlural"—said the media coverage of the case seemed hyper-focused on the students' athletic prowess. Some news outlets used the word "lacrosse" more than "murder or tragedy," the poster wrote. Why was the couple's lacrosse connection any more relevant than, say, their majors?

Megan Pringle, the *Good Morning Maryland* anchor, found herself agreeing. Months after Yeardley's death, she said she never saw Yeardley as a lacrosse player first and a young woman second. Yeardley's impending graduation and strong ties to her family and friends were as much a part of her as her love of lacrosse, Pringle noted.

"It's not like lacrosse was all she was," Pringle said. "She led a very nice life and was a beautiful woman. It was more than that. And it was profoundly sad."

In the days after Yeardley's death, the fate of the UVA lacrosse season was quietly weighed. The postseason was nearing, but Athletic Director Craig Littlepage said everyone was in too much shock by the loss of Love, who he said was "described as an angel by teammates and friends." The players yearned for normalcy, and wanted desperately to get back into the rhythm of their grueling practices and adrenaline-pumping games—but they didn't want to return to the field if it would upset Yeardley's family. It was only after Sharon Love gave her blessing that the university officially announced the continuation of both the men's and women's seasons. There was no doubt in anyone's mind that Yeardley would have wanted them to continue, women's

coach Julie Myers told reporters. Players returned to Klöckner Stadium for stretching and practice. Media reporters
were kept away to give the still-mourning athletes their privacy as they readied for NCAA battle.

Chapter 16

The UVA men's lacrosse team was the first to step on the field after Yeardley's death. It was a somber homecoming. The team was down one player, as George Huguely continued to sit in the Albemarle-Charlottesville Regional Jail, but his teammates weren't outwardly mourning the murder suspect. Rather, it was Yeardley's name on their warm-up shirts. Printed in a cursive font, set in orange type against blue fabric, it read ONE LOVE.

The combination of Yeardley's jersey number and last name had come to symbolize the way she had vowed to live her life in the wake of her father's death. "One Love" had quickly been adopted by everyone who knew her, and many who didn't. Her name and number seemed too perfect: It was inclusive, hopeful, even elegant. The men also wore orange and blue ribbons, adorned with a simple white emblem that read LOVE.

"She's out there with us when we're playing," sophomore attackman Steele Stanwick told a *USA Today* reporter.

Before game day, sportswriters had questioned how the team would hold up. Sure, their record was 14–1 before Yeardley's death, but it was impossible to predict how such a blow would affect the team psychologically. And it wasn't the first tragic loss the team had endured: In November 2008,

just shy of Thanksgiving Day, word spread that teammate
Will Barrow had committed suicide. Barrow, twenty-two, had
completed his four years of lacrosse eligibility but still lived
in Charlottesville as he wrapped up his sociology degree.
He'd burst from the high school scene having been named
the best athlete at Baldwin Senior High School in New York,
and his reputation had only improved in college as he helped
lead his team to its 2006 national championship. His senior
year, he finished with a career-high twenty-eight ground balls,
scoring seven goals and assisting in three. Considered one
of the top defensive midfielders in the country, he already
had been drafted eleventh overall by the Chicago Machine,
a Major League Lacrosse team, and had scored three goals in
the five games he had played. He aimed to shatter stereotypes,
reaching out to other young black men in hopes of teaching
them lacrosse.

Coach Starsia called Barrow a leader, and his death a
shock to his teammates.

"I can only begin to describe adequately the agony within
the Virginia lacrosse community," Starsia told reporters.
"Will is a dear friend, respected and admired universally by
his peers and the staff. He was a leader in our program, on
and off the lacrosse field."

Though few talked in-depth about Barrow's death, it had
a profound impact on his teammates and the lax community
as a whole. Just as news of Yeardley's death filled the forums, so too did questions about Barrow's. "When one of us
passes away, we get affected by it," one poster wrote. "Most
of the members here didn't know him personally, but because he was on . . . the greatest stage within the sport of
lacrosse, we feel it." Some questioned whether Barrow had
really killed himself; the university had kept the cause of
death so quiet that some circulated rumors online that the
broad-smiled athlete must have died at someone else's hands.
Though small in comparison to the outcry that would follow
Yeardley's death, online memorials popped up for Barrow as
well, including a Facebook page that two years later would
still have more than 2,000 members. Most of the recent

posts on the page, however, were obscene spam messages; the last real message that was posted came in October 2010 to promote the second annual Will Barrow Memorial Flag Football Tournament.

Despite the university's silence about Barrow's death, fourth-year players on the 2008–2009 lacrosse team, who had played alongside Barrow the previous year, took turns talking in private about him and the impact his life and death had on them.

"Will is someone who we think about every day and night," Max Pomper, one of Barrow's closest friends, told a reporter. "Before the game, we talk about Will. We talk about how we want to play like he did—play hard, play fast, play strong. He was an incredible leader and we'll never forget him. We want to honor him by playing well and playing hard."

Barrow's death had been mourned publicly, but in subtle ways. Many players wore special T-shirts during pregame warm-ups with "Will" embroidered on the sleeve.

Eighteen months later, they'd be donning remembrance T-shirts again, this time bearing Yeardley's initials. And they'd be joined by thousands. One CBS affiliate reported that tickets and T-shirt sales surged in the wake of Yeardley's death for both men's and women's teams.

"I think now, especially, they're going to show their support and their love for the teams and all the players and support what they're going through right now," UVA student Michael Parente told a television reporter.

Ken Clausen, a team captain, painted "Y.L." in eye black under one eye and "W.B." under the other. This game was in honor of both the fallen lax players.

It was Saturday, May 15, twelve days after life stopped for Yeardley and changed for everyone else. The Cavaliers were pitted against unranked Mount St. Mary's University, an 1805-founded private university in Emmitsburg, Maryland. Players from both teams bowed heads while Yeardley's picture appeared on the scoreboard for a moment of silence before the first-round NCAA tournament game began.

For Coach Starsia, the official return to Klöckner Stadium was his first following two gut-wrenching emotional blows: The same week Yeardley died, the coach's father succumbed to cancer. In the weeks that followed, he had to serve as a pillar to his dazed team, while at the same time nursing his own psychological wounds. For men like Starsia, and for the team that revered him, the best way to cope with pain was to unleash it on the field.

The Cavaliers exploded from the gate. Shamel Bratton, who wore No. 1 for the men, was fittingly the first to score. Seven more goals followed before Mount St. Mary's had a chance to respond. The 'Hoos were electric, seeming to exhale after nearly two weeks of bated breath. They were raw from mourning. Their sport had been scrutinized, their characters assassinated by association. They came ready to pummel.

"We wanted to play with a whole lot of heart and passion," Ken Clausen said after the game, "and I think we did a great job of doing that."

No. 1 Bratton scored two more goals for three total, tying for a game high with Brian Carroll and Chris Bocklet.

The 18–4 blowout had been cathartic, players said. Lacrosse had been both the team's bond and its sanctuary.

"By escaping and releasing some emotions and getting back to something we all love, I think that definitely helped us heal," said Clausen, who just a week earlier had been among Love's pallbearers and considered her one of his best friends. "But by no means has it healed. I don't think anything is going to go away anytime soon."

"Emotionally, it's been a tough ride for us," said junior goalie Adam Ghitelman, who added that "the best thing we've got going is the community of our teammates. . . . It's been a roller coaster. We've had to step up and kind of have iron hearts this past week. I think our team has come together, as well as the girls, helping each other out."

The men had won their comeback game. Next, it was the women's turn to take the field.

Chapter 17

Pressure ran high for the women as they geared up to battle Towson University on Sunday, May 16. The men had already come back to slaughter their first opponent. Now, everyone's eyes were on their female counterparts. News outlets that never before paid attention to lacrosse—much less women's lacrosse—sent reporters and photographers. Fans brought signs bearing heartfelt messages and Love's name.

It was a home game, again at Klöckner Stadium, meaning the women 'Hoos had the same home field advantage that the men had just a day prior. They made it no secret that they wanted to win this one for "Yards."

And there were reminders everywhere. Colorful flowers lay in memoriam by the game sign. Beneath the players' jerseys were shirts that read ONE TEAM. ONE HEART. ONE LOVE. The women, too, wore black patches on the front of their jerseys with the word LOVE in white letters.

Even Towson, the competition, paid their respects, honoring Yeardley with orange wristbands with Y.L. written in dark blue. Just as the community had united in mourning after Barrow's death, they were united now. The Towson players wished the 'Hoos well for the rest of the season, and gave each of their opponents a pin of an angel carrying a lacrosse stick.

A season-high crowd of more than 2,200 people filled Klöckner's stands.

"I just felt like I needed to take time out and show some support," Bob Mattie, a local lacrosse coach and UVA fan, told a reporter. Added Cricket Capucci, a Towson fan: "We're all parents and it could happen to any one of our kids. You feel helpless when you see something like this happen."

Fans and players alike acknowledged a moment of silence for Yeardley and her family. Several wiped away tears.

Cavalier player Whitaker Hagerman, a pretty but fierce blond who started in eighteen contests in the 2009–10 season, dropped her head and spoke to Yeardley in the stillness.

"Be out here with us," Hagerman quietly pleaded.

The silence was shattered by a Cavaliers fan in the grandstand, whose raucous "Let's go UVA!" seemed to energize both sides.

"We had to go out there, we had to play a game, we had to play lacrosse, and we had to play well," Hagerman later told reporters.

Like the men, the women seemed to explode with ferocity, scoring three goals in the first three minutes. But unlike the men's game, the fervor wasn't unmatched. Towson quickly responded to every goal. By the fifty-minute mark, the game was tied at eleven goals apiece. The crowd had erupted with every Cavalier goal—especially two netted by Caitlin Whiteley, the roommate who had discovered Yeardley's body in their shared apartment—and Towson's perseverance seemed as much in honor of Yeardley's competitive spirit as her own team's.

Megan Pringle, the *Good Morning Maryland* anchor, walked downstairs in her Baltimore home to find her husband, a sports reporter, watching the match at home. Tears streamed down his face. Rob Carlin, who had covered a few Yeardley-related stories as a freelancer for Comcast, was leveled not only by the players' tenacity, but also by the obvious outpouring of support by the fans. They wore ribbons and held signs. The camera regularly returned to shots of

Sharon and Lexie Love in the stands. Lexie, her eyes hidden behind dark sunglasses, was clearly in tears.

The camera seemed to focus in on one player, No. 14, more than others, Pringle recalled. When she asked why, her husband told her the player's name: It was Whiteley. Pringle suddenly understood.

As the game remained tied with ten minutes remaining, Coach Julie Myers noticed two pink-clad women in dark sunglasses making their way to the Cavaliers' bench. The younger of the women had Yeardley's beaming smile and, one teammate said later, even Yeardley's laugh. After a moment, the players on the field spotted the women, too. Yeardley's mother, Sharon, and sister, Lexie, had stepped forward to show the team their support in the game's waning minutes.

"When they came down, and I saw them kind of walking up behind our team, I felt like we were going to suddenly be OK," Myers later told reporters. "I felt like they were going to kind of be our extra emotion on the side."

The boost worked: Cavalier Brittany Kalkstein scored, giving her team a 12–11 lead. Next came Whiteley, whose third goal of the contest seemed the most powerful, pushing the team to a two-goal lead. Each team scored once more, and as the buzzer sounded on the 14–12 Cavaliers win, the team players stood together and held into the air white cards bearing Love's No. 1.

Lexie Love's head dropped as she cried.

After the game, the players spoke publicly for the first time since Yeardley's death. While they were careful not to discuss the case or their feelings about George Huguely, they described their friend and teammate—and the horror they had experienced over the previous two weeks.

"For me, it's been really hard, but I don't know where I'd be without my team and all my close friends," Whiteley said. "Playing today meant a lot, and it's obviously not normal, but I feel like each day we're getting stronger, finding out what we need from each other."

Though their season ended with the loss, Towson's players seemed satisfied.

"It was hard coming here knowing everyone was rooting against us a little bit," Towson senior Jackie Kendell told reporters after the game. "I think in respect to the Virginia team, it was our duty to play as hard as we could against them. I think that's what everyone would have wanted. On the field, that's where all that drama goes away, and it was our job to give them a really good game—and we definitely did that."

Yeardley was "an absolutely unforgettable person," UVA player Marye Kellermann told reporters. "When you met her, you just loved her, she was great. My very best friend . . . I am going to try my best to make sure the world doesn't forget what a good person she was."

Brittany Kalkstein, who scored the all-important, tie-breaking twelfth goal for the Cavs, said the previous two weeks had been "unbelievable."

"Our team is going through it together—and, no, I can't compare this to anything," she said, responding to a reporter's question. "It was just a crazy last two weeks, and I think being together and trying to stay focused and coming out to practice is the strength we needed to be with each other and get through it."

Kaitlin Duff, another fourth-year player who also roomed with Yeardley, said the community outpouring had been invaluable.

"Seeing everyone being so positive and so nice just really helps our team and helps our team get stronger," she said at a post-game news conference.

"We are one team," added Lauren Benner, the team's goalie. "We have one heart, and we're doing it for one purpose. And it's for Yeardley."

For Coach Myers, the Sunday afternoon victory was more than a simple lacrosse win. It was life affirming.

"I know I wasn't ready to be done," she said. "I don't think the girls were close to being ready, either. Partly because we're really competitive, and we really love playing lacrosse, and we feel like we're a good enough team to still be alive, but also because we still need to be together as we take these next steps.

"This was obviously much more than just a game today," she continued. "An NCAA game with obvious consequence of not being able to move forward if you don't win. Just a huge hurdle for our team to clear through. You hear that you always want to try to find some kind of normal, and to be back on a game field, I think is something that's normal at this point in the season. I'm very proud of the way they were able to play, especially during the circumstances we've been in."

The win marked the first in the NCAA Tournament for the 'Hoos since 2007, and it advanced them to the quarterfinal round the following weekend.

"Emotionally, we've been through an awful lot," Myers said. "I think the girls really were phenomenally inspiring this week. I felt like they played really hard with lots of attention and just emotion—positive emotion."

As the team celebrated its win, a song began to blast over the Klöckner's sound system. It was Cher, belting her 1998 hit "Believe."

"Do you believe in life after love?" began the chorus. The team exploded in excitement.

They believed indeed.

Chapter 18

Six days later, the fourth-seeded UVA women's lacrosse team faced third-seeded University of North Carolina. Some of the remembrances that had graced Klöckner Stadium carried over to Chapel Hill's Fetzer Field: wristbands worn in Yeardley's honor, a pregame moment of silence, Love's name adorning the UVA team's jerseys. The intervening days had been a whirlwind of grueling practice hours, commencement rehearsals, and mourning. The women tried to reignite the fire sparked during the game against Towson, but the vibe was different. Sharon and Lexie Love didn't attend this game. Instead, they sent players text messages, including one to Kaitlin Duff that read *1-2-3-4, Go Hoos*. Love's uncle, the former UVA lacrosse player in whose footsteps Yeardley had followed, told the women that their team was "everyone's team, the country's team right now." Heading into the contest, it was clear the Cavaliers were the sentimental favorites.

UNC Coach Jenny Levy sought out Coach Myers before the game to offer condolences. The two were lacrosse teammates at UVA years before and had stayed good friends as they moved on to teach competing teams. Levy's team had a game the day of Yeardley's funeral; her players wore wristbands with YL1 embroidered on them, and Levy sent Myers a text message and photograph of her captains wearing the bands before the game.

Myers told reporters that, aside from giving players a day off after the previous win to recuperate, they prepped for their Chapel Hill appearance as hard as ever.

"We're making sure our game is sharp and taking breaks when we need to," she told a reporter. "We're still in the healing process, but still trying to get ready for the game. We're trying to make sure we're doing enough to be ready but not too much to overwhelm."

But as the match began, it became quickly clear that some of the electricity had dulled. This time, as the Cavs gave up the first goal, it appeared to onlookers that the roller coaster of the past three weeks had finally caught up with the team. Instead of attacking, the players limped. They seemed drained, unfocused. Even the crowd had lost its fervor. Instead of a packed stadium with thousands of spectators, fewer than 700 people had gathered at Fetzer Field.

The Cavs found the scoreboard three minutes into the game, but UNC responded with eight more goals, jumping to a 9–1 lead. By halftime, the score was a painfully lopsided 11–2. In the end, the Tar Heels doled out a 17–7 loss— the biggest deficit the 'Hoos had endured all year—ending the mourning team's season.

After the buzzer sounded to end the sixty minutes, the Cavaliers stayed on the field. Some slumped onto the grass, breaking into tears. Several clutched each other in hugs. They simply weren't ready to walk away, to have the season end. They had survived so much together; the close of the season seemed to symbolize that they would now have to face things alone.

"The end of any season is a really hard, sudden ending," Coach Myers told reporters after the game. "I think that the end to this season, given all that we've been through, makes it especially hard."

Myers said she knew it wasn't an easy victory for North Carolina, either.

"Emotionally, it was hard for them to play a hand in the

ending of our season. I give them credit. I think they did a nice job with a lot of poise and a lot of competitiveness in making sure they won this game today."

After the 'Hoos finally left the field, the coach gathered with the young women and told them she was proud of them.

"The message was that I love them," Myers said. "And I couldn't have asked them to do anything more—not on the field, and not off the field. They've been really outstanding. Our first few days we literally took it hour by hour and, eventually, we were able to think as big as two days away. I don't think I ever thought where we would be three weeks down the road."

Kaitlin Duff again was a stellar scorer, securing three of the Cavaliers' goals. Caitlin Whiteley, whose three-goal performance less than a week prior had galvanized the crowd, was scoreless.

"I think we had a great season, and we had a lot of ups and downs, but we really stuck together," Duff told reporters. "It shows there's a lot more to the game of lacrosse than winning. We didn't play our best today, but I think we feel great about the season."

Reporters asked the inevitable question: *What next?*

Brittany Kalkstein answered thoughtfully.

"I don't think that there is any way you can really move on from this," she said. "Obviously, it's going to be in our thoughts forever. We will try and stick in town for a few days and be with each other . . . It's been a huge learning experience these past few weeks, and I think it taught us about life."

The women's season had ended, but the curtain hadn't fallen on UVA lacrosse entirely. Up next: the men.

Coming off the women's loss in North Carolina, the first-seeded men's team faced eighth-seeded Stony Brook University. The Seawolves, as the Cavaliers' counterparts were named, got home field advantage at the 1,000-acre campus on Long Island's North Shore in New York, about 500 miles north of Charlottesville.

By then, the intense media attention had shifted. The

women's run was over. While news photographers and cameras still lined the field at LaValle Stadium, the outlets were mostly familiar again—ones that normally would have paid attention to an NCAA quarterfinal match.

Shamel Bratton and Chris Bocklet again scored three goals apiece, helping the team eke past the Seawolves with a 10–9 win. While the women's team had halted, the men headed to another round.

"Watching the scores yesterday, finding out the girls didn't get the win they wanted, you really want to get to the end for them," Adam Ghitelman told reporters afterward. "For me personally and for the team, those girls deserve everything. We're going to play the rest of the season for them; they deserve it."

Captain Ken Clausen echoed the sentiment.

"With everything that's been going on, and lacrosse aside, we want to be able to stick together as a team and going out there and playing for the girls and playing for Yeardley," he said. "That's been in our minds and it's been some motivation for us. We're ready to keep playing hard and stick together for another week."

The men, like the women, had "been through a lot," Clausen added.

"Kind of our motto has been that we don't want this thing to end."

Six days later, it did end.

The Cavaliers faced fifth-seeded Duke in another away game—this time in front of 44,238 fans at M&T Bank Stadium in Baltimore. The turnout made the game the sixth-largest attended semifinal game in NCAA men's lacrosse tournament history, according to VirginiaSports.com.

Bocklet again led in team scoring, netting four goals, but the effort fell short. Thanks to Duke's stellar third quarter, during which they outscored UVA 4–1, the Blue Devils snuck past Virginia with a 14–13 win.

Coach Dom Starsia, wearing a patch that read Y.L. 1. on his shirt, somberly told reporters that the team had played hard and showed courage both on the field and off.

"The final score is probably the least important part of what has transpired here," he said.

Bocklet wiped away tears as Starsia spoke. Several players couldn't stomach the season-ending press conference and instead sought solace in the locker room. They were "upset the final result wasn't what they hoped for."

"Emotionally, it was hard. Emotionally, I think it's a lot to handle," sophomore Steele Stanwick, who tallied three goals and two assists in the game, said. "The season may be over, but we're still a team. We're going to stick together through this thing and make sure everyone's OK."

Again, George Huguely's teammates never mentioned his name, which by then had even been deleted from the team's official 2009–10 roster online.

It was as though he hadn't existed all season.

PART III

"You'll Get Nothing From Me, Pal"

Chapter 19

Students on the university's campus tried to get their lives back to normal, but it wasn't easy. The media scrutiny, while perhaps waning, was still pervasive. With every university milestone came another round of reporters looking to cover it from the "Yeardley Love" angle. On May 13, *People* magazine hit newsstands and mailboxes with Love on the cover. In bold letters, layered over the team photo that had run in newspapers nationwide, the cover text asked: "COULD SHE HAVE BEEN SAVED?" An inset photo of Huguely in jail garb hovered over the ominous title: "Virginia Lacrosse Killing." It was heavy fare, juxtaposed alongside a photo of actress Sandra Bullock with her new adopted child and an announcement that country music artists Blake Shelton and Miranda Lambert had gotten engaged.

By the time freelance writer Matthew Power showed up to cover the university's graduation, the whole town of Charlottesville seemed exhausted by what he described as a "shark frenzy" of media attention.

Power, a contributor editor to *Harper's Magazine* whose works have been published in dozens of high-profile magazines, including *Men's Journal*, *Mother Jones*, *Slate,* and *Maxim*, got a surprise phone call from *Rolling Stone* magazine. Editors there had been slow to pick up on the Love

slaying, but following the cover story in *People*, they seemed
interested in providing readers with a more detailed takeout
than they'd seen to date. Power hadn't paid much attention
to the case until he was asked to cover it. But his mother
knew all about it.

"It had been an oversaturated media circus since" her
death, Power later recalled. "I knew I was going into a tough
situation, and *Rolling Stone* knew it, too. I was so far behind
the curve of the rest of the media coverage."

Power wasn't thrilled with the assignment, but he accepted
it anyway—largely, he acknowledged, because he didn't
want to pass up a gig with *Rolling Stone*. Plus, despite his
distaste for the way Americans eat up grisly murder tales, he
had been assured that the magazine would allow him the
time and space he would need to tell Yeardley's story in a
respectful, insightful way. Perhaps some good could come
from telling the story thoughtfully, he reasoned.

"With *Rolling Stone*, you have the great fortune of space
and time and context and nuance," he said. "It didn't have to
be boiled down to 'dead, cute girl.' You do have the potential of doing it right without it being as sensational a story."

Armed with as many story clips and contact phone numbers as he could quickly gather, Power rented a car and drove
from his home in New York City to Charlottesville, crashing
at the home of a journalist friend. He tracked down Brendan
Fitzgerald, the reporter with *C-VILLE Weekly* who had covered the death from the very first hours. Power tried to reach
Yeardley's family, but to no avail. Sharon apparently had
spoken briefly to *People* but was declining further requests.
Attorneys from both sides weren't speaking, either. Power
then reached out to Yeardley's friends, most of whom were
polite but clearly unwilling to assist with the piece.

None of that shocked Power, but what did surprise him
was the reluctance of people who didn't know Yeardley but
who could have nonetheless helped tell the tale of her life at
UVA. It was as if the whole city was on lockdown, as though
some directive had been passed out community-wide in-
structing people to shrug off all media inquiries. It didn't

matter what outlet the reporter was from or how earnest he or she was about telling the story properly. Yeardley's death had united the city in silence.

The Sunday after Power arrived in town—about three days into his trip—an attempt at a profile piece on Huguely was published in the *Washington Post*. The story largely was based on public court records, some of which already had been made public, and unnamed sources—a noticeable lack of substance in a story that boasted three reporters in its by-line and several more as contributors. One unnamed source was a bartender at Boylan Heights, the bar down the street from Yeardley and George's apartments, an establishment that reportedly had been busy on the night of the slaying. Even though the source wasn't identified, Power learned that the bartender who blabbed had been fired after the piece ran. And when Power himself reached out to the bar, a different bartender snarled, "You'll get nothing from me, pal."

Power half-smiled, handed over his business card, finished his subpar $3 drink of well vodka and soda, and left.

"The fact was, there was no upside for anyone to talk," Power said. "They had been completely swarmed over by the media. Most of them were young kids about to graduate, and they suddenly found themselves in the deep end of a media pool. Every kid on both of the teams had been swamped with calls and calls and calls from reporters. Imagine your whole life is ahead of you, and you're suddenly thrust into a sordid murder investigation."

Power paused, then mused the university's colors.

"There was an orange wall of silence," he said.

Power reached his contact at *Rolling Stone* and told him the story might be tough to deliver. Somehow, the case was the talk of the town—but no one was actually saying anything. Still, Power decided to stay on through the university's graduation ceremonies in hopes that he might find two or three people to help him tell an appropriate story. The story he felt he was uncovering, even in people's silence, was one about wealth and connections in an insular high society. In fact, he said, it was an "insular culture within an insular culture within

an insular culture"—a group of wealthy young adults admitted to the prestigious University of Virginia who belonged to
the cloistered lacrosse culture. The story made headlines not
just because Yeardley was young, beautiful, and white, Power
said. It garnered international attention in part because of
the "shock that trailer park behavior would occur" within that
society.

Behind the scenes, Yeardley's family was hard at work trying to distance the young woman from the image of a domestic violence victim. While John Casteen's heartfelt words
at Yeardley's on-campus vigil had garnered national praise,
the family, by many accounts, was not happy with her being
depicted as a victim—or, as in the lyrics of the haunting
Pink Floyd song, among the "weak and the weary." As the
family's displeasure became known, university employees
were cautioned not only to avoid media questions, but to
particularly shy away from any phrasing that might depict
Yeardley as the victim of intimate partner violence.

One employee felt this was a mistake. Frances Godfrey*,
whose name has been changed because she fears she will
lose her job by speaking publicly, said the university missed
an opportunity to reach out to young adults by acquiescing
to the family's request to stay silent.

"It might seem honorable within the university to honor
the family's wishes, but I can't help but wonder if it's the
right way to go. There are ways to talk about the incident that
don't make Yeardley look like this was somehow her fault,"
Godfrey said.

Others at the university agreed. Some wanted to use the
case to reach out to young women in unhealthy relationships, but they were forbidden. Publicly, only Casteen had
been granted permission to speak about the case, and even
he fell silent within a week of Yeardley's death.

"He was considered by many to have made very eloquent
statements," Godfrey recalled. "Everyone at the university
was consoled by that. But then even he stopped talking. Everything got quiet."

Asked via phone message and e-mail about the university's response to the tragedies, UVA spokeswoman Carol Wood refused to reply. To some, it seemed reflective of the university's decision to fall mute. The pall cast over the university was palpable, employees said. The academic year had been so difficult. People felt sucker punched and drained, and now they felt they had to walk on eggshells around campus when so many were ready to scream out.

This had been a year when students kept hopeful vigil on the bridge where Morgan Harrington was last seen, only to be devastated with the discovery of her body three months later. A year when the peak of lacrosse season was marred by the brutal slaying of one student, and the unfathomable arrest of another. A year when six other students—three of them seniors, on the cusp of graduating and entering the so-called real world—died suddenly. For many, these instances marked their first introductions to death, serving as a wake-up call that the world they were entering could be unthinkably sinister and heartlessly random.

"It had been a terrible, terrible year. Just god-awful," Godfrey said. "This genuinely isn't a place that we think of as being violent. It was so shocking—profoundly, profoundly shocking."

Outside of Yeardley's vigil, students involved in the White Ribbon Campaign—meant to raise awareness for violence against women—passed out the looped material, but Godfrey said she later learned that they had already been asked not to directly link Yeardley with domestic violence. Instead, the volunteers—mostly young women—passed the ribbons out quietly to people approaching the campus lawn.

Sharon Love acknowledged to one reporter that she was tired of the media portraying Yeardley as a domestic violence victim. The reporter, a woman, said that she was personally familiar with such violence and saw Yeardley's story as a chance to illustrate how even smart, strong women could be victimized. Maybe some good could come from the story, the reporter suggested.

"Yeardley was no shrinking violet," Love interjected.

The reporter was taken aback. "Neither was I," she answered.

"The family did not want it to be called domestic violence because that meant particular things about Yeardley, and that was the end of that," Godfrey said. "It could no longer be called that. We were not to link these two things."

Liz Seccuro, the UVA alumna and victims' rights activist, noticed that people shied away when she called it domestic violence as well.

"That is what it is: Domestic violence," she said. "People don't like that moniker because it doesn't speak to 'nice kids' who go to 'nice schools.'"

The family's decree colored how—and whether—Casteen and others would discuss Yeardley from then on.

Though Yeardley wouldn't be there to cross the stage, she was still set to graduate from the University of Virginia. The school announced that she would receive her degree posthumously, allowing her to achieve in death what she'd set her sights on years prior: the UVA degree her father never got.

The first graduation was on May 23, and it was the one most university students attended. Yeardley would not have crossed the stage in that ceremony had she lived because she would have been traveling with her teammates 180 miles away in Chapel Hill, North Carolina, after playing in the final lacrosse match of the year. Still, her absence seemed to weigh down the crowd, recalled Matthew Power, who, like Brendan Fitzgerald, attended the ceremony.

Tens of thousands of people gathered to watch the sea of graduates, garbed in black gowns and colored hoods, make the hour-long trek across the stately lawn to their seats. As they walked, the heartache of the past few weeks lifted slightly and gave way to high-fives, hugs, and laughter. Students snapped photos of themselves on their cell phones and texted them to friends. Images from the ceremony were posted to Facebook profiles before the commencement even began.

As soon as the class was seated, however, the crowd quieted for a moment of silence to honor the four members of the graduating class who did not live to see graduation. Though Yeardley was just one of four, her death seemed to overshadow the others. Perhaps it was just timing as hers had been the most recent, or maybe it was the lingering what-ifs, the senselessness of it—and the feeling that it could have, and should have, been avoided.

As Charlottesville's streets clogged with commencement-goers, volunteers again quietly passed out their white ribbons—reportedly 25,000 of them—in hopes of raising awareness. Caitlin Donaghy, a UVA student, was one of only a few to agree to speak to reporters.

"The reality is, domestic abuse is prevalent everywhere, and people really need to talk about it and know that there are resources out there," she told CBS's *Early Show.*

But the reality was, no one was talking about what killed Yeardley Love. As the commencement speeches began, there would be some allusions to, and a few direct mentions of, Yeardley, but there would be no discussion of what caused her death. Nor would there be any mention of Huguely, who had also been set to graduate that day.

John Casteen, looking even more like an academic than usual, approached the podium, wearing a traditional black robe. He "appeared both timeless and unshakeable before a crowd of thousands," Fitzgerald wrote in the May 25 edition of *C-VILLE Weekly.* For the university president, the day weighed heavy for more reasons than Yeardley's death. He had announced prior to the academic year that 2010 would mark his final commencement before an August 1 retirement, bringing to an end a twenty-year legacy at the school. He had arrived amid a budget crisis, navigating through complicated changes to how the state would fund the university. In 1990, the university had been smaller; Casteen helped it grow, both in terms of its facilities and in student enrollment. In his two decades as president, the university had built or bought 134 new buildings, increased female undergraduate enrollment from 50 to 56 percent, increased minority enrollment by nearly 7 percent, and increased overall enrollment from about 18,000 to nearly 21,000. Casteen had been lauded for creating the Office of Diversity and Equity at the university in the wake of racial incidents between 2003 and 2005, during which black students reported experiencing racial epithets scrawled in bathrooms and screamed at them as they walked down the street. Largely, Casteen was praised as a university president. Some said he would likely go down in history as its best.

But his last year on campus had been remarkably dark. Seven of his students had died, four of whom were on the cusp of graduating and beginning new lives, and the murder of Morgan Harrington had also disquieted the town.

"This is, in a sense, a daunting moment for me," Casteen began as he faced some 6,000 graduates. "Just as the University has not been perfect in your time here, the world to which you go is flawed and, in some senses, corrupt."

Casteen admitted that he was more accustomed to watching commencements rather than speaking at them, and he struggled to find the right words and advice. Jokingly, he passed along his wife's tip—"don't sweat the small stuff." But his real message was wrapped in references to John Keats, the nineteenth-century poet whose life was cut short at age twenty-five by tuberculosis. For Casteen, it was Keats's theory of "negative capability"—or the capacity to accept the uncertain and unresolved—that resonated most.

"Here we must decide for ourselves whether or not to act—whether we will step out courageously to explore those dark passages," Casteen said.

Though he didn't say Yeardley's name at that point, those attending were sure he was referencing her.

Casteen mused about the things he would miss hearing most when he left the campus: "The sounds of children on the lawn during Halloween. The chapel's bells. Cheers at games, no matter what the sport. And the name of Yeardley Love."

It was the only time he uttered her name, and they were the final two words Casteen spoke. His message seemed clear: Yeardley must not be forgotten.

For those familiar with Keats's life and death, that message was especially poignant. The young man, whose poems and letters were only appreciated after his death, was both afraid and certain that his existence on earth would be forgotten. The epitaph he wrote for his tombstone reads: "Here lies one whose name was writ in water."

Casteen seemed to be urging the campus to make sure Yeardley's name was written in stone.

Department chair Jeffrey Legro presided over the ceremony for Yeardley's 250 political science classmates. It seemed a bittersweet day for those crossing the lawn to receive their diplomas. The death was too fresh—just three weeks had passed—for students to feel ready to selfishly celebrate their own accomplishments. A sense of survivor's guilt hung thick in the air.

After what seemed to be the last name was read and the final diploma received, Legro said he had one remaining.

"As you know, Yeardley Love was killed just weeks short of this ceremony," he told the crowd. "Today, we are not mourning Yeardley. We are celebrating her achievement as a member of the class of 2010 at this University of Virginia."

Several members of Yeardley's family sat in the audience, including an aunt and uncle and some cousins, Legro said. He called on Lawren McChesney, Yeardley's cousin and a 2006 UVA graduate, to accept the diploma on Love's behalf.

"It is a privilege to recognize all that Yeardley achieved as a student at UVA and all the potential she had in life by awarding a posthumous degree of bachelor of arts in government," Legro said.

He paused, then called her name the same fashion as everyone else who had received a degree: "Yeardley. Reynolds. Love."

The crowd erupted in applause. It lasted a raucous forty-five seconds, tempered only by Legro's prompting.

"You are now officially alumni," Legro told the graduating class. "You will be missed."

* * *

On Monday, the university held a special graduation for the men's lacrosse and softball players who had missed the previous day's ceremonies. The athletes filed into Old Cabell Hall, one of three buildings designed by Stanford White for the south end of the Lawn in 1898. Originally known as the Academical Building, it was stately and grand, with an auditorium stage lined with giant organ pipes and adorned on the north wall with a copy of *The School of Athens* by Raphael.

Several members of the men's team wore buttons bearing Yeardley's name and the date of her death on their robes. Ken Clausen, the men's captain who had worn both Yeardley's and Will Barrow's initials on his cheeks, was introduced as a stellar athlete, one of the men's lacrosse team captains. He took the microphone to uproarious applause and thanked the university, its faculty, his coaches, his teammates, and all the lacrosse parents. He shared in the university softball team's solid 2010 showing, and said that they gathered this day not only to celebrate the athletes' accomplishments in the classroom, but also their accomplishments on the field.

The weeks leading up to graduation had tested everyone, he added.

"The untimely death of Yeardley Love sent shockwaves through our program, the university, and the country," he said, reading from a speech. "This tragic event forced our teams and the university to stick together to come out stronger rather than fragment and fade away.

"Well, I can assure you the latter has not occurred, and that our university has come together like no one could have imagined."

The coaches, staff, students and parents had all supported the team immensely, he added. He thanked them on behalf of his whole team.

After his speech, as the applause began to quiet, Clausen stepped down. Matthew Power, who had already e-mailed and called Clausen before the graduation, tried to sidle up to him in hopes he would elaborate. Power's approach was respectful and a bit laid-back—more "please consider calling me" than the stereotypical microphone-in-the-face approach that some attach to journalists. He knew the kids were hurting. He knew, too, that they already seemed banded together in silence. Clausen had come across as a stand-up guy, and it seemed he had a lot more to say on the matter than what he presented in his seven-minute speech. But Clausen declined, as did Caitlin Whiteley and the other members of both the men and women's teams. No one was willing or able to shed light on either Yeardley's or George's personalities or their relationship.

Power had repeatedly run into the same refrain. After about a week of in-person and phone research, he gave up and alerted *Rolling Stone* that the story had stalled. It was the first time in his professional career that he had ditched a story because no one would cooperate. He assured *Rolling Stone* that the failure wasn't caused by any personal shortcoming.

"I said they could be comforted in the knowledge that no one else would have the story, either," he said.

A few months later, as he recalled the experience, Power said he couldn't blame anyone for refusing to cooperate. He suspected that many felt complicit in Yeardley's death—and he didn't disagree. There had been several public run-ins between Yeardley and Huguely, and for whatever reason, apparently not one of those instances had been reported to the authorities.

"Everyone should have known it was a huge problem," Power said. "I'd be surprised if many weren't aware, which makes them complicit in some way."

Chapter 20

If the people involved refused to talk, perhaps the documents could speak for them. Reporters had already started filing requests under state and federal Freedom of Information Act laws, which ensure that public documents are actually made available to the public. The laws perhaps seem like no-brainers, but they were enacted for a reason: Government agencies had a long history of refusing to release information that they thought might make them look bad.

The federal Act was signed into law by President Lyndon B. Johnson on July 4, 1966. While the president said flowery things at the time—"this legislation springs from one of our most essential principles," and "a democracy works best when the people have all the information"—he actually had fought against the bill, which was pioneered largely by a group of journalists, a Democrat creator (congressman John Moss), and a Republican co-signer (then-congressman Donald Rumsfeld—yes, the same one). The goal was to make the paper trail behind democracy accessible to the people. Built in were three paragraphs of cautionary language about military secrets, personnel files, confidential advice, executive privilege, and investigative files.

As with any high-profile case, reporters on the Yeardley Love case sought as many documents as the law allowed them to have: police reports, court records, and search warrant requests. All could help flesh out a story that otherwise would be told only by opposing sides with decidedly biased outlooks. Reporters filed, too, for copies of the nine-one-one call in hopes of learning why the death at first was flagged as a possible alcohol overdose, and they asked for the autopsy reports that would indicate exactly what caused Yeardley's heart to stop pumping.

Sometimes, journalists need do nothing more than ask. That depends on the source, the state, and certainly the reputation of the reporter. With criminal cases, of course, things can get tricky: What the public wants to know can pit one constitutional guarantee (freedom of the press) against another (innocent until proven guilty). Circulating details about a crime could compromise inquiries, undercut cases, or hamstring investigations. Thus, many documents are redacted or even sealed, citing "ongoing investigation" as the exemption from FOIA.

Within days of Yeardley's death, it was clear that access to police reports and court documents would be contested. Some of the initial search warrants had been released, and then, within days, suddenly sealed by court order even after they had been posted on the Internet. No doubt the sealing was meant to set a precedent in the case, establishing that most, if not all, of the records pertaining to the commonwealth's case against George Huguely V were exempt because of the ongoing investigation.

The *Washington Post* balked. Joined by Media General (publishers of the *Charlottesville Daily Progress* and *Richmond Times-Dispatch*) and the Associated Press, the *Post* filed a petition on May 11 asking that the search warrants and other documents in the case be unsealed.

Circuit Court Judge Cheryl Higgins presided over a hearing Tuesday, May 18, during which the media outlets' lawyer acknowledged that the judge might have "a very valid reason for closing the search warrants." Higgins had previously worked as a partner at Huguely's lawyer, Francis McQ. Lawrence's, Charlottesville law firm. The two focused on litigating divorce cases with St. John, Bowling & Lawrence, LLP (which later added Quagliana to its name). Perhaps sensing that the media might ask Higgins to recuse herself because of her past relationship with the defense, Lawrence and his new partner, Rhonda Quagliana, preemptively released a statement insisting they had not been part of any hearings regarding the order to seal the documents, nor had they sought materials related to the search warrants sealed by the court. In fact, they said, they hadn't taken a position yet as to whether the documents should be sealed or open.

Not so the prosecution. Warner "Dave" Chapman said in court that the widespread media attention was potentially damaging to the case and could make it difficult come jury-selection time to find people who hadn't formed an opinion on Huguely's guilt or innocence. He had long been known as a prosecutor who refused to talk about open investigations, and this case would not break his resolve.

"We have a duty that this is a proceeding that can take place in the city of Charlottesville," Chapman said. "We have a duty that this is a trial that can take place in front of unbiased jurors."

According to the media's petition, the *Daily Progress* obtained a search warrant inventory from the court clerk's office two days after Yeardley's death. When a *Washington Post* reporter went to the same office to view the same records, the reporter was told that it and all other records had been sealed. Even the order sealing the documents had been sealed.

The media groups' lawyer was flabbergasted. How could they argue against the judge's reason for sealing the documents if they weren't allowed to at least know the reason?

Higgins wasn't ready to rule. She wanted to review the briefs submitted by both sides, she said, and she would share her decision on May 26.

And she did. Higgins ruled that the news groups hadn't filed their petition in the proper format. She kept the documents sealed, as well as the order sealing the documents, and dismissed the petition.

The media outlets weren't ready to admit defeat. They

protested again, re-filing the petition in the manner that the court clerk had deemed proper. In early June, Higgins released partially redacted orders explaining why the search warrants and affidavits had been sealed. But the records themselves were still hidden.

The orders, boasting thick black marker over many words, stated that "public dissemination at this time of highly detailed information such as contained in the affidavit, the search warrant, and any return made thereon may prejudice the ability of law enforcement authorities to continue their investigation."

Additionally, they said, the release of the information "may prejudice the ability in any subsequent trial to select an impartial jury."

David Lacy, one of the lawyers representing the media consortium, told reporters that it wasn't enough to say that potential jurors *might* be tainted. The judge had to show that there is a "real possibility" of harm to a jury pool, he said.

Chapman declined to comment on the documents battle. He made it clear in court that he wanted them sealed to protect his case—which, in fact, was "the people's" case. He and the media were at odds over whether the release of details would derail justice.

Leonard Niehoff, a law professor at the University of Michigan and a media law expert, said the sealing of search warrants isn't unusual. Niehoff, who isn't connected with the Huguely case, said such warrants pose a peculiar set of problems.

"In one sense, they're related to a specific event—a search—and in another sense, they're related to what may be an ongoing criminal investigation, and they could contain evidence that might be admitted against a defendant if the case goes to trial," he said.

Once the search is over, some argue that the documents connected to the search should be released. The event has passed, so there no longer is a worry that releasing the information might tip off the parties and prompt them to destroy potential evidence. But law-enforcement officials have sound reason to hesitate, Niehoff said.

"The full disclosure of a search warrant might tell more information than the police are willing to disclose at that particular time," he said.

Some of the items that had been sought might still be pursued in later search warrants at different addresses, he said. And some of the sought items that weren't found could taint the defendant unfairly if the details were released publicly before a trial. Take, for example, a warrant seeking bomb-making materials or child pornography. Even if police don't find the items, they could stick in potential jurors' minds and forever paint an innocent person as a terrorist or pedophile, Niehoff said. In trial, judges have a ruling for keeping that kind of impossible-to-ignore information away from jurors' ears: "more prejudicial than probative." But when such information has already been released, it's sometimes tough damage to undo.

The argument of jury tainting is a battle fought time and again in high-profile cases. One side or the other worries that releasing information about a case will make it impossible to find jurors who can set aside their previously formed opinions and listen only to the evidence presented at trial. But, Niehoff said, jurors have repeatedly proven that they're willing and able to dismiss what they've heard or read and weigh only what the judge deems admissible. Take, for instance, the Charles Manson case: It was beyond question one of the most-publicized mass murders in U.S. history, and a paperback book containing confessions from one of Manson's so-called "girls" had hit bookstores long before the trial began. Then-President Richard Nixon declared Manson and his cohorts guilty of murder before a verdict was rendered. Still, lawyers from both sides signed off on a jury they felt would be fair, and Manson's conviction has withstood the obligatory onslaught of appeals. Then there was the case of O. J. Simpson, who some people believe got away with murder. He had been declared a killer by some news outlets before charges were even filed, and his attempt to flee police had been broadcast live on television. Despite all that seemingly damning publicity, his jury acquitted him based on the evidence presented in his trial.

"I'm very rarely persuaded by the argument that it's impossible to seat an impartial jury," Niehoff said. "Most judges aren't moved by it, either. When judges do things" in the name of protecting the jury, "they're usually being extraordinarily careful in how the case is handled pretrial so as not to give the defendant a good grounds for appeal."

No matter how pervasive the pretrial publicity is, Niehoff said, there are plenty of people who neither read the news nor watch news on television.

"It is much easier than people think to find jurors who have not heard about pending controversies," he said. "People are not all that well informed. You find jurors often who don't read newspapers or watch television, or if they watch television, they don't watch television news."

And that doesn't mean they're not intelligent, jury-worthy people, he added, describing a college-educated and successful friend of his who proudly boasts that he has neither watched TV news nor read a newspaper in twenty years. The friend finds it too depressing. And he's not alone, Niehoff remarked.

"It actually turns out that tainting a jury pool through pretrial publicity is harder than you might imagine," Niehoff said.

The threshold isn't whether a potential juror has heard of the case, but rather if she can set aside what she'd heard or read before and weigh only the evidence presented in the courtroom. A lot of jurors take those instructions to heart, and not simply because they're supposed to by law.

Still, the Yeardley Love case had stirred deep emotions in Charlottesville and Albemarle County. It seemed likely to legal onlookers that the defense would request a change of venue.

For most cases garnering even moderate publicity, the request is more or less pro forma, and it's more often than not denied. There are exceptions, however, when a judge feels a defendant simply has no chance of getting a fair trial in his or her backyard. In 1992, the case against four white Los Angeles police officers accused of beating Rodney King, a black man, was moved from Los Angeles County to neighboring Ventura County. The defense argued that the enormous pretrial publicity, matched with the defendants being police officers, had outraged Los Angeles residents so much that they weren't likely to be fair. (The riots that ensued when the officers were acquitted perhaps bolster that theory.)

Convicted terrorist Timothy McVeigh also was granted a change of venue in his trial on charges he shattered the Alfred P. Murrah Building, a federal office, in 1995. One hundred and sixty-eight people were killed, another 450 injured, making it the deadliest act of terrorism on U.S. soil until September 11, 2001. In McVeigh's case, it seemed a no-brainer that the trial should be moved: The United States District Court for the Western District of Oklahoma, where the case was to be heard, was located directly across the street from the Murrah building. Jurors would have to pass by the demolished building each day as they geared up to decide McVeigh's fate. More than that, the courthouse itself had been damaged, and people inside the courthouse were injured. The case was transferred to U.S. District Court in Denver instead. McVeigh ultimately was convicted of eleven federal crimes, including use of a weapon of mass destruction.

Virginia defense lawyer John Zwerling, who has handled many cases in Charlottesville, thinks that jurors within the college town are among the most open-minded and fair in the country.

"The jury pool there is excellent," said Zwerling, who is not connected with the Huguely case. "You can wind up with a bright, highly educated jury—or at least predominantly one—and there's always going to be a cross-section who understands the case, understands the importance of the law, and follows the law."

Zwerling speaks from experience. Not only did he represent Andrew Alston, the college student convicted of manslaughter rather than second-degree murder by a Charlottesville jury, but he also represented Valentina Djelebova, a self-described Bulgarian countess who had been charged as an accomplice in the 1997 murder of Charlottesville jewelry dealer George Moody. Though her lover had been convicted in the high-profile case, Djelebova was acquitted of all but an after-the-fact accessory charge.

"There was tremendous hatred for her in the press," Zwerling recalled. "The jurors were able to separate that out."

But it's easy for onlookers to dismiss fears of tainted juries when they're not in the hot seat. To people whose lives hang in the balance—in their hope for either a conviction or an acquittal—it seems too great a risk to have potentially prejudicial information released before a case reaches trial. As Sharon Love told reporters seeking comment, her only remaining concern in life was to make sure that Yeardley got a fair chance in court.

The media continued to fight, and finally, on July 1, they won.

Sort of.

Judge Higgins released documents that shed some new light on what happened inside 222 14th Street NW in the early-morning hours of May 3, but the documents were heavily redacted. In her ruling to grant the media's "motion to unseal search warrant records," Higgins vacated three of her previous four orders sealing the records based on "consideration of the pleadings filed, the exhibits and evidence received" and "the argument of counsel." The slew of blacked-out information would include witness names and Huguely's Social Security number. Also, the inventory list itemizing what had been taken off Huguely's person would not be released.

In one search warrant affidavit, dated May 5, Detective Lisa Reeves requested the following:

Any paper, cloth, clothing, shoes or other item that may contain blood or other bodily fluid; trace evidence such as, but not limited to, biological fluids and fingerprints; photographs, writings and documents related to Yeardly

[sic] ~~Love; computers and electronic storeage~~ [sic] devices

In another warrant request filed the same day, Reeves
also requested "cell phones, digital cameras, financial records, and any other electronic devices; any weapon that may
have been used to include firearms, firearms components,
firearm documents or manuals, and ammunition; any other
evidence associated with the death of Yeardley Love at 222
14th Street NW, apartment number 9."

Both requests included a page titled "search inventory
and return," which, between the two, spelled out thirty-nine
seized items. Based on the array of items gathered into evidence, it was clear that investigators were combing through
both Huguely's and Yeardley's apartments carefully.

Still, they would miss one important item, for which they
would need to return later with an additional search warrant.

Among the items gathered inside Yeardley's apartment:

Swabs of red stain
Hair and fibers
A golf tee
The door to her bedroom
A mobile phone
A digital camera
A backpack containing miscellaneous books and papers
A purse
Towels with red stains
A Natural Light beer can
A pink laptop case
A comforter with red stains
Sheets and pillow (including the pillowcase), all with
    red stains
A note in a desk drawer
A possible fingerprint lift
A bedskirt, also with red stains

Just one item of the fifteen removed from Huguely's apartment was described as having a "red stain"—a white UVA lacrosse T-shirt. The rest of the items—two white Apple laptop computers, blue cargo shorts, a green spiral notebook, two socks, a letter addressed to Yeardley Love—seemed to indicate that officers were trying to narrow down what Huguely had been wearing during the confrontation, and what communication he had had with Yeardley before he walked into her apartment's unlocked front door. Additionally, officers grabbed items from his bathroom—a rug, the shower curtain, swabs from the bathtub—which suggested, at least to case watchers, that officers hoped to trap any potential evidence before it, quite literally, went down the drain.

Among the most detailed information released was contained in a May 6 search warrant affidavit that requested access to a black 2002 Chevrolet Tahoe. Reeves wrote that she hoped to find "any paper, cloth, clothing, shoes or other item that may contain blood or other bodily fluid; trace evidence such as, but not limited to, biological fluids and fingerprints; any property identifiable as that of Yeardley Love."

In trying to sway Judge Higgins to grant the request, Reeves described some of the scene she and her investigative cohorts had come upon when they entered Yeardley's bedroom three days prior. The witnesses at the scene (their names redacted) "described finding Yeardley Love face down on her pillow in her bedroom. There was a pool of blood on her pillow. Love had a large bruise on the right side of her face which appears to have been caused by blunt force trauma. Love's right eye was swollen shut and there were bruises and scrapes to her chin."

Reeves described the battered door—the one that had been bashed in, and from which hairs had been pulled as evidence. The detective also detailed her conversation with Huguely at the Charlottesville Police Department, how he admitted he had been in a fight with Yeardley, and that as they fought "he shook Love and her head repeatedly hit the wall."

The standard search warrant affidavit form sets aside enough space for a lengthy paragraph in which to describe probable cause. Reeves needed much more than that. On an additional sheet titled "Continuation of Paragraph #4," Reeves, referring to herself as "your affiant," laid out even more.

> Huguely told your affiant that he had communicated with Love by email. Huguely admitted that he took Love's computer from the residence and disposed of it. Huguely provided the location of Love's computer and it was recovered. Huguely stated that he and Love had been in a relationship and that the relationship had ended.
> Your affiant was told by (name redacted) that George Huguely operated a black Suburban. Your affiant walked the parking lot of 230 14th Street NW and observed a black Chevrolet Tahoe with Maryland registration. Your affiant ran the registration through the Maryland Department of Motor Vehicles. The registration returned to George Huguely IV. The parking space of the Chevrolet Tahoe is in close proximity to the apartment of George Huguely.

After describing some of the items already seized from Huguely's apartment, Reeves continued in her stilted police talk to say that she knew from investigative experience that sometimes trace evidence and bodily fluids can be transferred from a victim to a suspect's car and, in short, she wanted permission to search Huguely's vehicle. Also, she wanted to see if anywhere inside the vehicle were items that Huguely had once given to Yeardley but then reclaimed.

The request was granted by the judge the following day. From the vehicle, police seized some handwritten notes, a Canon digital camera, and a Verizon flip phone. It was unclear what, if any, evidentiary value the items had.

Within the documents was also a description of an item that police had missed. When medics arrived at Yeardley's apartment, she had been topless. Huguely, however, insisted she was clothed, and even described the T-shirt she had been wearing. The shirt hadn't been collected by crime scene investigators, but when detectives scoured the crime-scene photographs, they spotted it on the floor. The warrants released showed that police had searched her apartment again in a vain attempt to find it.

News stories across the country included the oversight in the reports: Could Charlottesville police have jeopardized the case with shoddy evidence gathering? Before the question could gain ground, Charlottesville Police spokesman Ric Barrick allayed the concerns. Love's family had turned in the T-shirt a few days after the police's unsuccessful search for it, he said. Hopefully, whatever trace evidence it might have had embedded in its fibers was still intact.

Just because Higgins had acquiesced and released some of the public documents didn't mean the media could now smooth their hackles. In August, more heavily redacted affidavits were released. This time, the judge gave a reason for the omissions: The investigation was ongoing, the affidavits identified by name people who had been cooperating with police, some information had not yet been made public and may or may not be admissible at trial, and the public dissemination of some of the information could hinder authorities' efforts to find a prejudice-free jury come trial time.

What was released of the request, however, was this:

Apple laptop computer, white in color. This laptop has a sticker located on the corner with the following inscription "University of Virginia-2006 Desktop Computing Initiative ITC Helpdesk: (434) 924-3731." There is also a barcode under this inscription with the number 600431 underneath. This laptop is currently being stored [at] The Charlottesville Police Department in The Forensics Department under evidence tag #245472. This computer is one of two computers siezed [sic] by police during a search warrant executed at 230 14 Street NW, Charlottesville Virginia.

In short, police already had the computer in storage.
What Reeves wanted now was permission to look inside.
The affidavit also sought:

> Any emails sent, received, stored or deleted referencing
> the email addresses (redacted). Any emails sent, received
> stored or deleted referring to Yeardley Love between the
> dates of April 3, 2010 and May 3, 2010.
>   Any stored or deleted documents referring to Yeardley
> Love or referring to past events involving George Hu-
> guely and Yeardley Love.

In her two-and-a-half page probable cause summary,
Reeves wrote that one of Love's friends had seen an e-mail
the week before Yeardley died that seemed to show the two
had been fighting. Detective Jim Mooney interviewed the
friend, who had shared a hotel room with Yeardley in Chicago. Yeardley told her friend that Huguely had sent an
e-mail to her, and she read it out loud. The next day, she read
it aloud again.

Reeves wanted to find that e-mail. Judge Higgins granted
her request, and both laptops—first Yeardley's, then
George's—were sent to Fairfax, Virginia, for a forensic examination.

Chapter 21

Detectives suspected that some of the most important evidence would be discovered not in the bloodstains on Yeardley's floor, but in the e-mails stored on her computer. They figured that something housed in the hard drive struck Huguely as potentially damaging enough that he went to the trouble of stealing the laptop and tossing it in the trash, where two detectives discovered it just before his arraignment.

Reeves got permission from Yeardley's grieving mother to forensically inspect the computer's contents. With Sharon Love's permission, the white Apple laptop was shipped to Fairfax, about 100 miles northeast of Charlottesville.

Detective Albert Leightley, a computer investigative specialist who was also involved with the U.S. Secret Service Electronic Crimes Task Force, was tasked with searching both Yeardley's and George's computers. He declined to be interviewed while the investigation was ongoing. According to several experts not connected with the case, but with extensive backgrounds in recovering evidence from computers, the process typically used is both complex and precise, designed to protect the computer's hard drive from tampering while giving investigators a mirror copy to search.

Casey Hiser, a forensic consultant at a litigation support firm and a graduate in computer and digital forensics from

Burlington, Vermont's Champlain College, said there are several processes that investigators can use. ("It is actually one of the problems with our field, lack of standardization," she said.) But the identification and seizure phase is fairly universal.

The computer system is collected using an anti-static bag for safe transport of its electronic components. The bag protects the hard drive from static electricity, which can discharge enough voltage to sufficiently destroy internal microchips. A person walking across a rug can produce up to 12,000 volts of static electricity; as little as 10 volts can damage the delicate innards of a computer system. (Humans can't even feel a static electricity zap until it reaches about 1,500 volts.) Once the item is bagged, the investigator is charged with recording its chain of custody, meaning that the components' whereabouts have to be catalogued with every move to show a judge and jury that the evidence found within is reliable.

To actually peruse the computer's contents, a mirror copy must be made. Most computer users know how to back up their hard drives, but making a forensically sound copy is much more complicated. The investigator has to use a write blocker, which ensures that he's only reading information from the drive and not writing information to it. (Writing onto the hard drive would be akin to scribbling across an incriminating note found at a crime scene; it would be deemed tampering with evidence and tossed from the trial.) Most forensic investigators use software such as EnCase or Forensic Toolkit (FTK), which create a bit stream image—or mirror-image backup—of the hard drive.

"It convinces the computer locally that the drive is accessible, but in effect it's read-only," explained Doug White, a computer forensics expert based in Rhode Island. "It protects it from modification by us."

White, who has testified in both criminal and civil trials—but is not connected with the Huguely case—is a professor at Roger Williams University, where he's considered an expert in security, computer technology, electronic crimes, and computer forensics. He also works for the International Society of Forensics Computer Examiners.

He explained that when he creates a copy of a hard drive, he starts "at byte zero, and I go to the last byte on the hard drive and duplicate the whole thing."

To prove that the copied drive is identical to the original, the investigator uses a hash, which is a mathematical algorithm that serves as something of a fingerprint for a hard drive. If even the tiniest bit of information—right down to a deleted period or an added space in a document—is tweaked from the original compared with the copy, those algorithms won't match, and the analysis of the copy won't hold up in court.

And that's paramount. Evidence gathered from computers hasn't always been welcome in trials. Just as DNA evidence was scrutinized when it was first introduced, computer technology has just in recent years been consistently deemed admissible—but only when the examiners can prove that the data they found is from an untainted, mirror copy of the original.

John B. Minor, a Texas-based communications expert and member of the International Society of Forensic Computer Examiners, said that creating a mirror image does more than capture information that's easily accessible to laymen on the hard drive, such as one's documents folder. It also captures random bits of data, or flotsam, floating around the free space of a hard drive. Named after the debris left behind a shipwreck, that data can prove to be invaluable to an investigation.

"It's an area littered with bits and pieces of files," Minor, who is not connected to the case, explained. "It's often where we find the gems of evidence. It can be part of a chat stream, part of an e-mail or an instant messenger chat exchange."

Take, for example, an average e-mail: The recipient opens it, reads it, and perhaps deletes it. Even though the message has been deleted, it's stored on a free area of the hard drive. If a computer user doesn't regularly use specialized software to clean out the flotsam—and few people do—the information stays until it's eventually written over by other information stored in similar fashion. The free space becomes a hodge-podge of bits and pieces of random data—flotsam—that an investigator can collect, organize, and then carefully search.

White also described discovering information in cache files: "Say you're looking at the weather. The information is old, so you hit the refresh button. When you hit refresh, the Web browsers want to speed things up, so they write copies of stuff to the hard drive. Things you're looking at may be stored physically on the hard drive. When you hit refresh, your browser dumps that cache and gets a new one."

Modern computers tend to update more often than older computers, he added, but investigators still find tons of information hidden inside the hard drive.

"We've grabbed screen shots of e-mails, texts, chats, child pornography you were looking at yesterday or last year or who knows when," White said. "It might just be fragments of it, too. We might just see an e-mail address."

Another gold mine of information can be found in what's called file slack, or the unallocated space between the end of a file and the end of the disk cluster it's stored in. It occurs when a computer gets a new file that overwrites a previous file. Rarely are the two files exactly the same size, so there often is a smidgeon of space leftover where residual data can collect. Investigators sometimes find meaningful data hidden inside.

"Sometimes the information is intelligible, sometimes not," Minor said. "It could be an entire e-mail. In some cases, it's an entire PDF file. There might be bits and pieces of a live text chat."

And then there are the partitions that some crafty computer users try to delete entirely. White translated it as such: Let's say a bookshelf contains an entire set of encyclopedias, but you as the owner want to hide one of the books. You take its cover off, and someone viewing the shelf will likely notice that your collection is missing one volume. With a computer, a user can delete an entire drive, and it will look as though it's missing—but forensics investigators know how to find it. That information usually is a jackpot, White said, because investigators not only discover what the user was trying to hide, but they also can prove in court that he took great pains in trying to keep it hidden—providing prosecutors with circumstantial evidence of a guilty conscience.

According to the search warrants initially released by the Charlottesville Police Department, law enforcement wanted to search Yeardley's computer for e-mails between her and Huguely. Leightley, the examiner, likely would have first looked through Yeardley's available e-mail account, and then carefully sifted through the data in hopes of finding more about her doomed relationship. After that, experts said, he probably would have started the daunting task of sorting through all of the gathered information. It's no easy job, Minor said: An e-mail account showing perhaps just 400 messages might actually turn up 14,000 when the hard drive is thoroughly examined.

"There's not a practical way to look through all of those, though sometimes we do," said Minor, who regularly works with law-enforcement agencies and testifies in criminal and civil trials. He has not been asked to work on the Yeardley Love case.

To more easily track down specific information, investigators organize the data into a searchable database, then run keyword searches. They might look for nicknames or monikers to find all the e-mails sent from a particular person—sometimes this points investigators to additional e-mail accounts used by the same person—while other times they might look for words that seem likely to turn up threatening messages ("kill" or "hurt," for example). When looking up browser history, they might stumble upon some incriminating searches. Hiser said that's "a great source of info if your killer happened to look up 'how to hide a body' . . . Don't laugh; it has happened."

In the Love case, detectives curtailed their hunt by searching through just one month's worth of e-mails—from April 3, 2010 to May 3, the morning Yeardley was killed. The search warrant request on Huguely's laptop asked for "any stored or deleted documents referring to Yeardley Love or referring to past events involving George Huguely and Yeardley Love."

During his search of Yeardley's computer, Leightley discovered fragments of an e-mail that Reeves said appeared to be "in response to an e-mail sent by George Huguely," according to a court document dated Aug. 17. The media filed requests hoping the e-mail fragment would be released. They received a document that included a chunk of text, measuring about a dozen lines long, completely blacked out with dark marker. But Reeves's words surrounding the mystery text were telling: "Further examination of the fragmented e-mail . . . is evidence of a prior incident between Huguely and Love," she wrote. That incident, she said, was the one in which Yeardley had hit George with her purse, causing her belongings to spill out, including her cell phone, which she believed Huguely held on to.

But while detectives suspected the fragmented e-mail found on Yeardley's computer was in response to an upsetting one from George, they couldn't find the original e-mail on her hard drive. Leightley set off to search George's laptop in hopes of finding it.

He came up empty.

Reeves tried another tack: After talking with Leightley, she learned that sometimes, when an e-mail is written on a person's smart phone rather than on a computer, the messages could be retrieved from the phone long after the message was written. She asked Judge Higgins for permission to search Huguely's phone to see if any additional messages could be recovered.

Minor said such a request isn't unusual, especially these days when few people use their phones simply for making calls. With smart phones, it's difficult to completely erase data. Forensics experts can extract the memory of the entire cell phone, then go into that information and carve out pertinent data.

"Smart phone evidence can be corroborating evidence, or it can be key evidence," Minor said. "Smart phones can be sometimes be dead giveaways" that a crime has been committed.

Higgins granted Reeves's request. The search for more e-mails was under way.

Chapter 22

Every bit of evidence collected, and everything still being sought, seemed directed at helping authorities understand Huguely's state of mind when he made that fatal visit to Yeardley's apartment. Had he threatened her beforehand? Did he say he meant to hurt her? Was there any hint she might be in peril?

With the first public denial by Huguely's lawyer, it was clear that at least one prong of the defense would be that George never meant to hurt Yeardley, that he went over to talk and things got out of hand (an accident, as Lawrence had described it). As more search warrants became public, it seemed clear that police were looking for evidence to obliterate that defense or create a new one altogether.

The search for evidence of intent came as no surprise to Gregory Mitchell, a self-described "evidence guy" and professor at the University of Virginia's law school, who found himself questioned by reporters about the case even though he had no direct involvement in it.

"The dispute here is about state of mind, how much harm he inflicted on her at the time, and whether it was foreseeable that this"—her death—"was the kind of result that would happen," Mitchell said. "Everything I saw about the case through the media indicated the prosecution was trying to make the case that this was an intentional killing, that he could have stopped but he didn't."

In movies and on television shows, much is made about motive: Why did the killer do it? In real life, prosecutors don't have to establish motive. It's not their job to get inside the heads of the accused and figure out why they do the things they do. They just have to prove *that* they did it. Sure, painting the "why" picture is helpful, and it often can sway a jury to convict when evidence is otherwise so-so—even if lawyers and the jurors themselves don't admit it. But establishing motive is not legally necessary.

In Yeardley's case, according to her friends, the motive could have been that George Huguely was the jealous type, and far too controlling to let the relationship end. But even having the motive question out of the way wouldn't keep prosecutors from having to climb inside his head to anticipate the defense they would likely face at trial.

The questions they had to answer: What was his intent? Did he mean to kill her? Could he have stopped?

The Hook, a weekly newsmagazine, ran a story titled "Playing defense: Legal eagles prognosticate on Huguely strategy." Fifty-cent headline aside, the piece drew comparisons between Huguely's case and that of another UVA student who had been charged with murder, Andrew Alston.

Alston was a twenty-one-year-old third-year student in 2003 when he headed out for drinks with some friends and his older brother, who was in town visiting. During a night of bar hopping and booze, his path intersected with twenty-two-year-old Walker Sisk, a volunteer firefighter, near the Corner—the same area Yeardley and George lived near and where they regularly bar hopped. What happened next became hotly debated during trial a year later: Alston, who regularly carried a pocket knife, testified that Sisk grabbed the knife and lunged, and in the struggle, Alston wrestled back the weapon and stabbed Sisk twenty times in self-defense. He claimed he learned his knife-redirecting skills in an eight-week martial arts course he had taken. Police arriving at the scene followed a trail of blood to, ironically, 222 14th Street

Northwest, Yeardley's apartment complex, where they arrested
Alston. He stood trial on a second-degree murder charge in
November 2004.

Sisk's family balked at Alston's explanation of the fight,
and the only possible defense wound Alston suffered was a
cut that the testifying medical examiner said could have come
from his hand slipping on the blood-slicked knife. Still, the
jury weighed both his testimony and the evidence of substantial drinking—Sisk's blood-alcohol content was at least .19%
when he died, more than twice the amount needed to be considered legally intoxicated—and came back with a surprising
verdict: voluntary manslaughter. Their agreed-upon sentence:
three years in prison.

"I looked at all the evidence, and didn't think it was
malice—just tragic on both sides," one juror told *The Hook*.

Alston, dubbed the Corner Killer by some media, was
released from prison in 2006 after serving two-thirds of his
sentence, as is typical if the prisoner has behaved behind
bars. Sisk's family filed a wrongful death suit against Alston
upon his release and was awarded $600,000—of which
Alston paid just $3,600 after filing for bankruptcy.

The Hook, which had run a series of prosecution-favored
stories during and after the trial, pointed to Alston's light
conviction when presenting the "legal eagles" story forecast-
ing Huguely's likely defense.

"So what can a shocked community expect when Huguely
eventually comes to trial?" the paper asked, then turned to
area defense lawyers for some predictions. The consensus:
that Francis Lawrence, Huguely's attorney, was well respected and highly skilled and wouldn't have stated that
Yeardley's death was a tragic accident unless he felt certain
of it.

"I won't second guess him," said defense lawyer John
Zwerling, who had represented Alston seven years earlier. "I
would think he has information that the intent of the client
was not to kill her, and that it was accidental."

Perhaps Huguely meant to slap, punch, or shake, but that
doesn't mean he meant to kill, Zwerling continued.

Unlike Alston, Huguely wasn't charged with second-degree murder. He faced first-degree murder. And that hinged on him having intended to kill his victim, or at least having had ample opportunity to slow down and halt his actions. Second-degree murder is more a crime of passion—not unintentional enough to be an accident (and downgraded even further to perhaps a manslaughter charge), but, typically, quick and rage-fueled. Perhaps the killer walked in on her husband with another woman, and she snapped. That scenario is more likely to fall into the second-degree category, while the woman who leaves her apartment, buys a gun, and returns the next day to kill her husband is far more likely to be charged with first-degree murder in most U.S. states.

Of course, there are many gray areas, and outcomes vary not only state by state, but jury by jury and judge by judge. One jury might rule that a strangulation, which takes on average at least three and a half minutes to complete, is a snap, impulsive action, and perhaps that jury would only convict a suspect of second-degree murder. A jury in the same court-house might determine that those final minutes dripped like molasses, giving the assailant plenty of time to stop himself and reassess whether his anger warranted taking another human life. That jury, perhaps, would convict him of first-degree murder. Same circumstances, same courthouse, but different verdicts.

In Virginia, there's the added complexity of capital murder—or a murder that qualifies for death-penalty consideration. The Commonwealth of Virginia, in fact, has a storied history with hangings, electric chairs, and lethal injection. The colonies' first formal execution occurred in 1608, when Captain George Kendall, living in Virginia's Jamestown colony, was hanged for spying for the Spanish government. According to Espy, a database that tracks executions, Virginia to date outranks relative U.S. newcomer Texas as having executed the most people since 1608 (though its numbers have dropped significantly since 1976, after the federal government lifted a four-year ban on state executions).

Not every murder qualifies for capital consideration. Second-degree murder is out entirely, and only certain premeditated murders qualify. For example, a premeditated murder committed while in the commission of an abduction, a robbery, a rape, or an attempted rape would qualify. So would the premeditated murder of someone under age fourteen by a person over the age of twenty-one, and the premeditated murder of more than one person within a three-year span of time. Also, premeditated murder of certain types of people could land a culprit on death row—such as a pregnant woman, a law-enforcement officer, a judge, a juror, or a witness.

Whether Huguely qualified was debated not by prosecutors and the defense, but by the media. On *Good Morning America*, Robin Sax, a former Los Angeles County district attorney, pointed to Huguely's theft of his ex-girlfriend's computer as a possible nail in his capital-punishment coffin.

"This is Law School 101," Sax said. "This is a felony murder that happened in the course of a burglary."

Mark Geragos, a defense attorney also not connected with the case, said he doubted prosecutors would seek death.

"This is not the type of case that generally prosecutors will seek the death penalty in," he told *Good Morning America*. "He's going to argue, 'Well, I had no intent to kill and I didn't have malice. I never wanted to kill her. I loved her.'"

If District Attorney Chapman was weighing the death penalty, he wasn't saying so publicly. But his actions in court at least indicated that he had no plan to heed the defense's claim that Yeardley's death was nothing more than a tragic accident. That proclamation by Francis Lawrence, which came while he addressed reporters after his client's arraignment the day after Yeardley's death, seemed to lay the foundation for Huguely's defense.

In short, it's the "I didn't mean to" argument.

Lawyers weren't the only ones struggling to get inside George Huguely's head. The case sparked interest among domestic abuse experts nationwide, some of whom used it and its notoriety to highlight the dangers of dating violence.

On paper, Huguely was the antithesis of the stereotypical abuser. He was charming, educated, talented, and wealthy. And Yeardley seemed one of the unlikeliest victims imaginable. She was smart, strong, ambitious, and, by all accounts, emotionally well adjusted. On top of that, she had no reason to stay—she wasn't bound by marriage vows or forever tied to Huguely through children.

But while the case left many perplexed, Huguely appeared to some to fit a mold: that of a man with narcissistic personality disorder. On talk and television programs, as well as on mental health blogs, domestic violence experts and psychiatrists posited that Huguely's behavior could be attributed to the disorder. The condition is hotly debated among psychiatrists, and its future as an official personality disorder is gray: The *Diagnostic and Statistical Manual of Mental Disorders,* published by the American Psychiatric Association, has targeted NPD as one of several personality disorders to be axed when its fifth edition is released in 2013—not because people don't have it, but because some scientists are looking to revamp the labels psychiatrists and psychologists use. (One Harvard psychologist described the potential elimination as "draconian" and "unenlightened" to a *New York Times* reporter.)

Narcissistic personality disorder is a clinical diagnosis, one that can't be made by reading police and court documents alone. Named for Narcissus, the handsome hunter in Greek mythology who fell in love with his own reflection in a pool, narcissists are preoccupied with their own self-importance. They believe that they're special and should associate only with other special people, and they harbor disdain for people they feel are inferior. They have a sense of entitlement and expect nothing short of adulation and admiration from others. They exploit other people to further themselves, their arrogance is undeniable, and their fragile egos make them quick to become jealous of others.

When breaking down the red flags reported in the wake of Huguely's arrest, the definition could fit, some experts said.

He lashed out at a police officer, threatening to kill her.

He beat a fellow teammate for walking Yeardley home and supposedly trying to kiss her.

In a fit of self-indulgent rage, he jumped into the ocean to swim to shore because his father refused his request to turn the family's yacht around.

He attacked Yeardley at least once in public, choking her until he was pulled off by fellow lacrosse players.

And even his high school behavior, as reported by the *Washington Post* in 2006, pointed to potentially unhealthy self-aggrandizement that at the time was laughed off as Huguely being a jokester: He stole his coach's car keys, then drove the vehicle to the coach to show off behind the wheel. He bet another coach he'd make a play in exchange for a kiss from the coach's girlfriend. When he indeed made the play, he went a step further, asking for the woman's phone number.

But Levy said there's a difference between being narcissistic and having a diagnosable disorder.

"Certainly someone who is so wrapped up in himself that he could hurt someone he loves is only focusing on himself," Levy said. "He's not seeing the consequences of his own behavior, and he's not empathizing with how she might feel. But that's during the abuse. He may go back and forth. He may be attentive at other times.

"You do see narcissism often in people who are abusive," she continued. "But whether they all fit a clear diagnosis for narcissistic personality disorder, that's a stretch."

Even if Huguely had NPD, a jury likely would never be told. Occasionally defense lawyers try to use the diagnosis to trim time off a client's sentence post-conviction, but NPD is not grounds for an insanity defense. For the insanity claim to stick, the culprit must be unable to tell the difference between what society deems is right and wrong. Narcissists know the rules; they simply don't want to abide by them.

And if Huguely's drinking was nearly as heavy as his neighbors told police and reporters, it could have made it tough for Yeardley to see his eruptions as something more sinister than booze-fueled outbursts.

Domestic violence studies have shown that women are more easily able to blame drugs or alcohol for their partner's moody behavior. According to statistics compiled by the Marin Institute, a self-described "alcohol industry watchdog," two-thirds of victims of intimate partner violence reported that alcohol was involved in the incident, and women whose partners abused alcohol were more than three times as likely than other women to be assaulted by their partners. In 2002, more than 70,000 students between the ages of eighteen and twenty-four were victims of alcohol-related sexual assault in the United States, according to a study published in the *Journal of Studies on Alcohol.* In Huguely's case, most of his legal run-ins reportedly came during booze fests. Friends and relatives seemed to have trouble understanding how a young man who appeared so likeable and charismatic one minute could be accused of such outrageous behavior the next. Some apparently blamed the alcohol and reportedly asked him to curb his drinking.

But according to some substance abuse experts, that would have been a naïve—if well-intentioned—request. Levy has for years dealt with the misconception that alcohol is the sole cause of violent behavior.

"With men who batter and also drink, they were violent before the drinking and they're violent after the drinking," Levy said. "It's just an excuse."

Rather, alcohol abuse is considered a complication of narcissistic personality disorder, according to the Mayo Clinic. The disorder is rare, affecting more men than women, and its cause is unknown. According to the clinic, some evidence links the disorder to excessive pampering and extremely high expectations in childhood. Other evidence indicates it's prewired in the brain.

For a young man like Huguely, whose upbringing was posh and whose athletic prowess was routinely praised, it might have been difficult for those around him to recognize his behavior as possibly indicative of a personality disorder. After all, he wasn't the only lacrosse player known to occasionally act superior or cocky. It was only in hindsight that

people seemed to string together the series of outbursts and
wonder if they should have recognized Huguely as a lit powder keg.

By friends' accounts, Yeardley was growing tired of it all.
It's not clear if Huguely had physically abused her before he
choked her in public—she can't speak out, and he so far has
refused interview requests—but research indicates that it's
unlikely for someone to escalate from zero to murder in just
a few weeks. Perhaps there were put-downs or verbal threats.
Maybe he had grabbed an arm or pushed her. It might be that
he showed some signs of troubling behavior that Yeardley
initially dismissed as being out of character or forgivable.

Whatever happened, one thing seems clear: Yeardley
couldn't have known that the young man she had let into her
heart and introduced to her family would one day be arrested
in her violent death. Had she any clue, she certainly would
have summoned the strength to ask for help.

Yeardley was nothing if not strong.

Chapter 23

Months after Huguely's lawyer declared Yeardley's death an accident, John Zwerling, an onlooker, acknowledged he had been taken aback by the lawyer's first public comments. He suspected that Francis Lawrence had been asked by Huguely's family to give the statement; Zwerling felt it was premature.

"I wasn't expecting that comment," he said. "He was in a time and place where he didn't know what his defense was going to be. He still might not know for sure."

The word "accident" drew Lawrence a lot of criticism. At the same time he described Yeardley's death as such, the media were just beginning to report details of Huguely's alleged statements to police. Nancy Grace wasn't the only analyst who scoffed at the notion of someone "accidentally" bashing a woman's head against the wall until blood poured from her nose.

Zwerling said Lawrence likely meant that Huguely perhaps intended to hurt his ex-girlfriend, but had no intention of killing her. "Which is different," Zwerling said. "It's subtle, but wording it that way is a way to avoid some of the criticism."

For Gregory Mitchell, another legal onlooker, Lawrence's "accident" statement was not a surprising declaration. Nor was Mitchell shocked when, months after the slaying, defense lawyers asked for access to years of medical records in order to explore whether Yeardley's death was caused by more than her fight with Huguely.

"From the defense's perspective, you're basically trying to do the mirror image thing" with the prosecution, Mitchell said. As prosecutors tried to pin blame for Yeardley's death solely on the brutal head trauma, the defense would try to spread the blame. Was Yeardley drunk? On drugs? Did she provoke Huguely somehow? Mitchell expected all of those questions to be posed to jurors. No doubt, the defense would counter any prosecution expert witnesses with experts of their own. Like so many cases in the American court system, it would likely become a showdown between specialists on the stand.

For outsiders, however, the specifics of that battle remained a mystery even months after Yeardley died. While autopsy reports can be released under Freedom of Information Act laws in some states, Virginia law considers them part of a person's medical records even after death, according to Stephen Murman, an administrator with the Medical Examiner's Office. Thus, requests to see the pathology reports detailing what injuries Yeardley had suffered were denied. Police had announced her cause of death as "blunt force trauma" after her autopsy, but, according to outside pathologists, that definition was far too vague to shed light on exactly how Yeardley Love was killed.

Though court documents pointed to blunt force trauma as Yeardley's cause of death, Police Chief Timothy Longo was cautious when it came to officially releasing the cause. Early media reports had suggested she might have been both beaten and strangled, and though Longo certainly knew there were no obvious signs of the latter—none of the telltale bruising around her neck or tiny hemorrhage spots (called petechiae) in her eyes or mouth—he declined to set reporters straight in the days immediately after the death.

Even when the commonwealth's medical examiner released a preliminary cause of death to police in mid-May,

Longo delayed announcing it until he and detectives had a chance to read the final report, which was still weeks from being completed.

Finally, in early July, police announced the cause. It indeed had been blunt force trauma to the head.

Though no other details were released, the two months that had passed had given authorities enough time to get toxicology reports back from state labs. It would be months before a defense motion released some of those findings: a blood-alcohol content of 0.14%, meaning Yeardley was drunk when she was attacked, as well as the prescription drug Adderall, designed to treat people suffering from attention deficit hyperactivity disorder. Dr. Bill Gormley, the medical examiner who performed Yeardley's autopsy, determined that the alcohol/Adderall combination did not cause her death. Rather, he decided, it was the repeated beating of her head against a wall.

The brain is a delicate organ, a soft, mushroom-shaped bundle of arteries and veins, nerves and fluids. Kindly, evolution provided vertebrates with not one, but two layers of protection for the brain: the skull, of course, and in between that and the brain itself, a system of connective tissue membranes to serve as a sort of cushion between soft tissue and tough bone.

Despite those protective encasings, about one million people a year visit doctors because of blows to the head. Of those, upwards of 50,000 (with some estimates being closer to twice that) suffer prolonged problems. News reports in recent years have placed great emphasis on head injuries sustained in sports—especially those affecting kids and young adults—but in reality, the bulk of head injuries are from car wrecks. Even a seemingly minor fender bender can cause the head to whip to and fro, bruising both the front and back sides of the brain. With bruising can come swelling, and that's when the unforgiving skull can turn from ally to enemy.

While the medical examiners involved in the case declined

to elaborate on their findings while the trial was still looming, Dr. Daniel Spitz, a Michigan-based pathologist not connected with the case, offered some insight. Yeardley's skull wouldn't have to have been fractured for the beating to be fatal, he said.

When someone sustains a head impact, there's an acceleration and a deceleration: the movement of the brain inside the skull (acceleration), and then its abrupt halt when it hits the skull (deceleration). Because the brain is made of a different substance than is bone—similar in consistency to gelatin—it moves at a different rate than its encasing. So as the head is slammed, the brain moves within the cranial cavity and strikes the skull.

And that, Spitz explained, causes what's known as traumatic axonal injury (also known as diffuse axonal injury). In layman's terms, the brain gets compressed and stretched as it slams around inside the skull. Axons, which conduct nerve signals, can get disrupted or even torn, and thus the brain can't continue to send out those all-important instructions to the rest of the body: keep breathing, keep pumping blood, keep living.

"Basically, you have disruption of the brain at a cellular level," said Spitz, co-author of *Differential Diagnosis in Surgical Pathology*. (Spitz also contributed as an author and editor of the 4th edition of the so-called Bible of forensic pathology, *Spitz and Fisher's Medicolegal Investigation of Death: Guidelines for the Application of Pathology to Crime Investigation*—though the Spitz in the title refers to his father, world-renowned pathologist Werner Spitz, who is now retired.)

"If the brain doesn't function, you have disruption of heart rate, breathing, and everything else," said the younger Spitz.

Multiple impacts are "of greater concern than a single impact," he added. George Huguely had described Yeardley's head hitting the wall repeatedly, meaning that she potentially endured the axonal shearing several times. Imagine taking a hammer to a melon. Hit it once and you cause *some* damage. Hit it repeatedly in the same spot and you're guaranteed to destroy it. Unlike a melon, the brain can heal—but only if given the chance.

"That's why so many are concerned about kids in sports and pro-athletes who suffer concussions," Spitz explained. "You don't want to put them back in the game right away because if they sustain another impact such as the first one, it could be really detrimental. . . . *Any* impact could be potentially serious or even fatal, but when you have repeated blows, the effects are exaggerated."

Upon finding Yeardley's body, Detective Reeves had immediately noticed external injuries: the facial bruising, the right eye swollen shut. Neither of those injuries would help determine exactly when in the beating Yeardley likely fell unconscious, said Spitz. Yeardley perhaps could have been knocked unconscious immediately, or she could have remained alert until the final throes.

Huguely told police that at some point, he noticed blood pouring from his ex-girlfriend's nose. It was soon after, he said, that he finally pushed her back onto her bed, stole her laptop, and fled.

He claimed he didn't know how badly she was hurt, and that he certainly didn't know she was dead. According to Spitz, with the viciousness of the described attack, immediate efforts to save Yeardley might have been in vain—and even if she had lived, the damage done to her delicate brain could have impaired her forever.

Chapter 24

Dr. Daniel Spitz has testified in hundreds of court cases, many of them involving homicides. As a medical examiner in suburban Detroit and a former pathologist in homicide-heavy Miami-Dade County, he has sat on both sides of the courtroom, often testifying for the prosecution, but occasionally, usually when he has been hired privately, for the defense.

Without doubt, he said, the defense in the case against George Huguely V would aim to minimize the damage the repeated head bashing had caused the twenty-two-year-old athlete. One way, predicted Spitz, would be to minimize the number of impacts. If the prosecutors say she banged her head seven times, the defense would likely look for evidence that it could have been as few times as two or three.

"Of course, I'm sure they'd try to get it down to one," he said.

But to Spitz, "it doesn't really help. You don't accidentally hit your head against the wall to the point of causing [the] kinds of injuries [that police had described in the case]."

UVA Professor Gregory Mitchell said he expected the defense to attack Yeardley's behavior with whatever information they could gather.

"From the defense's perspective, they're going to try to

say that he was intoxicated and that impaired his view of things—or that she provoked him," Mitchell said. "Whatever the prosecution says, they're going to try to show the flipside of that."

If Yeardley had been drinking, that would open the door for defense lawyers to argue that the depressing effects of alcohol were the real reason her life ended.

And that's where Yeardley's supposed "Sunday Funday" would likely come into play.

Sunday night was usually a social one for both the men and women's UVA lacrosse teams. Game days typically fell on Saturdays, Sundays, and Tuesdays, meaning that Sundays offered the one night in a weekend in which players were usually guaranteed not to have a game the next day.

Like many college students, the lacrosse players were known to mix alcohol with their "fun," according to neighbors and area bartenders.

On May 2, as on so many other nights during the academic year, the beers were tossed back at Boylan Heights, just down the street from Yeardley's apartment. It was the perfect kind of establishment for a gathering of sports-minded college students: a bit dingy, with a worn concrete floor inside and the type of battered stuffed chairs you often spot on front porches in college towns. But the place had a hint of chic as well, with loft-style exposed brick and ambient lighting.

The beer-and-burger joint thrived off its college patrons. Even its signage was written in the same heavily outlined block font so often associated with universities. Instead of standard menus, customers were given checklists with which to create their burgers (patty options: beef, turkey, veggie or chicken). Fries were of course a mainstay, though Boylan Heights offered an option with a twist: sweet potato fries.

A deck area surrounded by blue railing provided outdoor seating—ideal for people watching—while inside, patrons could gather around a massive projection television screen usually tuned in to one sports competition or another. As one online reviewer wrote, Boylan Heights's pros were its thick burgers, pool tables, and happy-hour specials. Among its cons? Being packed with college students during the school year.

Indeed, it was a regular hangout for the lacrosse teams. The players often arrived late and stayed until closing, sometimes watching sports on the TVs inside. (Yeardley was said to have insisted on complete isolation during Baltimore Ravens games, but on this Sunday in early May, the Ravens were still months away from taking the field.) Caitlin Whiteley, Yeardley's friend since the sixth grade and UVA roommate, later testified that the gathering May 2 was altogether ordinary. A group had gathered in the early evening for a friend's birthday party, but Yeardley didn't feel like staying long. Caitlin walked her friend home, then went back to Boylan Heights about 11 p.m.—without Yeardley.

"She was tired," testified Whiteley, who added that Yeardley drank beer at the bar but didn't seem drunk.

Caitlin testified that her roommate and Huguely's relationship had been on and off for years, but, according to other friends who spoke to reporters in the days after the death, not everyone knew. The *Washington Post* quoted one unnamed friend who said, "I still didn't know they had broken up. Everything seemed fine." And another friend said she approached Yeardley at the Boylan Heights birthday gathering and asked, "What's going on with you and George?" Yeardley replied, "Same old stuff. Everything is good."

As it turned out, Huguely was headed to Yeardley's apartment soon after. Friends testified that he had spent the day at a father-son golf tournament at the Wintergreen Resort, a mountainous retreat about forty-five minutes southwest of Charlottesville. After spending the day golfing and drinking, Huguely was "definitely drunk," his roommate, Kevin Carroll, would testify months later. At 11:40 p.m.—not long after Whiteley left Yeardley alone in their apartment—Carroll said he left to buy more beer before the stores closed at midnight. Huguely stayed behind. When Carroll got back, Huguely was gone.

About ten minutes later, Anna Lehman, who lived downstairs from Yeardley, heard "very loud" banging noises coming from upstairs, according to testimony she gave months later. Next, she heard footsteps come down the stairs and spotted a man wearing a blue shirt leaving the building. Soon after, Huguely returned to his apartment and told Carroll that he had gone downstairs with two friends for a few minutes. Carroll called one of the friends, Will Bolton, to suggest he join the upstairs crew for a few beers, but Bolton said he wasn't there, immediately disputing where Huguely said he'd been.

The other downstairs friend also said he hadn't hung out with Huguely that night. In fact, he testified, he was so busy studying that when Huguely knocked on his door earlier in the evening, he told Huguely to go away and locked his door.

Caitlin got back to the apartment she shared with Yeardley about 2 a.m., she testified, and spotted the hole in the door to Love's bedroom. She peeked in the room and noticed her hair, which had earlier been pulled up, splayed in that unnatural fashion.

"I saw Yeardley in bed facedown with a comforter over her," Whiteley testified. "I shook her shoulder. I moved her hair to the side and touched her shoulder."

That was when, she said, she saw blood on Yeardley's neck and face. She and Oudshoorn called police, and as Oudshoorn lifted Love out of the bed to attempt CPR, he saw more blood on Yeardley's face and eye. Soon, the apartment filled with police and medics and the once-calm home was transformed into a crime scene.

Yeardley's body, found around 2:15 a.m., offered investigators something they were less likely to be able to obtain from Huguely: a relatively accurate reading of her blood-alcohol content. While police wouldn't tell reporters whether Huguely voluntarily submitted to any Breathalyzer or blood tests to determine whether he was intoxicated—and if he was, how much—Detective Reeves's search warrants seeking bodily fluids and DNA samples wasn't signed until 11:52 a.m., presumably more than eight hours after Huguely would have last had a chance to drink. And even if the sample had been taken earlier, he might have had more to drink after Yeardley's death, thus raising his BAC, or perhaps he had stopped drinking, which would have given his body time to process the alcohol and lower his reading by the time Reeves caught up with him.

Yeardley, however, would likely have been tested soon after her death.

If police had a BAC for Huguely, they didn't release it to the public, leaving many to speculate. A high BAC could work in favor of his defense, bolstering Lawrence's assertion that the death was an accident. If Huguely had been significantly impaired, his ability to form intent was questionable, his lawyers could argue. *He's a generally good man with an unfortunate illness*: It was a sometimes-successful argument to jurors. It worked in Andrew Alston's case, after all. As far as the jury in that case knew, Alston had no significant criminal history. (In reality, he had been previously charged and acquitted of assaulting his girlfriend. The judge ruled that to be inadmissible in the murder trial.) He was the son of a well-respected lawyer, and he'd just two years earlier suffered the tragic loss of a brother to suicide.

On the other hand, Huguely was well aware of his ongoing alcohol issues—the blackouts he reportedly told friends about, and the public service sentence he got after threatening to kill an officer trying to arrest him. If jurors were told about those incidents, they could lose sympathy for someone who should have known better, even if he was too drunk to at the precise moment of his crime.

Yeardley's drinking could theoretically have played a role in her death, Spitz said ("Anything's possible," he regularly testified in trials), but the issue would likely become a contentious one between the prosecution and defense. Spitz had seen it before.

PART IV

"It's the Elephant in the Room"

Chapter 25

After George Huguely V appeared via closed circuit television on May 4 for his arraignment, he was entitled to a speedy preliminary hearing. Apparently, he didn't want one.

By law, the preliminary hearing—basically a baby version of the trial, meant for prosecutors to lay out just enough of their case to convince the judge that there is sufficient probable cause for the case to move forward—is supposed to be set soon after arraignment. Very often, however, suspects agree to postpone the date to give their lawyers enough time to collect and digest the evidence and prepare themselves for a defense. After the preliminary hearing, the judge decides whether the case should be forwarded to a grand jury, which then determines whether the defendant should face trial. With a case like the one against Huguely, there was no reason for defense lawyers to rush.

Huguely had admitted a fight with Yeardley, and his lawyer had stopped short of denying any culpability, instead calling it a tragic accident. If Lawrence was preparing to fight for a lesser charge, as legal onlookers expected, he faced the difficult task of convincing a judge that the prosecution didn't have enough evidence to justify the first-degree murder charge. At the preliminary hearing stage, the judge doesn't need to be convinced beyond a reasonable doubt. Rather, she must be swayed only enough to believe there is probable cause that a crime was committed. And that standard is far lower. Most states define probable cause as a "reasonable belief" the person committed the crime. Thus, the standard from preliminary hearing to trial shifts from "he might have done it" to "it's unreasonable to think anyone else did."

Huguely's defense would be significantly helped if his lawyers were able to nix the first-degree murder charge before it ever reached a jury. And that's typically why a defendant in a high-profile murder case might waive his right to a speedy preliminary hearing—to give his lawyers as much time as possible to gather evidence before both sides begin presenting their cases in court. The defense's job, while not easy, was simple: undermine the prosecution's case at every turn. If Chapman planned to argue that Huguely had murder on his mind, Lawrence needed to be ready to prove that his client had just meant to sit down for a chat.

Predictably, Huguely waived his right to speediness, and his preliminary hearing was scheduled for Thursday, June 10.

Less predictable was his lawyer's decision to not request bond. In many cases, it's perfunctory, even if it's unusual that a judge would grant someone charged with first-degree murder the freedom to roam the streets while murder charges loomed. Many lawyers at least request that their clients be allowed to go home under house arrest, monitored by Global Positioning Satellite technology to track their whereabouts. Lawrence skipped the request.

Some speculated that in May, so soon after the slaying, the vitriol was too intense. Perhaps Lawrence would try to secure Huguely's release after his scheduled June preliminary hearing.

John Zwerling, for one, didn't question Lawrence's decisions. He knew his colleague as a fine attorney with a stellar reputation.

"He has developed a reputation over the years as being very competent," Zwerling said. "So is his partner."

Liz Seccuro, the UVA alumna whose rapist had been defended by Lawrence and Quagliana, had a different take.

"They are paid to plant a tiny seed of reasonable doubt into the mind of just one juror," she said. "It's business. That's all."

Francis Lawrence had been selected as one of Virginia's so-called "Super Lawyers" by the magazine of the same name every year since 2006. *Super Lawyers* is a rating service for lawyers; those chosen are selected based on peer nominations, peer evaluations, and independent research, according to its mission statement. Lawyers aren't able to buy themselves onto the list, the organization insists, and the final list may represent no more than five percent of the lawyers in the state.

Lawrence graduated from Washington & Lee University in Lexington, Virginia, first for his bachelor's degree, which he obtained in 1971, and then for his juris doctorate, which he got in 1975. He lectured at the University of Virginia School of Law from 1989 to 1999, according to several online profiles, and once served as president of the Thomas Jefferson Inn of Court, an organization of attorneys, professors, and law students "who have an interest in litigation," and judges who hear cases in Albemarle County. Rhonda Quagliana, nearly sixteen years Lawrence's junior and a later addition to the 1974-established law firm on Charlottesville's Park Street, had graduated from the University of Virginia School of law with her juris doctorate in 1995; she'd previously earned a PhD from the college in 1992. She worked as president of the Charlottesville Albemarle Bar Association, a not-for-profit professional association meant to improve the Charlottesville area's legal profession.

The duo's firm claims to offer "individualized and courteous attention essential to effective legal representation," according to its online profile (www.stlawva.net). "Our attorneys have the experience and resources to handle complex cases."

As word of Yeardley Love's death spread through Virginia, the legal community began to speculate which lawyer would be tapped by Huguely's wealthy family. That they chose Lawrence and Quagliana was no surprise, Zwerling said.

* * *

Journalists from throughout the East Coast, as well as those with national operations such as ESPN and TruTV (formerly CourtTV), began gearing up for the planned June preliminary hearing. So did Brendan Fitzgerald, the *C-VILLE Weekly* reporter, who had followed the case from its onset. When perusing the court docket, Fitzgerald noticed that on the same day in the same courthouse, another young man charged with murder was also set to have a preliminary hearing. He couldn't help but be intrigued: The courthouse would teem with reporters covering Huguely's case, while the other went unannounced and uncovered in a courtroom just down the hall. Fitzgerald decided to write about it.

"It was characterized by an entirely different dynamic, a different economic dynamic, a different racial dynamic," he recalled. "And, because it involved a person involved in a completely different walk of life than George Huguely, we thought it an interesting project to put those two things side by side."

Unlike Huguely, whose name and face had flashed across television screens and in newspapers nationwide, relatively few people had heard of nineteen-year-old Demonte Burgess. Physically, he and Huguely both stood six foot two and weighed about 200 pounds. Both had been charged with ending another human's life. Both would see their cases begin in Charlottesville General District Court.

That's where the similarities ended.

Burgess was black; his listed address, "homeless;" his income, "zero." Huguely, meanwhile, came from a family owning second and third homes in the Outer Banks and Palm Beach.

Burgess's alleged victim, thirty-two-year-old Miguel Salazar, was shot in the head on January 22 in a trailer park after what police described as an "altercation" between four Hispanic men and two black men. Salazar's name is likely still unknown to many in the Charlottesville area; he certainly never graced the cover of *People* magazine after his death.

Huguely and Burgess lived just three miles apart, Fitzgerald noted in a June 8 story comparing and contrasting the men's predicaments, but "during the four years since Huguely moved to Burgess' hometown of Charlottesville to go to school, it seems unlikely the two would have crossed paths."

Fitzgerald wrote the piece, he said, because as the national media swarmed Charlottesville to cover Huguely's court hearings, he grew increasingly bemused at the picture they painted of the city. Writers used flowery words like "pastoral" and "bucolic." Meanwhile, the area in which Burgess lived was far from pastoral. It was, basically, a rundown slum literally on the other side of the tracks from UVA's well-to-do college kids. If ever there was a concrete example of town versus gown, this was it.

Fitzgerald compared the upbringings of Huguely and Burgess, and *C-VILLE* ran photos comparing the crime scene locations and the defendants' original homesteads. While Huguely attended an expensive private school for boys, Charlottesville High School had no record Burgess ever attended. Questions about Huguely's case were directed to, then ignored by, high-priced lawyers. When Fitzgerald approached the dilapidated duplex where Burgess had reportedly once lived, a man answering the door told him that Burgess "didn't do that shit," and threatened that he would "lump up" the next reporter to knock on his door.

Fitzgerald's point was that Charlottesville couldn't be summed up with pretty adjectives, and that while the whole nation might envision it as far removed from drugs and violence, people who really lived there knew the city had an underbelly that wasn't reflected in the crime statistics. (Burgess's case was forwarded to a grand jury, which determined in October 2010 there was enough evidence to send it to trial. As of now, Burgess is still awaiting trial.)

Fitzgerald's story, posted on *C-VILLE*'s Web site and featured on the front page of the weekly print publication, sparked some heated debate. Some applauded him for pointing out the disparities; others accused him of "stirring the pot." Readers of his story began commenting online just past midnight the morning it went to press. "I'm offended by your thinly veiled, baseless, and at this point quite cliché criticism of the UVA community just because of its privilege," one commenter wrote. "Please stop indicting all of UVA in this terrible tragedy."

It was telling, perhaps, that, despite Fitzgerald describing two separate slayings, the commenter referred to a "tragedy"— singular rather than plural.

As it turned out, neither Burgess nor Huguely actually had their hearings on June 10 as planned. While Burgess's was postponed until mid-August, Huguely's was delayed even longer, until October 7. Neither the defense nor the prosecution commented to reporters when asked why, though such delays aren't uncommon. The wheels of justice can sometimes turn agonizingly slowly.

Huguely reportedly awaited his court dates in isolation inside a 4-foot-by-8-foot cell inside the Albemarle-Charlottesville Regional Jail. Officials said he was segregated from the rest of the jail population and released about an hour a day for exercise, phone calls, or bathing. The jail, set off I-64 east of the 5th Street exit, is sprawled on a rural chunk of land away from the bustling UVA campus. Its locale, perhaps ironically, is among the most bucolic in Charlottesville. The jail was built in 1974 so that Albemarle County could shutter its outdated city and county jails. The staffs from those facilities were combined, and the Albemarle-Charlottesville Joint Security Complex was born. Its name was changed to the Albemarle-Charlottesville Regional Jail twenty-two years later, in 1996.

Aside from lawyer visits, Huguely was allowed a maximum of two visits per month, as per jailhouse rules. His family could send money to his "canteen fund"—an account from which he could buy commissary items such as shampoo, body wash, cough drops, or candy bars. Because he was segregated, he couldn't take part in some of the jail's inmate activities, dubbed "Beyond the Bars," such as its art show in

January 2011. Nor could he enroll in the jail's many classes, which ranged from culinary arts to crocheting.

Jail officials declined to say why Huguely was segregated from the others. Asked by Fitzgerald, Major Adam Rodriguez vaguely replied that "it could be either for disciplinary" reasons "or for his own protection—the safety and security of him." Despite early reports to the contrary, officials insisted Huguely had never been on suicide watch.

By mid-August, the October 7 court date had already been changed. Anticipating a mass of media, Charlottesville officials decided to push the date by one day and move it to the Charlottesville Circuit Court, which contained a larger courtroom than would be available in the district court.

Police Spokesman Ric Barrick told reporters that Charlottesville had turned to other cities that had handled high-profile cases for advice on how to handle the crush of journalists who surely would descend on the city come trial time. For example, they had contacted Chesapeake and Virginia Beach to find out how those cities handled the hundreds of reporters who arrived to cover the 2003 sniper trial. (In that case, John Allen Muhammad and Lee Boyd Malvo were linked to twenty shootings, resulting in thirteen deaths in Virginia, Maryland, Alabama, Georgia, Louisiana, and Washington, D.C. Both men were ultimately convicted.)

"We're not exactly sure what's going to happen through the trial, or how much interest we're going to have, but the interest has remained since the beginning of this incident," Barrick told one reporter. "We're going to need more space, and we're going to need to coordinate things a little bit more carefully and strategically than we currently do in Charlottesville."

While reporters waited to cover the preliminary hearing, bits of details in the case slowly trickled out thanks to the media consortiums' constant pressure to have public documents released. Every few weeks, some of those details would appear under headlines such as "New info released in

Huguely-Love case." The stories would invariably be short and direct, with no quotes from family members, lawyers, or even friends of the victim or suspect.

Josh Bowers, a UVA associate law professor, said that with each new story came reinvigorated interest in the case around Charlottesville. The lulls in between developments were so lengthy that it gave people who might otherwise have grown tired of the story time to regroup and get re-invested.

"Even if they were getting sick of the massive coverage, by the time a new development occurred, the story was somewhat fresh again because the last development had occurred some months ago."

Summer brought the first sustained breather. Aside from a smattering of quarter-turn updates, the case parties fell quiet, as did Charlottesville as a whole. The TV trucks and spotlights had been packed up and hauled away. About one-fourth of the student population had graduated, and a new crop of freshmen were enjoying that contemplative recess between high school graduation and college matriculation.

Bowers was impressed that so little leaked out.

"The parties have been somewhat admirably tight-lipped," he said. "We want our justice system to be transparent, but we want it to be transparent during the trial process. We don't want our cases litigated in the courts of public opinion, and by newspapers and other media. That kind of public judgment has the tendency to flip the presumption of innocence on its head. We see an exacerbation of reputational harm simply from the levying of charges itself. Ideally, you want at least to let the process play out in court without too much in the way of guilt and innocence arguments being made through media outlets. I'd rather see those arguments made in an open court."

Plenty of journalists would have agreed with Bowers, but in August came the realization that Huguely's first day in court might not come by year's end.

Chapter 26

The summer break wafted through Charlottesville like a lazy afternoon, and by Saturday, August 21, thousands of students crowded the streets as they moved into their homes away from home both on and off campus. While orientation wasn't required, it was offered from Saturday through Monday, with courses beginning that Tuesday. The town's temporary serenity gave way to the all-too-familiar horn-honking SUVs and parking-garage nightmares of another academic year.

Huguely's constantly changing court date loomed overhead, and though the summer had offered a reprieve, the case cast an ominous shadow across the again-bustling campus. Students filled the bookstores stocking up on academic supplies—notebooks, textbooks, and, of course, UVA sweatshirts and hoodies. Parents helped their youngsters move in to residence halls and apartments during the day, then flooded the city's family-friendly restaurants at night. Some young adults dragged their folks to the bars, bracing for their months-long separation over some beers.

The university had scheduled a weekend's worth of orientation events, including a so-called "move-in day 'oasis' fair" at the Aquatic & Fitness Center. Complimentary drinks were served while parents and students toured the recreational facilities and programs, enjoying some air-conditioned relief from the ninety-degree scorcher outside. Inside O-Hill Dining Hall, it seemed easy to pick out the fresh faces from the returning students—one group looking wide-eyed and slightly lost, the other a bit more comfortable with the routine—as hundreds flocked to have their photographs taken for their all-important student identification cards. Minority students were invited to a bevy of events, from ethnic-targeted meet-and-greets to a gathering for lesbian, gay, bisexual, and transgender students. One evening wrapped up with a Welcome Back Concert at John Paul Jones Arena.

Teresa Sullivan, UVA's newly minted president, welcomed the students in an hour-long speech. Though Sullivan had just three weeks prior moved into her new home at Carr's Hill—which had housed every UVA president since its completion in 1909—she already had made plans to address Yeardley's death in what she dubbed a "Day of Dialogue" on September 24.

In public speeches, Sullivan addressed Yeardley's death, even if she didn't always mention the young woman by name. In one speech to the Student Council on the first day of classes, she tasked the student representatives with empowering their classmates.

"You will help change the patterns of bystander behavior," Sullivan said. "Of course, we are each responsible for our own actions, but as members of this community, we also have responsibilities for one another. We are responsible for being aware, for recognizing threatening situations and behaviors, for reacting appropriately, and for respecting each other."

Mostly, however, Yeardley wasn't mentioned at all that first weekend back on campus.

"We really haven't heard anything," said the mother of one Baltimore-born first-year student. "It's the elephant in the room. Everyone is thinking about it, but no one is saying anything."

They weren't yet, anyway.

* * *

Sullivan had left her job as a provost at the University of Michigan to become UVA's first woman president. Round and cheerful, she came to campus with her husband, Douglas Laycock, and brought a different vibe to the post than the men who preceded her. It was no doubt a daunting legacy to continue. Casteen had the helm for two decades, and despite the many successes he boasted, his last year without question was shadowed by sorrow. Sullivan's efforts to bring people together to talk about the previous year's tragedies were applauded by some who had worried the administration had so far fumbled the human side of the tragedies.

Sullivan touted her Day of Dialogue as a "first step in building the caring community we all want to have." She began the day with a speech, taking the stage after the Virginia Belles and Virginia Gentlemen student groups sang the same songs they had performed at Yeardley's vigil more than four months earlier.

"In a very real sense, we are picking up from where we left off last May," Sullivan said.

The university and its community were different now than they had been the previous May, she told the crowd. The fourth-year students had moved on, and 25 percent of the undergraduate student body—the incoming first-year class—was new. Some faculty hadn't been there the spring before, and neither had Sullivan, she acknowledged.

"Some faculty weren't here last spring; I was not here last spring," Sullivan said. "Those of us who weren't in Charlottesville last May experienced Yeardley's death from a distance. Even from a distance, it was heartbreaking," Sullivan said.

But this day was to be about more than Yeardley, she added. The year prior was unusually tragic, marked by the deaths of seven students, as well as the slaying of Morgan Harrington. While some of the deaths happened elsewhere and seemed unpreventable, others haunted the university grounds.

"We are left to wonder if we might have done something differently to change what happened," Sullivan told the somber crowd. The question was especially impossible to ignore in Yeardley's case, when a young life was, by police accounts, ended by repeated and vicious blows to the head. Sullivan said that those who knew Yeardley even peripherally had to be wondering if they could have done or said something to change the trajectory of tragedy. To save a life.

Not everyone wanted Sullivan to go through with her planned day of discussion. The new president's staff had fielded angry phone calls from concerned parents who wanted her to call it off.

"Some expressed the opinion that we should not talk about these issues, that these issues are depressing or upsetting, and that young people should not have to consider things that are depressing or upsetting," Sullivan said. She understood the hesitancy. They were difficult matters to discuss and ponder, and she was as uncomfortable as anyone having to talk about them in her first weeks as university president. It would be easier to ignore the subjects, and certainly more palatable for parents sending their beloved children away from home to think they'd be inherently safe.

The Victorians, Sullivan said, had no qualms talking about death, but they wouldn't dare to talk about sex. Though the word "sex" triggered laughter in the crowd and allowed Sullivan a brief moment of levity, her point was this: "In our society, we talk constantly about sex but don't dare talk about death."

People have unique perspectives on violence and death, their standpoints painted by life experiences. Some in the crowd had experienced abuse only from a distance, Sullivan said. Some had never experienced death. Others had witnessed both first-hand, and perhaps even been the victims of violence or abuse themselves.

"We need to understand and respect reality, that these are intensely personal matters for some of us," she said.

Unlike Yeardley, whose face and story were splashed across newspaper and magazine covers, most victims suffer in silence and anonymity, Sullivan added.

"We gather today for those people, too," she said. "Although we have seen horrible events right here in Charlottesville, we acknowledge that violence, bias and abuse are national and global problems. All over the world, victims of hate and abuse are suffering, many of them with no recourse for help or even for making their suffering known."

She encouraged those who gathered to speak openly with each other about Yeardley's and Morgan's deaths, as well as Huguely's arrest. With Sullivan's arrival came a new student-led program called the Let's Get Grounded Coalition that focused on so-called bystander behavior. The group united representatives from thirty-five student organizations across the campus to work with the university administration on creating a safer community. Will Bane, a University Judiciary Committee member and member of Let's Get Grounded, told the *Cavalier Daily* that the initiative encourages students to seek help when needed.

Let's Get Grounded played a big role in Sullivan's Day of Dialogue, during which faculty members led small group discussions in rooms across campus. The talks had lofty titles like "Am I my sister's/brother's keeper?" and "Are we a caring community?" Student groups such as the Minority Rights Coalition set up booths on the campus grounds and chatted with passersby. Fewer students showed up for the discussions than expected, and male students were particularly underrepresented, according to reports, but organizers considered the event a success.

"It's not so much a day for solutions as a day for questions to keep the conversation going," Sullivan had said. "The solutions will come later. Today is the first step in building the caring community we all want to have."

Sullivan promised to follow up the daylong discussions so that the ideas and concerns presented wouldn't end up as wasted words. Let's Get Grounded went a step further and began developing training programs to combat the so-called bystander effect. As of late September 2010, more than 500 students and faculty members had been trained, and the

group was creating pledge cards to pass out to students who
promised to "recognize, react and respect" problems that
they might otherwise have seen and ignored.

The same day as Sullivan's dialogue, Judge Downer decided
to again postpone Huguely's court date. Instead of appearing
in October, Huguely was to have his preliminary hearing
January 21, 2011. Again, there was no explanation for the
decision, though it wasn't a particularly surprising one. No
one in the Huguely camp appeared to be in a rush. Even if
Huguely ultimately was convicted of a lesser crime than
first-degree murder, as his lawyers clearly wanted, he still
could face a hefty amount of time behind bars, and he would
be credited for time he had already served. It was more important that his lawyers be completely prepared rather than
rush to trial. And at this point, Huguely remained in solitary
confinement, apparently safely removed from other prisoners
who might want to make a name for themselves by harming
the high-profile suspect.

Downer made it clear, however, that despite the intense
media scrutiny of the case, there would be no cameras allowed inside the courtroom once the preliminary hearing got
underway. Ric Barrick, the police spokesman, said reporters
would be given room to write and record their stories in a
space near the Charlottesville General District Courthouse.

To John Zwerling, the Charlottesville-area defense lawyer, this was good news. Downer had made it clear he would
ban the gavel-to-gavel coverage that some news outlets undoubtedly had requested.

"Putting a trial on television changes the dynamics," said
Zwerling, whose firm handled the CourtTV extravaganza
that was the Lorena Bobbitt trial. ("That put CourtTV on the
map for a while," the lawyer mused.)

"First of all, the judge becomes extremely cautious and
puts his or her instincts away, which is usually bad," he said.
It's tough on attorneys, too, he added, because even the best,
most experienced lawyers can start doubting themselves

when they know people will be commenting every day on every little thing that occurred in the courtroom.

And, with an audience watching, sometimes lawyers feel pressured to perform—even when the best move for their client is to sit down and shut up.

"Some of the best cross-examinations are 'No questions, your honor,'" he said. "I've seen famous lawyers destroy a witness who had actually helped them. They destroyed the value of all the good stuff they gave. The lawyers may want to shine and sometimes that's consistent with effectiveness, but sometimes it is not. It makes you shake your head."

Even the jury feels pressured with cameras in the courtroom, Zwerling said. People outside of the trial pass judgment on the verdicts handed out inside because they feel they have real insight into the case thanks to the TV coverage. In reality, however, TV viewers of a trial are able to see and hear arguments for which the jury isn't present.

Despite the repeated delays in the preliminary hearing, the case itself still appeared before Downer for occasional motions. It was during one such motion in December 2010 that Huguely's lawyers dropped a bombshell—one that cast aside the "tragic accident" defense and instead attempted to exonerate Huguely altogether.

Chapter 27

The newspaper headlines on December 16 were sensational:

"Yeardley Love died from drugs, not assault, defense says."

Some even nixed the attribution, so the headline read as fact rather than conjecture.

The day prior, Dr. Jack Daniel, a pathologist from Richmond, Virginia, in private practice and hired by the defense, shocked the courtroom when he testified that he disagreed with the commonwealth's medical examiner and believed that Yeardley Love didn't die from blunt force trauma to her head. Rather, he said, the young woman died of cardiac arrhythmia caused by her consumption of alcohol and the prescription drug Adderall. The arrhythmia in turn caused insufficient blood flow to her head, Daniel said.

The doctor said the lack of oxygen caused "ongoing damage" that proved fatal.

Toxicology tests revealed that Yeardley had .05 milligrams of Adderall per liter of blood in her system—considered a therapeutic amount—as well as a blood-alcohol content of .14%—nearly twice the legal limit to drive in most states. In searching the coed's room after her body was discovered, police recovered a prescription bottle in her name for Adderall, which contains amphetamine.

Daniel said he examined Yeardley's brain and found that she suffered no lethal injuries. Any damage that did exist, he said, could have been caused while emergency responders administered CPR in their efforts to save the young woman's life. This was counter to the opinion of Dr. Bill Gormely, who had conducted the initial autopsy. Gormely told the court that the Adderall and alcohol "were not enough to have contributed to her death."

Yeardley's skull was not fractured, Gormley acknowledged for the first time in open court, but he noted a two-to-three-inch hemorrhage on Yeardley's scalp.

"It wouldn't necessarily cause death, but it could in conjunction with other injuries," Gormley told the court.

Add that to bleeding deep inside her brain, and Gormley said his findings pointed to "some sort of force."

Daniel disagreed, insisting that the patterns Gormley said were caused by a beating were "unusual for blunt force."

"Vigorous CPR caused these injuries interpreted by Dr. Gormley as primary traumatic injuries," Daniel said.

The battle of experts had begun earlier than expected.

Adderall is the brand name for a stimulant marketed largely to people with attention deficit hyperactivity disorder and narcolepsy. Designated a psychostimulant, it's thought by scientists to work by increasing dopamine and norepinephrine in the brain to make the taker feel more alert and better able to concentrate. It is also supposed to increase libido and reduce fatigue. Many psychiatrists prescribe the medication and find it a godsend for certain patients.

"There are people with [attention-deficit disorder] who can be on big doses and function just fine, and in fact need it to function well," one psychiatrist said. "I don't think of it as a drug with a very narrow window of dosage, like Lithium. Lithium has a narrow window between what's therapeutic and what would be toxic. Adderall isn't that way."

Generally, ADHD drugs aren't considered very dangerous when taken as prescribed. Some doctors even prescribe the medications to elderly people suffering from acute depression.

Seniors who previously refused to get out of bed have been known to rally back from the blues when given Adderall, Ritalin, or other ADHD drugs.

"They're not the beastly drugs that some people make them out to be," according to one psychiatrist.

Still, since its introduction in the 1990s, Adderall has caused controversy. Some people have complained that their heart seems to race after a dose, and the drug's advertised risks—glossed over in both print and TV ads with fine print and rushed voice-overs—include sudden death among people with heart abnormalities, stroke, heart attack, hypertension, psychosis, seizures, and aggressive behavior.

Adderall is abused plenty, too. People who take it when it hasn't been prescribed to them—or who take more than is recommended for them—can get a speed-like rush, one that can prove to be as addictive as cocaine.

At universities, it's sometimes dubbed a performance-enhancing drug, and not necessarily for athletes. Some misuse it as a study drug as users claim it keeps them awake and focused much longer than usual, providing much-needed fuel for their all-night cram sessions. Entire Web sites are devoted to young adults praising the drug's effectiveness.

"I love Adderall," one poster, identifying himself as Andrew, wrote on www.squidoo.com. "If I need to pull an all nighter, all I have to do is pop more pills and I'll be good to go, concentration and everything. Regular people can go for up to seven days without sleep if they take Adderall two to three times a day because it eliminates fatigue." Wrote another: "It has helped me through some of my darkest days. I wouldn't come down so hard on college students or anyone who uses it to enhance their performance. Most professionals and athletes all use some kind of enhancer."

In February 2005, Health Canada, the government department responsible for national public health in Canada, suspended sales of Adderall after twenty reported deaths. Of the deaths, twelve were from strokes, two of which were in children. In a letter to Shire Pharmaceuticals, which manufactures Adderall, Health Canada wrote that the "identified risk of sudden death following recommended doses cannot be managed by label changes." Shire shot back that the suspension came as a complete surprise. The U.S. Food and Drug Administration didn't follow Canada's lead, finding that the data wasn't definitive enough to merit a change in either Adderall's labeling or marketing in the United States. Six months after the ban, Health Canada agreed to allow Shire to resume its Adderall XR sales, provided it agree to some conditions: The company had to revise its patient information to reinforce that using the medicine could cause sudden cardiac death; it had to send letters to healthcare professionals explaining the risks associated with the product, and it had to commit to improving its post-market surveillance of the drug and update safety information to Health Canada.

But that hardly quieted the debate surrounding Adderall. Director for the Center of Alcohol Studies Robert Pandina conducted a study in 2007 that focused on Adderall use among Rutgers University students who did not have a prescription for the drug. The study found that nearly twelve percent of the 122 students surveyed said they used Adderall, while nearly 90 percent said they used alcohol. When asked why they used the ADHD drug, most said it was to beef up their academic performance. The study also found that more than three-quarters of the students found the use of Adderall without a prescription was socially acceptable.

According to Sober Living By the Sea, a treatment community based in Newport Beach, California, up to 25 percent of students enrolled at competitive universities have taken Adderall as a study aid. Another study, administered by the federal National Survey on Drug Use and Health, found that while just 6.4 percent of students said they had used the drug in 2008, college students between the ages of eighteen and twenty-two were twice as likely to abuse Adderall as nonstudents.

By all accounts, Yeardley did not fall into that category. According to court documents, her prescription for Adderall was valid. But her doctor likely would have warned her about another potential Adderall pitfall: the way it interacts with alcohol.

Studying aside, there's another use of Adderall rampant among college students: to keep the party going. Users report that they take Adderall before drinking to stave off the effects of alcohol, allowing them to drink longer without feeling drunk. Plenty of online forums discuss this effect, complete with descriptions of crushing the pill and snorting it to get even speedier results. Mixing alcohol and Adderall can even lead to alcohol poisoning, according to the Office of Alcohol and Drug Education at the University of Notre Dame:

"The stimulant effect can cause students to prolong use resulting in consuming unhealthy amounts of alcohol, which has lead [sic] to cases of alcohol poisoning. Stimulants in the system can block the depressant effect, shutting off the warning signs to a person's body that they may be drinking too much."

Instead of feeling drunk and drowsy, someone mixing alcohol and Adderall might well end their night by passing out, having been able to fend off the typical symptoms of drunkenness for longer than is healthy.

The complaints are similar to the ones circulating around drinks that mix caffeine and alcohol. Take the Four Loko controversy: The caffeinated drink had a 6% or 12% alcohol by volume content, depending on which state it was sold in. After a series of college students landed in hospitals because of Four Loko benders, the federal Food and Drug Administration put pressure on the drink's makers, finally forcing them to remove the caffeine from the product.

Francis Lawrence and Rhonda Quagliana, Huguely's lawyers, seemed prepared to argue that mixing Adderall and alcohol could have been the sole cause of Yeardley's death. During a December court hearing, they asked to see all of Yeardley's medical records from her time at the University of Virginia. They argued it could prove crucial to their defense strategy.

"This is an important time to have available to us very important information," Lawrence told the court.

Judge Downer, however, declined the request. It took him a week to make his ruling, during which time he said he reviewed all of the medical records Huguely's lawyers had sought.

"I find nothing even remotely material to his case in there, with the exception of what has already been described previously," the judge said from the bench on December 22, referring to the Adderall/alcohol levels the night Yeardley died.

"I'm not going to permit a fishing expedition," Downer said.

Lawrence pressed further. He wanted to know if Yeardley had any "diet or weight" issues—both of which could also weaken her heart and perhaps make her more susceptible to an Adderall-sparked cardiac arrhythmia. The judge said she didn't.

"There is nothing remotely embarrassing or unusual for a woman who is a student-athlete," he said.

The new Adderall defense caught many off guard. Death is rare even among those who abuse the drug; onlookers wondered how Huguely's lawyers planned to convince a jury that an appropriate dose killed her.

"It's not likely that the alcohol and therapeutic Adderall played a role in the death," speculated Daniel Spitz, the Michigan forensic pathologist not connected with the case. "Repeated head impacts are the real issue and seem to be what caused her death. The etoh [ethanol in alcohol] and Adderall are of course helpful to the defense because it gives them something to put in front of the jury as a potential cause. Also, it will help cloud the real issue and allow them to try and minimize the severity of the head trauma."

John Zwerling saw the Adderall hearing as possible insight into Lawrence and Quagliana's defense strategy. They had seemingly shown their cards early on when they described the death as a tragic accident—a move that left many assuming they wouldn't deny Huguely's role in the death, but would do their best to argue the charges down. But with this latest turn, it seemed possible that they had an ace up the sleeve.

"It could be that it's a two-prong approach," Zwerling said.

He likened it to the strategy his firm had laid out for Lorena Bobbitt, who infamously maimed her husband in 1989 by cutting off his penis and tossing it in a field.

"The defense there was 'self-defense, and in any event, I was temporarily insane,'" the lawyer recalled. The jury bought one of the two defenses, and found Bobbitt not guilty by reason of insanity.

Megan Pringle, the *Good Morning Maryland* anchor, said the newsroom was aflutter with the Adderall development.

"It's crazy what's happening now," she said shortly after the defense's revelation. "Every intern at our station said, 'Oh, everyone takes Adderall.'"

Liz Seccuro, the UVA student whose 1984 rape on campus finally resulted in a conviction twenty-two years later, was especially outraged by the turn of events. She called the "Adderall defense" disgusting, and characterized the defense's attempt to peruse all of Yeardley's medical records as particularly disturbing.

"They'd want to find anything—birth control, antidepressants, suicide attempts, abortions, eating disorders, cutting, alcohol abuse," she said. Luckily, she added, "the judge said 'no.'" He'd allow the inclusion of Adderall, which was found in her backpack and was allegedly being taken for the right reason (ADHD) and in the correct dosage.

"But it's their job to defend Huguely, not to make the dead girl look good," Seccuro said. "That said, I do think there is a broader issue of 'blaming the victim' at stake and it's become more permissive in courts, even when we speak of a deceased victim. Even when we have a defendant who admits to shaking her around the neck violently, causing her head to repeatedly strike a wall. So, yes, I do think that there's a fine line between defending a client and making a victim out to be the one who somehow caused her own death by associating with such an alleged perpetrator. She broke up with him. He bashed in her door with his foot. She had every right to feel safe in her own home with a locked door. That is domestic violence."

Seccuro took to the Huffington Post, considered by many to be among the most powerful news Web sites in the world, to write an opinion piece about the case. To her, she wrote, the defense "might as well be saying [Yeardley] is a speed junkie."

"It's unorthodox, even shocking, but not surprising," she wrote. "They must go after the cause of death and try to remove their client, who allegedly confessed to hitting Love, from the full responsibility for his actions."

Chapter 28

In mid-December, the Washington *Examiner* posted a story headlined "No death penalty for Huguely, cops say." The lead paragraph said exactly that: "Prosecutors have no plans to seek the death penalty for George Huguely V. . . ." But it was the second paragraph that was picked up by the Huffington Post Web site and reprinted around the world:

"And there is a growing consensus that the case will be settled in a plea deal before trial, said persons close to both the prosecution and the Huguely family."

The story, written by journalist Hayley Peterson, wasn't unexpected. Anytime a case drags out in court, there obviously exists the possibility that the defense and the prosecution could be negotiating behind closed doors. After all, the vast majority of convictions aren't the result of trials, but of plea deals, Bowers said.

"Ninety-five percent of convictions are the result of guilty pleas, and the overwhelming majority of those guilty pleas were the result of some explicit or implicit plea bargains," he said. "Very few—five percent or fewer—end up being litigated at trial."

With murder cases, the figure drops a bit for a few reasons. For starters, there is more at stake. Defense lawyers are fighting for more than a few years of their clients' lives;

they're sometimes fighting for life itself. And prosecutors aren't as willing to let a murderer plead to a lesser crime as they are, say, a first-time dope dealer or a robber. Then you add in the wishes of the accused, and things get even more complicated.

"Criminal defendants are sometimes quite present-focused and don't always take the long-range view," Bowers said. "If you have a twenty-five-year-old confronting the possibility of fifty years in prison or life, he or she might go ahead and try to get an acquittal because the results of a conviction by either trial or plea seem intolerable."

Still, he added, about two-thirds of murder convictions are historically the result of guilty pleas.

"Trials are a relative rarity even with murder charges," he said.

It wasn't a surprise then that Peterson found sources willing to say that a plea deal was likely in the Huguely case. What *was* shocking, however, was that one of the sources was a Charlottesville police spokesman.

Lieutenant Gary Pleasants had helped field the early media onslaught in the Huguely case, appearing by phone on Velez-Mitchell's CNN show two days after Yeardley's body was discovered. It was an unusual step into the limelight for a man who typically was interviewed about Charlottesville's petty crimes: Not two months before the murder, he was the prime police source for a story about a rash of motor scooter thefts throughout Albemarle County. As the immediate crush calmed, however, most media calls were shipped to spokesman Ric Barrick, who declined to say much on the record.

So it was a surprise to most when Pleasants was the *Examiner* story's main source on the plea-deal discussion.

Peterson wrote that prosecutors would lay out just enough evidence at Huguely's preliminary hearing to convince a Charlottesville judge to send the case to trial: "But Pleasants says it is unlikely the case will make it to opening arguments. . . . He said he believed it is likely that [District Attorney] Chapman and Huguely's defense will instead negotiate a settlement."

~~Charlottesville~~ defense lawyer David Heilberg chimed in, telling the paper that he believed prosecutors would want to settle if the commonwealth's case was strong enough. "[Prosecutors] are getting what they want out of the case by agreement: Angling for Huguely to plead to something, whatever it might be, [for a sentence] not less than forty years, and then let a judge decide," said Heilberg, who was not connected with the Huguely case.

To some, a plea deal seemed the best option for both sides—especially the Loves. Bill Mitchell, who buried his daughter Kristin in 2005, couldn't have fathomed having to sit through weeks of gut-searing testimony at trial.

"I feel terrible for what the Love family is going through," he said. "Unless Huguely pleads and goes away, the Love family will be dragged through hell all over again. Unfortunately, the legal system is not about getting to the truth and then administering a sentence. It's about either 'sending him to a life sentence' or 'making it seem as if he wasn't the responsible party'—as if he were the victim."

Mitchell wanted to see his daughter's killer spend as much time behind bars as possible. But he also believed that families traumatized once by heart-breaking loss could face even more trauma once mired in the judicial system.

"[P]eople who kill people don't belong around innocent women. Ever. You can quote me," Mitchell said. "That life of freedom should be forfeited. I don't believe in 'serving time and paying a debt to society' any more than my daughter will come back to life after she serves a term as a dead person in fifteen to thirty years. His life isn't worth more than hers. If anything, for what he did, it's worth so much less."

But the news of a possible plea sparked outcry from some, especially victims' rights activists. Liz Seccuro again wrote an outraged piece that ran on Huffington Post. She couldn't help but connect the recent unveiling of the Adderall defense with the heightened talk of a plea arrangement. Were Huguely's lawyers providing a sampling of the character assassination to come?

"What Huguely and his team are doing is trying to allow a frisson of reasonable doubt to creep into the mind of just one sympathetic and uninformed juror in order to set him free, hang the jury or have a mistrial," Seccuro wrote. She found it insidious and disgusting, she wrote, as well as a red herring. Instead of focusing on Huguely's behavior, they instead were aiming to sully the reputation of a young woman "who, by all accounts, was extraordinary in every way."

In a later interview, Seccuro said she wrote the piece to rail "against any sort of plea deal that blamed the victim."

"In this case, Rhonda and Fran [the defense lawyers] are trying to say that Yeardley's perfectly safe and prescribed use of Adderall caused her death," Seccuro said. "Um, yeah, I'd have a heart attack too if my 200-plus pound . . . exboyfriend kicked in my door. She died of blunt force trauma," she said, echoing the autopsy.

Seccuro compared it to the defense Lawrence and Quagliana provided her own attacker: They had argued that Beebe's attack was a "thoughtless college sex encounter" during which Beebe behaved in an "ungentlemanly manner."

"Yes, the 'Twinkie Defense' for the ages," Seccuro said. "So, nothing new for these two. They are just doing their jobs."

The Charlottesville Police Department tried to repair the damage.

"As for talk of a plea deal, I believe that officer spoke out of turn," Barrick said in an e-mail. He assured reporters that the January 21st preliminary hearing was going ahead as planned and "I anticipate the upcoming court date to be important to attend."

From then on, getting answers to even the most mundane what's-next questions in the case became all but impossible.

Chapter 29

Yeardley's family kept quiet in public about the young woman they had lost, declining interviews from Oprah Winfrey and Piers Morgan, according to some close to the case. While Sharon Love said she worried that any pretrial publicity might hurt the case against Huguely, she also said that her sister—Yeardley's aunt—planned to write a book about the ordeal and that she preferred to let the book speak for the family. But while she and Yeardley's sister said nothing to the media, they and other loved ones toiled tirelessly behind the scenes creating an organization designed to both honor Yeardley's memory and help other young adults, regardless of the outcome of the criminal trial.

In mid-September, Yeardley's family and friends unveiled the One Love Foundation, a nonprofit organization created as "a tribute to Yeardley Reynolds Love, who wore #1 as a lacrosse player at both Notre Dame Prep and the University of Virginia. Yeardley lived her life with one purpose: to make her world a better place." The foundation, online at www.joinonelove.org, includes heart-adorned messages such as "inspire others." It is a registered 501(c)(3) organization, meaning it is a tax-exempt charity.

One Love's creation made headlines across the country, including on ABC's *Good Morning America*. By the time of its unveiling, the foundation already had several fundraisers in the works, including a Baltimore Orioles game, a golf tournament, and a marathon. Notre Dame Prep, Yeardley's high school, announced it wanted to build a turf field in honor of their slain alumna, and funds raised by One Love would help offset the costs. The school also aimed to create a scholarship in Love's name. The Texas-based Charles T. Bauer Foundation offered a challenge match to donate, dollar-for-dollar, all gifts up to $500,000. The exchange would support a scholarship fund to provide a full, four-year scholarship every fourth year for a Notre Dame student.

Sharon Love released a short statement to the media about the foundation:

"The mission of the foundation is to encourage and develop in children and young adults four qualities of character that Yeardley exemplified—service, kindness, humility, and sportsmanship—that together add up to One Love. The foundation would like to 'bring out the Yeardley' in everyone. . . . It is our turn to make Yeardley proud, and we will do our very best."

The foundation's Web site spells out its lofty goals, which include encouraging young adults to "choose a path of goodness." Among its other aims: to help children and young adults participate in service programs, to draw attention to society's "unsung heroes," and to create a character-based program to bring sports, specifically lacrosse, into underprivileged communities. "In turn, the beneficiaries of such programs would be encouraged to 'pay it forward' and volunteer in their own communities." The site includes a brief biography, describing Yeardley's upbringing and ambitions, as well as a copy of the high school essay she wrote about herself that had been handed out to mourners at her funeral. The family also posted photographs of Yeardley from happier times—swimming with friends, at the beach with her family, dressed in her Sunday best with her sister, smiling broadly with friends. In one picture, she mugs to the camera in her lacrosse gear, jokingly jutting out her bright green mouth guard. In another, she stands alongside roommate and teammate

Caitlin "Caity" Whiteley, ~~who would later~~ discover her battered body. In the photograph, the girls are beaming; both are wearing #1 jerseys.

The foundation's site includes ways to donate, as well as links to One Love merchandise, from T-shirts to wristbands to bumper stickers. Donors are encouraged to leave messages, which the foundation posts online:

"Yeards, the girls play with your sticks and we feel you right here with us. Keeping you close . . ."

"For our children, may they always love and honor life like this young woman did."

"I keep a little bit of Yeardley with me every day, and I miss her so much! This is just a small tribute to the impact she had on me as a friend and mentor at UVA, and I just feel so lucky to have met someone as beautiful, caring and kind-spirited as her. I will always remember her."

The last message was signed by Boyd Vicars, a member of UVA's field hockey team.

The site closes with a quote from Mother Teresa: "So let us always meet each other with a smile, for the smile is the beginning of love."

Hoping to raise money for the foundation, the Timonium, Maryland–based Baltimore Coffee and Tea Company released a special blend in Yeardley's honor. The coffee mixed two beans—Costa Rican and Brazilian Santos—to create something "a little sweeter and a little softer, to emulate her," Norman Loverde, the company's executive vice president, told journalist Nick DiMarco. "It's a make-everybody-happy kind of coffee. That's what she was about."

For each $9.50 bag of "Yeardley's Blend" that it sold, the company said it would donate $5 to the One Love Foundation.

Loverde said his motivation was simple: He had sent his daughters to Notre Dame Prep, and his family had always placed importance on giving back to the community and the school. The company had been roasting and cultivating coffees at its 9 West Aylesbury Road location for fourteen years,

DiMarco reported, and had regularly developed private-label coffees for local businesses and fundraisers.

"This is our niche," he told DiMarco. "It's a part of our culture and philosophy. We've always done this."

But Yeardley's Blend hit closer to home, Loverde admitted. One of his daughters had been friends with Yeardley, and the slain girl had been to his home and played with his children.

"I don't think you need much motivation for this. I'm a parent," Loverde said. "My daughter being friends with her, obviously we're affected by it. It's tragic. . . . We're just trying to make something good out of something bad."

Catherine Barthelme, one of Love's best friends involved with the One Love Foundation, told DiMarco that the coffee was a "great personalized way to keep Yeardley's memory alive.

"It's one of the positive things that has come out of this tragedy, that everyone has come together to keep Yeardley's memory alive," Barthelme said. "I think that every single girl in my class could say this, but she had the most contagious laugh and smile."

Yeardley's Blend became a popular gift at Christmastime, allowing people to both buy coffee for loved ones and donate to the One Love charity. The foundation also planned a New Year's celebration marking January 1, 2011—or 1/1/11, an appropriate date for a young woman who had worn a #1 jersey. Tickets to the $75-a-person event sold out in late December and, just days later, the foundation announced that it had reached its first fundraising goal.

"Notre Dame Preparatory School is pleased to announce that a $500,000 challenge grant from the Charles T. Bauer Foundation has been met," read a news release from the high school. "With the funds, the school may begin two projects honoring deceased alumna Yeardley Reynolds Love: The Yeardley Reynolds Love Field, and a scholarship in Ms. Love's name."

Of the $500,000 raised, One Love donated $220,000 in gifts and pledges, the school reported.

"This challenge grant received tremendous support from the NDP community and beyond, locally and nationally, demonstrating the regard people hold for Yeardley and her family," said headmistress Sister Patricia McCarron in a released statement.

School spokeswoman Cami Colarossi told Patch reporters that school officials were taking "sheer delight in the fact that this one grant is really launching two projects. We are thrilled with that."

Sharon Love again spoke to the media through a released statement: "We are so grateful for the support of the community. We are thrilled that . . . future generations of need-based students will have the opportunity for a NDP education. We all know how special NDP was to Yeardley, and think this is an amazing tribute to her."

As the weather grew bitter, many of Yeardley's friends sent messages to the Love family offering support and prayers. Even strangers sent their version of comfort online—one such message, sent via the social networking site Twitter, called on people to pause and remember the Loves on Christmas Day. Their grief must have been crippling.

Outwardly at least, the One Love Foundation kept its messages upbeat and succinct. Through its own Twitter account, it posted thank-yous to followers as it promoted the foundation. As the holidays neared, its Twitter account, @JoinOneLove, posted photographs of college-age girls wearing One Love T-shirts and bustling crowds at events such as one held in a Baltimore bar called Pickles Pub. Notre Dame Prep hosted the Yard for Yeardley event Oct. 1, inviting supporters to watch the Baltimore Orioles take on the Detroit Tigers at Camden Yards. Tickets cost $15, and proceeds went to the Love fund. In another play on words, the "Every Yard for Yeardley" racing team formed, raising money through donations for a November run in Richmond. The team ultimately raised more than $60,000, according to the foundation, and as of late January, the team had re-launched in hopes of raising $10,000 more for the Charlottesville 8K, Half-Marathon, and Marathon to be run April 9.

On Christmas Day, One Love sent out a simple message: "Merry Christmas and Happy Holidays from the One Love foundation! Thanks for all your support!" Barely a week later, it sent an emphatic thanks to the 800 people who took part in the "1.1.11" fundraising event: "You are all amazing!!"

The benign comments and fundraising efforts highlighted how the Loves chose to outwardly mourn: by turning to activism. It was a method that Morgan Harrington's parents had used as well as they grappled with their daughter's recent murder. REMEMBER MORGAN T-shirts for sale at www.findmorgan.com helped support both a memorial scholarship at Virginia Tech, and the construction of an educational wing in an African village. But while the families were similar in their attempts at advocacy, they deviated when it came to sharing their grief. Gil Harrington, Morgan's mother, continued to turn to the Web to vent, to post poems, to describe how life was like a minefield around the holidays.

"There is a lot of pain in discarding family traditions that are fractured for us without Morgan taking her part in them," she wrote in January.

The Loves had endured two horrific losses in less than a decade: first John Love, then Yeardley. How many broken family traditions were they being forced to endure?

Nick DiMarco, editor of the Lutherville-Timonium Patch (an online news organization backed by AOL), had by then written several stories about Yeardley, particularly about the outpouring of community support in the months after her death. Out of respect for the still-pending trial, he refrained from asking questions about the criminal case but asked to learn more about Yeardley as a person. The most he had learned about her personality was that she was a "sweet, sweet girl," as Loverde had described. DiMarco was employed as a research assistant for this book.

He contacted officials with ~~Notre Dame Prep, Yeardley's~~ high school, and at first was greeted kindly by a public relations representative. Soon after, however, he received a terse e-mail from the school's headmistress, which stated that "no one affiliated with Notre Dame Preparatory School will participate in the research in any way." She demanded that DiMarco "cease" his research "regarding this project or any other information about Miss Love or her family."

While taken aback, DiMarco complied and reached out next to Karen McGagh, a Love family friend and self-described spokeswoman for the One Love Foundation. The two spoke amicably on the phone about DiMarco's intended research and agreed to communicate via e-mail. During one e-mail thread, McGagh abruptly replied, "Hi nick! (sic) I will not be speaking with you on this issue." The signature line on the email read, "Sent from my iPhone."

Then DiMarco received an e-mail from a woman with whom he had spoken for Patch's story about "Yeardley's Blend," the coffee whose sales had benefited the One Love Foundation. The woman thanked DiMarco for his story, then continued:

"I understand that you now have a new assignment. I would ask you not to use my name as a frame of reference for that or any other assignments. . . . Again, I appreciate your coverage of Yeardley's Blend."

DiMarco finally made headway with St. Joseph Parish, home of Yeardley's elementary school. Sister Anne O'Donnell, the school's principal, agreed to organize a gathering of Yeardley's former teachers to talk about the young woman behind the headlines. On Friday, January 14, she led Di-Marco to a work area of the school where about twenty-five teachers were sitting at tables after a work session. The students had been given the day off for an extra long weekend, thanks to the following Monday being Martin Luther King Jr. Day, a national holiday.

DiMarco again explained his intentions—that he wanted to assist in a manuscript meant to humanize Yeardley and describe what kind of person the world had lost with her untimely death. The teachers agreed and began to talk about Yeardley's younger years—her bright smile and blue eyes, her loving relationship with her father.

Four and a half minutes into his interviews, DiMarco was interrupted. O'Donnell pulled him out of the room, saying she had been contacted just then by someone with the One Love Foundation.

"It was like going to the principal's office," DiMarco described. "O'Donnell said that I could no longer be there and asked that all information I had collected be given back to her. I said I could not do that."

DiMarco collected his things and was escorted from the building.

It was a frustrating experience. DiMarco considered himself a sensitive reporter who had clearly spelled out his intentions both in writing and in person. Weeks later, one of the sources would reach out to him again to ask for help publicizing another fundraising event, and while she apologized for her earlier snubbing, she still declined to describe the young woman for whom the money was being raised.

Chapter 30

As January got under way, people began gearing up for the anticipated preliminary hearing set for the 21st. But the month had barely started before the prosecution made an announcement that would change everything:

Huguely faced new charges.

On Friday, January 7, District Attorney Warner "Dave" Chapman issued a memo on city letterhead announcing that five additional warrants were requested and issued against Huguely. Now he faced charges of felony murder, robbery, burglary, statutory burglary, and grand larceny. Until this point, Huguely had faced one charge: first-degree murder. George was to be arraigned via video feed the following Monday in the Charlottesville General District Court.

The memo reminded reporters—and the public—that the new warrants were still nothing more than allegations. "Every person is presumed to be innocent unless and until proof beyond a reasonable doubt is established before a judge or jury." And it suggested that Chapman expected the defense to ask that the preliminary hearing be delayed yet again.

Late in the day, Lawrence and Quagliana released a statement saying the new charges were not a surprise.

"These additional charges were not unexpected and we have been fully prepared to defend against them. We think it is significant that the amended charges acknowledge that there was no premeditation."

Word of the new charges piqued curiosity among the gadflies. Did this imply that prosecutors no longer felt they had enough evidence to prove Huguely had intended to kill Yeardley—a necessity for a first-degree murder conviction? Or were these new charges meant to offer the defense some wiggle room in which to reach a plea deal, possibly sparing Huguely from having to face trial?

John Zwerling guessed neither. Upon hearing of the additional charges, he said they seemed as though they would be more beneficial to Huguely's defense lawyers than to the commonwealth.

"There's plenty of punishment attached to murder," he said. "I imagine it would have zero effect on negotiations."

Felony murder is a form of first-degree murder that looks quite similar on paper. Both mean you're charged with killing someone, and if you're convicted, you'll likely spend life behind bars. But they differ when it comes to intent. While first-degree murder requires premeditation, felony murder means that someone died while you were committing a felony that generally is considered dangerous. For example, if a gunman robs a store and kills the resisting storeowner, he maybe didn't go to the store to kill anyone, making it tough to prove premeditation. But because he caused the victim's death while he was committing a robbery, he could more easily be convicted of felony murder.

Before January 7, Huguely hadn't faced other felonies. Now, he faced several, robbery among them. According to the search warrants, the only item taken from Yeardley's apartment during the attack was her laptop. That perhaps constituted burglary, but it raised another question of intent: Did Huguely go to the apartment to steal the laptop, or was that an afterthought? Unless prosecutors could prove that Huguely went to his ex-girlfriend's apartment intending to bash in her door and steal her laptop, they could risk handing a jury reason to reduce the charge significantly.

Josh Bowers, the UVA associate law professor, saw the

~~charges as a chance for the prosecution to come at the mur-~~
der theory from multiple angles.

"It's advantageous for a prosecutor to pursue a felony murder theory where such a theory is available," Bowers said. "It provides an additional opportunity to make out the top charge—the charge of murder—without having to actually demonstrate that the defendant had a guilty, culpable mindset as to the death itself. All the prosecutor needs to do is prove that the elements of an underlying felony were met, and a death resulted."

In short: felony plus death equals murder.

"It's better for a prosecutor to have two theories than one," Bowers continued. "You don't want to have so many theories that you leave the jury confused, but having two ways to make the case is probably reasonable."

Bowers laid out an example he teaches to students in his substantive criminal law class, a required course for first-year law students at UVA: Let's say a man steals a car. He wants to avoid drawing the police's attention, so he drives exceptionally carefully. He obeys speed limits, signals when he turns, and yields to passing ambulances. Despite all these precautions, a child jumps into traffic and is mowed down by the stolen car. The child dies, and the car thief is arrested. Bowers said that it would be difficult for the prosecutor to win a first- or second-degree murder case against the car thief, and it might even prove impossible to sway a jury to convict him of manslaughter because the thief was neither reckless nor grossly negligent. But it could be possible for the prosecutor to charge the thief with felony murder—because felony plus death equals murder.

"There are limitations, of course, and it varies from one state to another what felonies will serve as a predicate, as a trigger, for a felony murder charge, and there are also questions of causation," Bowers said. But in nearly all states that have felony murder on the books, burglary and robbery charges would qualify—and now Huguely was faced with both.

* * *

Though many inmates would have happily left the confines of their jail cell for a daytrip to the courthouse, Huguely waived his right to appear at the next Monday's arraignment in Charlottesville General District Court. Instead, his lawyers appeared alone—and indeed asked for more time to review the newly added charges.

"Judge, I can say that both sides have been moving with diligence, and the commonwealth certainly has been cooperative, but there is a bunch of stuff still out there," Lawrence said in court.

He and Quagliana still needed to analyze about twenty of the more than 100 pieces of evidence collected against their client in the case, Lawrence added. Judge Downer agreed to the continuance, saying that justice would be better served if the case weren't rushed to a preliminary hearing. The latest rescheduling marked the third time the defense won a delay, first from June to October, then from October to January, and now until April. No one ever accused the wheels of justice of spinning too quickly.

The sides couldn't immediately agree on a date that worked for everyone, but within a week, they had settled on April 11—three weeks shy of the one-year anniversary of Yeardley's death.

Chapter 31

With the rescheduling came a jolting realization: Both the men's and women's lacrosse teams would be immersed in their new seasons by the time the horror of the previous year even began to unfold in a courtroom.

The new academic year was well under way. Christmas break had come and gone. The twinkling strands of multi-colored lights had forced some festivity on the tragedy-weary town, and then were packed away for another season. Yeardley's jersey number was retired, and the roster for the women's lineup began with #2—freshman Lauren Goerz of California. She was one of eleven freshman players. It was a young team, featuring just four seniors. The previous year, the team had had seven freshmen and six seniors.

In contrast, Huguely's jersey number had seemingly been resurrected. In the days after the slaying, the official UVA men's Web site at www.virginiasports.com dropped him from the lineup. Suddenly, the online roster jumped from #10 Chris Bocklet to #12 John Haldy. Huguely's number, position, statistics, and photograph were outright deleted from each of the four years he had played on the team. For the 2010–2011 team, however, #11 reappeared, having been handed over to Pat Harbeson, a freshman from Annapolis,

Maryland, who undoubtedly knew well the history behind the number he now bore.

The women's team had played in a series of fall and winter scrimmages, but as late January approached, it was time to focus on the regular season. Their first game was set to be on February 19 at Loyola College in Baltimore, Maryland; the men's would be the same day against Drexel at home.

Together, both teams issued a statement acknowledging how difficult the time off had been:

> With both of our seasons about to unfold, the players and staffs of the University of Virginia's men's and women's lacrosse teams would like to take a moment to express our thanks and gratitude to all our families, friends, fans and alums for their support since the tragic event of last May. Yeardley Love and her family remain constantly in our thoughts and prayers.
>
> It is difficult to describe the emotions and feelings we have all experienced since losing a friend, teammate and fellow student. We are dealing with this loss as teams and individuals while also searching for ways to move forward. We are grateful for the support and counseling made available by the University and so many wonderful staff members.
>
> Some members of the media have expressed a desire to interview us about what we have experienced during the last nine months. We understand the interest in wanting to explore our healing process, our thoughts and our feelings in greater detail. As we move forward and out of respect for the ongoing legal process, we do not feel it is appropriate for us to answer those kinds of questions. We will instead focus on our continued healing, our teams and the upcoming seasons. We appreciate your understanding.

Clearly, the death still hung over both teams. There would still be the occasional public remembrances—a moment of silence before some games and the counting to four before the women took the field—but for the most part, it would remain the elephant in the room.

Outside of the locker rooms, as the case against Huguely slowly crept through the court system, Yeardley's death continued to make headlines. Governor McDonnell's talk of proposing a state law that would require police departments to notify universities when a student was arrested collapsed under what he called "logistical issues." But different legislation aimed to make it easier to get protective orders.

Love's death also sparked proposed legislation to change Virginia's protective order laws. As it stood, Virginia didn't allow couples in relationships to get protective orders unless the pair was living together or had a child—meaning that the laws didn't help people embroiled in what experts call dating violence. Virginia Delegate Joe Morrissey, a Democrat from Henrico County, introduced legislation that would nix the cohabitation requirement. A similar bill had been proposed the previous year by Republican Delegate Robert Bell, but it was debated by police officers, domestic violence advocates, and attorney general representatives, and ultimately failed to win approval.

Morrissey said Love's death "has brought this to a head."

"Everyone in law enforcement is concerned with providing protection without swamping the system to the point where they can't provide protection to those who need it," Bell told reporters.

Morrissey hoped his bill would strike that balance.

UVA kept its promise to revise its seven-year-old self-reporting policy. New president Teresa Sullivan announced that all students would be required to disclose in writing their criminal records before they'd be allowed to access course material information and school e-mail services. The question would be posed as each student accessed the university's computer system, followed by a prompt that reminded them of their obligation to report new incidents within seventy-two hours of the occurrence. The change greeted students as they gathered in late August for the 2010–2011 academic year.

Sullivan, gathered with reporters for a news conference about the policy change inside the campus's Madison Hall, said the background check requirement "has been changed from a passive notification system to a more active notification system," and that students caught lying about their criminal histories would be found in violation of the school's honor code. In short, like hundreds of test cheaters and thieves before them, they would be expelled.

Student athletes were required to inform their coaches of an arrest within twenty-four hours. If coaches found out that a player conveniently forgot, as Huguely apparently did, he or she would face sanctions from the athletic department.

"The one place where there is a difference is student athletes have additional obligations to the athletic program and their coaches," Dean of Students Allen Groves told reporters.

UVA's Division of Student Affairs also began reaching out to other colleges and universities in the commonwealth in hopes of devising a system that would enable them to alert one another if a student was arrested at another school.

Sullivan said she planned to walk the fine line between making the campus a sanctuary and forcing students to face a sometimes ugly reality.

"We cannot build a bubble around the Grounds," she said. "Things that happen, bad things that happen in everyday life, also happen on the Grounds."

Life moved on throughout the campus. The football season kicked off in early September with the team winning 34–13 over Richmond. The following month, as the leaves across campus turned vibrant shades of scarlet, thousands of alumni flooded the city and watched as the 'Hoos fell to their North Carolina rivals. Winter came and coated the city with snow just as students wrapped up the first semester of the academic year.

But there were signs, too, of Yeardley's impact. The

Women's Center on campus worked with university police to promote the Red Flag Campaign in October, also known as Domestic Violence Awareness Month. The campaign's goal—encouraging people to speak up when they saw signs of unhealthy relationships—fit perfectly with the "bystander behavior" training that Sullivan had been promoting. The Dean of Students also spoke to the school's daily newspaper to spread word that female students needing help could turn to his office for residence relocation assistance, no-contact orders, and no-trespass orders.

Yeardley's now-infamous apartment #9 no longer sits empty on 14th Street Northwest. One hundred days after the slaying, as a new crop of students crowded the Charlottesville campus, the apartment was rented out to four students who had signed the lease before the fateful day in May.

Katelyn Krause, a neighbor, told reporters that she helped the young women move into the apartment.

"It was just weird knowing what happened in that room, to be inside it," she said. "There's no way I could ever be so inclined as to take that lease . . . It's something that's going to be on your mind every night when you go to sleep. Just the thoughts of what happened in that room would keep me awake."

The battered door leading into Yeardley's bedroom, long ago removed by police as evidence, had been replaced. The blood stains and signs of struggle had long been cleaned away.

Huguely, too, was gone. He had celebrated his twenty-third birthday in a jail cell three miles away from the room where his ex-girlfriend's lifeless body had been discovered. New tenants had moved into his apartment two buildings away. The turnover would have happened regardless of the tragedy; both young adults would have left Charlottesville for their new lives as full-fledged adults. But standing at the Sadler Street T-junction, looking past the brick-and-cream apartment complexes toward the Corner businesses that bustled with students, it felt even months later as though something had irrevocably changed. Yeardley Love's death wasn't the first tragedy to bring the city to its knees, nor would it be the last. But for tens of thousands of students who had endured the heartache of May 2010, and for thousands more who would attend UVA in its aftermath, it would be the tragedy that defined their coming-of-age on a campus forced to acknowledge that its ideals didn't always match its reality.

Even if no one said so.

Epilogue

When it comes to criminal cases, time can change form, morphing from predictable metronome to mercurial ooze. Such is the case with the murder trial against George Huguely V.

Though the grand jury handed down its indictments in April 2011, Huguely's trial date was pushed off nearly a year to February 2012. The delay was prompted by many factors, including scheduling conflicts for the defense team. As of this writing, Huguely's lawyers have never asked that their client be released on bond. He remains in the Albemarle-Charlottesville Regional Jail awaiting his day in court. In a newly released mugshot, he bears the hallmarks of a prisoner: His once-shaggy hair—the en vogue look for a male college lacrosse player—is shorn off, his blue-and-orange jersey traded in for black-and-white jail garb. His face appears more angular, slightly hardened, but there's something still doe-like in his eyes, something that seems to ask, *How did I get here?*

One year after Yeardley Love's death, as spring slowly crept across the University of Virginia campus, the excitement of a graduating class was again tempered by bleak reminders of life's frangibility. The campus marked the May 3, 2011, anniversary quietly, but Yeardley's name again was forefront in the media, both mainstream and social. Thousands of Twitter users marked the day with the hashtag "#onelove" and asked that Yeardley's family be in their thoughts. At Notre Dame Prep, Yeardley's high school, family and friends gathered that day to remember her and to ask each other to "bring out the Yeardley."

"That's what we've encouraged people to do—a kindness for someone, make their day," Cami Colarossi, the school's spokeswoman, told a reporter.

Some of Yeardley's friends and family members spoke exclusively to *Good Morning America* to describe the friend they said saw the world through "sunshine-colored glasses" and to promote the One Love Foundation. Sharon and Lexie Love also broke their silence, speaking most in-depth to *Sports Illustrated*. Though they still refused to talk about the man accused of murder, they described the grief that threatened to level them—until they paused to ask themselves, "What would Yards do?"

"Nothing good comes from not being positive," Sharon Love told journalist L. Jon Wertheim.

It wasn't easy, she said. Sharon had grown accustomed to nightly phone calls with her youngest daughter, chats that always ended with "I love you." Lexie recalled sharing a bed with Yeardley in the days after their father died in 2003, just as the two had done growing up. The two felt like—and were often mistaken for—twins, despite their three-year age difference.

In some ways, life had moved on. Sharon returned to her job as a Baltimore schools teacher; Lexie worked as an IT specialist. But those were just day jobs compared to what had now become their mission—to do right by Yeardley.

The One Love Foundation had generated hundreds of thousands of dollars in donations. Its goal to build a lacrosse field bearing Yeardley's name at her high school alma mater was well under way, and in May, one male and one female Atlantic Coast Conference lacrosse player was to each receive the inaugural Yeardley Reynolds Love Unsung Hero Award. The foundation's Web site had grown and become more polished with each passing month, announcing new

events in Yeardley's honor and new goals aimed to keep her
memory alive.

The foundation and its success kept the women focused
and motivated, providing them with their "good days." So,
too, did the letters and emails that poured in from strangers
worldwide.

"I'm not sure people realize how much little things help,
how much of a difference it's made in our lives," Sharon told
Wertheim.

The bad days could be triggered by a holiday, a birthday,
or nothing at all, Lexie said.

"There are days when we're devastated," she said. "The
emotions come out of nowhere . . . and it hits you: *This is
real*."

On May 3rd, UVA posted on its Web site an article that
served both as homage to Yeardley and description of what
steps the university had taken since her death. It recapped
the Day of Dialogue organized in the fall by University President Teresa Sullivan and outlined other projects under way,
including the creation of five new groups to discuss issues
such as violence and socioeconomic class. The Let's Get
Grounded movement continued its "Recognize, React, Respect" campaign to supposedly provide bystander interven-
tion training, though its calendar of events was nearly empty.

The university said other measures had been taken as
well: Patricia Lampkin, vice president and chief student affairs officer, sent a memo in the fall of 2010 to faculty to help
them identify students who might be in abusive relationships.
Lampkin also reached out to 70 other colleges and universities in Virginia requesting courtesy calls when a UVA student behaved inappropriately while in their area. (Thirteen
institutions agreed to make those calls, and UVA reported
that it had received one notification in December 2010.) Student conduct records were revamped in October 2010 to give
officials room to store more data and documents and share
that information with outside agencies "when appropriate."

Most importantly, students seemed more determined to
intervene when they saw something amiss with a classmate.

"We are fairly certain that students are calling us more often and reporting incidents more frequently—something we want and encourage them to do," UVA Police Chief Michael Gibson said in the article.

"Students took the lead and have made important progress this year," Lampkin said. "I foresee that progress continuing as new leaders fill their shoes."

University officials still declined to discuss Yeardley or her case, however. One official told a journalist that workers had been warned not to talk with reporters near the anniversary of the death because the university had recently been alerted that Yeardley's family was considering filing a wrongful death lawsuit against the institution. As of this writing, no suit had been filed.

But Yeardley's memory is still honored at the university, most notably in the women's lacrosse locker room. There, long after Yeardley's #1 jersey was retired, her locker and nameplate remained.

"We all take a glance and very privately think for a few minutes when we see it," Coach Julie Myers told *Good Morning America*. "She still has a way of making us reflect back, but making us feel good about reflecting."

And Yeardley's story continued to reach strangers. Female lacrosse players at Perry Hall High School in Baltimore had never met the girl with the piercing blue eyes, but when their coach suggested a charity game, they immediately knew which charity they wanted to benefit. The girls sold bracelets, bumper stickers, and heart-adorned T-shirts that read "Lax for Love," raising hundreds of dollars for the One Love Foundation. During the game, the players lifted their lacrosse sticks and chanted, "One, two, three, Love!" each time they broke from a sideline huddle. The Perry Hall Gators won the game handily.

An overwhelmed Sharon Love attended the game. "We really didn't know anybody here before tonight, but they reached out to us to support a cause that we think is pretty important," she told a reporter. "It's just so nice of the girls."

No matter the trial's outcome, Yeardley's family and

friends said they would remain dedicated to preserving and promoting her legacy. It seemed to be the only way that anyone touched by Yeardley could assign meaning to the tragedy.

"The entire university still mourns her loss," Myers told *GMA*. "I think every month we try to get a little stronger, but what's happened in that time is she's gotten deeper and deeper into our hearts."

It's a legacy those who knew her say they want—and need—to live on.

The legacy of Love.